Sustainable AI

Tools for Moving Toward Green AI

Raghavendra Selvan

O'REILLY®

Sustainable AI

by Raghavendra Selvan

Published by O'Reilly Media, Inc., 141 Stony Circle, Suite 195, Santa Rosa, CA 95401.

O'Reilly books may be purchased for educational, business, or sales promotional use. Online editions are also available for most titles (*http://oreilly.com*). For more information, contact our corporate/institutional sales department: 800-998-9938 or *corporate@oreilly.com*.

Acquisitions Editor: Nicole Butterfield
Development Editor: Lauren Mine
Production Editor: Katherine Tozer
Copyeditor: Kim Wimpsett
Proofreader: Stephanie English
Indexer: Judith McConville
Interior Designer: David Futato
Cover Designer: Susan Brown
Cover Illustrator: Monica Kamsvaag
Interior Illustrator: Kate Dullea

October 2025: First Edition

Revision History for the First Edition

2025-10-08: First Release

See *http://oreilly.com/catalog/errata.csp?isbn=9781098155513* for release details.

978-1-098-15551-3

[LSI]

Table of Contents

Preface

Climate change is at our door step. It is causing heat waves, flash floods, droughts, and other erratic weather patterns. Addressing the challenges posed by climate change will be the defining project of our times. To do this, we should employ all the tools at our disposal. And one of the most powerful tools currently is artificial intelligence (AI), which has revolutionized tasks in many application domains. As such, AI can be indispensable in our efforts to combat climate change.

The recent class of AI methods, however, is growing to be extremely resource-intensive. Developing and using them requires powerful datacenters, which consume vast amounts of energy with correspondingly high carbon emissions. In addition, the datacenters used for AI require large volumes of fresh water in their cooling systems, rely on extractive mining to manufacture the electronics, and incur additional carbon emissions along their lifecycle. These factors, and other broader environmental impacts, pose a dilemma about using AI for sustainability.

The main argument in this book is that the material basis for any technology should not be discounted even in the light of their promised benefits. This is also true for AI. Even though AI has promised—and delivered on some—solutions to the sustainability challenges, the underlying resource cost of AI should not be ignored. If we don't pay close attention to these massive costs, the supposed benefits offered might be eclipsed by the negative impacts of AI; the trade-off between the cost and benefits should always be considered.

This book is an attempt to lay out these arguments so that we can make meaningful trade-offs that advance the sustainability of AI, while using it to improve the sustainability of our planet. To do this, the book presents practical tools and conceptual frameworks that will help us assess and grapple with the complex interplay between sustainability and AI.

Who Should Read This Book?

The book is primarily aimed at machine learning (ML) practitioners, which is by now a broad definition because almost all of us are using AI in one way or another.

The majority of the book focuses on stakeholders who are responsible for developing, deploying, and assessing the impact of AI. This includes engineers who develop novel ML models, managers who commission new AI applications, and policymakers who want to obtain a better insight into the technicalities and thus assess the trade-offs when developing and using AI models. Anyone who is broadly interested in the topics of sustainability and AI but not in algorithmic development can also get a lot out of this book by skipping some of the technical sections.

Sustainability and AI are the two most important concepts that will shape our future, and this book is positioned at the intersection of these ideas. I hope that ML practitioners will get a lot out of this book, while a general audience will still find it useful to draw upon statistics and discussion points that can influence their digital culture.

What This Book Is and Is Not

This is neither a popular science book nor a graduate-level academic textbook. This book tries to balance the needs of AI stakeholders by providing key arguments, formalisms, tools, and conceptual frameworks, so that we can foster informed discussions about the sustainability of AI.

Using This Book

The main questions about the sustainability of AI are framed in Chapters 1 and 3, and revisited in Chapter 10. Anyone who is broadly interested in AI can read these chapters and get a peek into the intricacies of the questions being addressed in the book.

The book does assume some background knowledge about the inner workings of ML models; however, readers who do not have this background can bridge some of the essential concepts using Chapter 2. This chapter is not intended to be a primer on ML for AI practitioners, but I do hope they will gain new intuitions about the technology behind recent AI models that are behind generative AI.

The remaining six chapters consist of a more technical look into the algorithmic workings of modern ML models. Each chapter focuses on a step in the AI model lifecycle using the gaze of resource consumption. In doing so, these chapters identify resource bottlenecks and suggest interventions that can improve the resource efficiency, and hence advance the sustainability, of AI.

Specifically, Chapter 4 addresses the question of data used in AI, Chapter 5 explores the vast space of model selection, Chapter 6 identifies improvements during training of AI models, and Chapter 7 provides suggestions for improving the resource efficiency at deployment. These four chapters are closely tied to the algorithmic choices that ML practitioners can make to exercise high-level control. Chapter 8 addresses the question of hardware efficiency, and Chapter 9 takes a system-level view of AI.

All the technical chapters have use cases that consider a real-world application of AI for sustainability. These use cases are presented several times within a chapter after introducing technical tools to show how the concepts can be put into practice.

The questions pertaining to the limitations of resource efficiency, limitations of focusing only on environmental sustainability, and how the path to achieving broader sustainability of AI are not addressed in any single chapter but form the general themes of the book.

Conventions Used in This Book

The following typographical conventions are used in this book:

Italic
: Indicates new terms, URLs, email addresses, filenames, and file extensions.

`Constant width`
: Used for program listings, as well as within paragraphs to refer to program elements such as variable or function names, databases, data types, environment variables, statements, and keywords.

`Constant width bold`
: Shows commands or other text that should be typed literally by the user.

`Constant width italic`
: Shows text that should be replaced with user-supplied values or by values determined by context.

> This element signifies a tip or suggestion.

> This element signifies a general note.

This element indicates a warning or caution.

Using Code Examples

Supplemental material (code examples, exercises, etc.) is available for download at *https://github.com/raghavian/sustainable_ai*. The GitHub repository also includes a bibliography with references and further reading listed by chapter.

If you have a technical question or a problem using the code examples, please send email to *support@oreilly.com*.

This book is here to help you get your job done. In general, if example code is offered with this book, you may use it in your programs and documentation. You do not need to contact us for permission unless you're reproducing a significant portion of the code. For example, writing a program that uses several chunks of code from this book does not require permission. Selling or distributing examples from O'Reilly books does require permission. Answering a question by citing this book and quoting example code does not require permission. Incorporating a significant amount of example code from this book into your product's documentation does require permission.

We appreciate, but generally do not require, attribution. An attribution usually includes the title, author, publisher, and ISBN. For example: "*Sustainable AI* by Raghavendra Selvan (O'Reilly). Copyright 2026 Raghavendra Selvan, 978-1-098-15551-3."

If you feel your use of code examples falls outside fair use or the permission given above, feel free to contact us at *permissions@oreilly.com*.

O'Reilly Online Learning

For more than 40 years, *O'Reilly Media* has provided technology and business training, knowledge, and insight to help companies succeed.

Our unique network of experts and innovators share their knowledge and expertise through books, articles, and our online learning platform. O'Reilly's online learning platform gives you on-demand access to live training courses, in-depth learning paths, interactive coding environments, and a vast collection of text and video from O'Reilly and 200+ other publishers. For more information, visit *https://oreilly.com*.

How to Contact Us

Please address comments and questions concerning this book to the publisher:

> O'Reilly Media, Inc.
> 141 Stony Circle, Suite 195
> Santa Rosa, CA 95401
> 800-889-8969 (in the United States or Canada)
> 707-827-7019 (international or local)
> 707-829-0104 (fax)
> *support@oreilly.com*
> *https://oreilly.com/about/contact.html*

We have a web page for this book, where we list errata and any additional information. You can access this page at *https://oreil.ly/SustainableAI*.

For news and information about our books and courses, visit *https://oreilly.com*.

Find us on LinkedIn: *https://linkedin.com/company/oreilly-media*.

Watch us on YouTube: *https://youtube.com/oreillymedia*.

Acknowledgments

On a spring morning in 2019, when riding the local train to work in Copenhagen, I was reading James Bridle's thought-provoking book *New Dark Age: Technology and the End of the Future* (Verso Books). Halfway through the book was a passage about the increasing energy consumption of datacenters. That passage was the seed that got me thinking about the energy consumption, and the corresponding carbon footprint, of deep learning. I conducted a literature survey, and there were no noticeable efforts in this direction. Later that year, in collaboration with two of my motivated bachelor students—Lasse Anthony and Benjamin Kanding—we developed Carbontracker (*https://carbontracker.info*). It is now widely used by the ML community (it has been downloaded 150,000 times as of this writing).

This was my first foray into the questions of sustainability of AI, which has resulted in the book you are reading now.

A book like this is written by standing on the shoulders of passionate giants. I would like to thank all the amazing researchers, thinkers, and creators who have made it their life's objective to work on sustainability and/or AI. I have referenced all of their influential works throughout the book, and I hope you will find as much inspiration as I do when reading those works. Also, I would like to acknowledge all creators at SVG Repo (*https://svgrepo.com*) for making amazing designs and permitting their usage.

Writing this book has been a tough but gratifying journey. It was tough simply due to the nature of work in academia with its ebbs and flows. There were many kind and passionate people along the way who have helped me stay afloat, navigating these tides.

I would like to thank Nicole Butterfield from O'Reilly for providing me with the opportunity to work on this book on sustainable AI. Thanks also to Katherine Tozer and the others at O'Reilly for their meticulous work in bringing the book to life. Most of all, I have the utmost gratitude to Lauren Mine—my editor—for being keen, insightful, constructive, and kind throughout the duration of the project and also for putting up with my never-ending delays.

The bulk of the content in the book is based in the research that I have been fortunate enough to be carrying out in the past years with a strong team of collaborators. I would like to thank all the former and current members of my team at SAINTS Lab at the University of Copenhagen (*https://saintslab.github.io*), especially Pedram Bakhtiarifard, Rasmus Løvstad, Jonathan Wenshøj, Tong Chen, Sophia Wilson, Frederik Johansen, Julian Schön, and Dustin Wright. I would also like to thank my colleagues at the Machine Learning Section at University of Copenhagen, for the constant motivation, feedback, and enthusiasm about this book, particularly, Erik Dam, who has championed and believed in me throughout my research career. I also thank Christian Igel for his excitement about the book and his regular feedback. I also thank all my collaborators who have worked on these topics, particularly the members of the European Horizon projects, EnrichMyData, SustainML, and DataPACT. Thanks are also due to all the students I have been fortunate to know and interact with over the years, who keep me inspired. Thanks also to my reviewers Gourav Bais, Mikio Braun, Abhishek Gupta, Dan Situnayake, and Bijo Thomas.

I want to express gratitude and affection to all my friends and family, who have been supportive and proud of me always, particularly all the women in my life: my incredible mother, Chitra; my amazing sister, Rekha; my lovely niece, Nissi; my inspiring Danish godmother, Merete; and my life partner, Sneha. I would like to use this opportunity to acknowledge how amazing a researcher, person, and partner Sneha has been. I would not have been able to do this, or anything else that is remotely meaningful in my life, without her support.

CHAPTER 1
Sustainability and Artificial Intelligence

There is clear consensus among scientists about the climate trajectory of our planet—it is warming at an alarming rate. The Intergovernmental Panel on Climate Change (IPCC) in their most recent report declared, "Human activities, principally through emissions of greenhouse gases, have unequivocally caused global warming, with global surface temperature reaching 1.1°C above 1850-1900 in 2011-2020."[1] Figure 1-1 illustrates these trends of a warming planet and rising sea levels. The clear rise in global temperatures and sea levels coincides with the Industrial Revolution around the 19th century and has been accelerating in the last couple of decades.

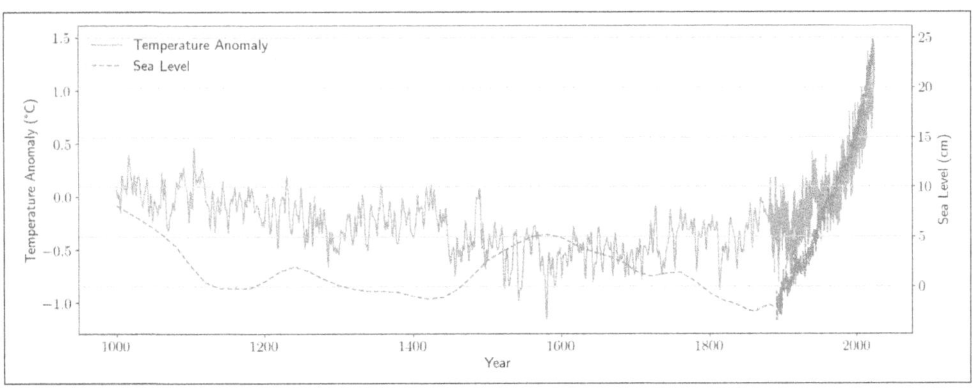

Figure 1-1. Historical trend of global temperature anomaly and sea levels. (Source: Two Degrees Institute (https://2degreesinstitute.org).)

1 IPCC, *Climate Change 2023: Synthesis Report. Contribution of Working Groups I, II, and III to the Sixth Assessment Report of the Intergovernmental Panel on Climate Change* (Geneva, Switzerland, IPCC, 2023) (*https://doi.org/10.59327/ipcc/ar6-9789291691647*).

The effects of planetary warming and climate change are increasingly unpredictable: erratic weather and intensifying natural disasters are becoming all too common, disproportionately harming vulnerable populations. While international agreements like the Paris Climate Accord have set emission targets, most fall short in either ambition or enforcement.[2] The result is a growing gap between what is needed and what is being done.

> **The Difference Between 1.5°C and 2°C Global Warming**
>
> Keeping global warming under 1.5°C, emphasized in the 2015 Paris Agreement, is considered the safer upper limit to avoid the worst impacts of climate change. At 2°C of warming, the risks grow substantially due to the nonlinear nature of climate impacts. The difference between 1.5°C and 2°C could be the difference between resilience and devastation. The planet is currently on track to exceed 1.5°C warming in the near term (by 2030).

Strategies to cope with climate change are currently categorized into two streams of efforts: climate change mitigation and climate change adaptation. *Climate change mitigation* refers to efforts of reducing or preventing greenhouse gas (GHG) emissions, aiming to limit the pace of global warming. *Climate change adaptation* involves adjusting systems, practices, and infrastructure to minimize the harm caused by the impacts of a changing climate. These are no longer future challenges; these are the defining crises of our time.

Faced with these daunting challenges, we need to draw on every tool at our disposal to advance these efforts. The scale and urgency of climate change demand a comprehensive approach, which includes policy, collective action, systems change, and, critically, technology. But for technology to play a meaningful role, it must be deeply rooted in sustainability.

We will adhere to the United Nations (UN) definition of sustainability: "meeting the needs of the present without compromising the ability of future generations to meet their own needs."[3]

Returning to the question of using technology to combat climate change, of all the recent advances in technology, few have defined the current zeitgeist as much as artificial intelligence (AI). The rapid proliferation of AI tools across domains including science, industry, and governance has opened new possibilities for addressing

2 The Paris Agreement (*https://oreil.ly/LiL5j*) was signed and adopted by 195 parties at the UN Climate Change Conference (COP2021) in December 2015.

3 World Commission on Environment and Development, *Our Common Future* (Oxford University Press, 1987).

large-scale, complex problems, and climate change is no exception. AI can be useful to tackle the climate crisis in several ways. However, as with other technologies used to tackle climate change, AI should also be rooted in sustainability.

Making AI more sustainable is important for several reasons. The most pressing one is the large-scale resources needed to develop and use some of the recent classes of AI methods. While these large-scale AI methods are promising, their reliance on vast amounts of data, hyper-scale compute resources, massive energy consumption, and the corresponding carbon emissions are concerning as they negatively affect the environmental sustainability of AI. Resources at these scales are fiscally expensive, which also deepen the digital divide in the AI era and hence hamper the economic and social sustainability of AI.

AI/ML/DL

The terms *AI*, *machine learning* (ML), and *deep learning* (DL) are often used interchangeably, though their boundaries are neither fixed nor universally agreed upon. One useful classification frames ML as a broad class of methods designed to learn from data, encompassing everything from basic linear regression to large-scale conversational agents. DL then refers to a subset of ML methods that rely on deep neural networks as the underlying model class, ranging from simple feedforward networks to convolutional architectures and transformers. AI, in turn, subsumes both ML and DL but extends beyond them to include the broader pursuit of machine-based intelligence. This includes not only technical approaches but also the social, philosophical, and cultural dimensions of what we consider "intelligent" behavior, which is often shaped as much by industrial ambition and public imagination as by scientific consensus. Figure 1-2 visualizes the relationship between these terms as a Venn diagram.

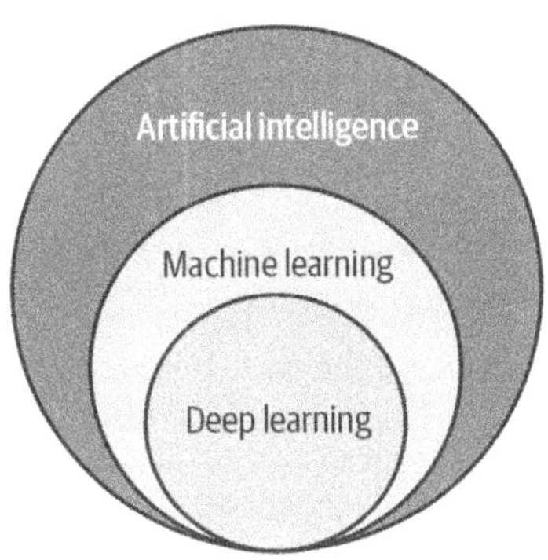

Figure 1-2. One possible classification of AI/ML/DL.

This book attempts to shine a light on the questions surrounding the sustainability of AI. It uses a lens of resource consumption, primarily energy and carbon. As AI practitioners, we can have the greatest impact by influencing the design and development of AI models to keep their resource consumption in check. While this alone will not make AI sustainable, it can be a step in the right direction.

In the remainder of this chapter, I will formalize some of the commonly used notions (including what it means to be sustainable and what we mean by AI), point out the pros and cons of pursuing resource efficiency, and outline the rest of the book. Sustainability and AI are two of the most important ideas defining our age. So, by definition, the ambitions of a book entitled *Sustainable AI* are grand. I hope this chapter will offer a glimpse into the promise of the rest of the book.

Scope of Sustainability

The most visible discussions around sustainability are focused on the environment. However, this is only part of the story as achieving true sustainability should also emphasize the economic and social aspects. We will use a real-world scenario to understand sustainability in all its complexity next.

The Samsø Sustainability Story

Step off the ferry to the Danish island, Samsø, and you will see a postcard-perfect view of Danish farms that, like any rural community, burned imported oil 25 years ago (see Figure 1-3). Then the islanders won a 1997 national contest to become Denmark's "Renewable Energy Island."[4] Within a decade they had installed cooperatively owned wind turbines and biomass district-heating plants so that today Samsø exports electricity to the mainland, and each resident averages about 3.7 tonnes (t) of carbon dioxide (CO_2) equivalent (e) of GHGs per year, which is roughly half of the Danish national average at about 7tCO_2e.[5] For more about tCO_2e, see "GHG Emissions and Carbon Footprint" on page 68.

Denmark's energy grid is one of cleanest in the world today, primarily due to the strong investment in wind energy.

Seen through the environmental lens, the transformation is striking. The grid runs on 100% renewables, mainly wind. It has shown a carbon drop of roughly 140% from its 1997 baseline, meaning by exporting surplus renewable energy to mainland Denmark, Samsø offsets more than its total emissions.

4 Jan Jantzen et al., "Sociotechnical Transition to Smart Energy: The Case of Samso 1997–2030," Energy 162 (August 3, 2018): 20–34 (*https://doi.org/10.1016/j.energy.2018.07.174*).

5 UNFCC, "Samsø: An Island Community Pointing to the Future," 2023 (*https://oreil.ly/S9_Sd*).

Figure 1-3. Windmills scattered in the picturesque Danish rural side.

Economically, those turbines double as community savings accounts. Farmers, fishers, and the municipal pension fund bought shares; dividends arrive whenever the wind blows, and surplus power sales bring fresh revenue. The renewable buildout, plus an Energy Academy (*https://oreil.ly/p5RJs*) that trains visiting officials, has created several new local jobs each year and nudged tourism upward.

Because 1 in 10 islanders now co-owns a wind turbine, hardware that might once have provoked not-in-my-backyard (NIMBY) protests instead signals collective pride.[6] Maintenance, future investment and political support all flow from that sense of shared stake.

"The Samsø Sustainability Story" illustrates the multifaceted nature of sustainability, which is usually translated to the three pillars of sustainability: environmental, economic, and social. Environmental gains persist because they generate income, and both depend on institutions that keep ordinary people in the decision loop. Figure 1-4 positions AI as a foundational technology, asking whether it can support the pillars of sustainability.

6 NIMBY protests are citizen protests against large-scale infrastructure projects that are perceived to adversely impact local neighborhoods.

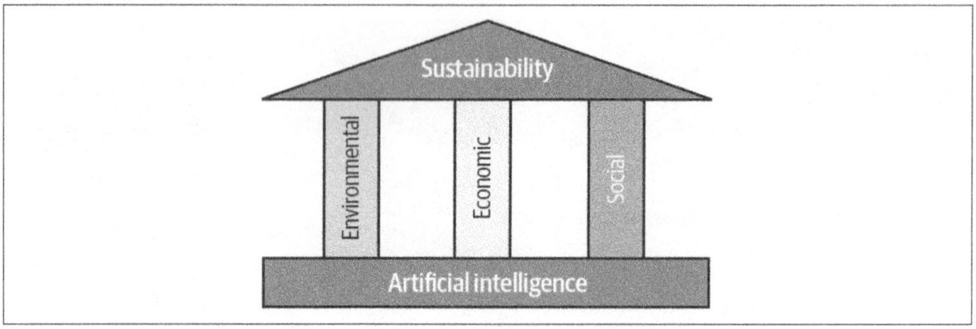

Figure 1-4. The three pillars of sustainability. Can AI support these three pillars?

The figure reflects the current enthusiasm toward using AI to tackle complex problems like climate change. Is this feasible? How far can AI take us? Does AI itself come at a cost? These are some of the questions this book will try to answer. Before doing that, let's settle on a definition of AI.

Artificial Intelligence: The New Electricity?

What is AI? We have been asking this question for more than 70 years.[7,8] And though the answers have shifted with time, our fascination has not faded. Figure 1-5 is a snapshot of some famous metaphors from eminent researchers and industry experts. These responses range from hype to doom, and everything in between.

Today, it even feels like we have crossed a threshold when it comes to AI: it is no longer just an abstract goal or a sci-fi idea. It is here, and it seems to be pervasive.

But AI is not what many imagined. We are not facing machines that outthink us or threaten to replace us wholesale. What we are seeing is something more subtle and arguably more transformative. It's becoming a foundational layer of how our world operates, shaping healthcare, education, entertainment, climate research, and more. It is not just a tool anymore; it is becoming part of the scaffolding of modern life. In this book, we will use the more mundane but useful description and view *AI as infrastructure*. And it's at this level that this book agrees with the comparison of AI to electricity, which is reliant on the interaction of complex resources, policies, and technology.[9]

7 John McCarthy et al., "A Proposal for the Dartmouth Summer Research Project on Artificial Intelligence, August 31, 1955," *AI Magazine* 27, no. 4 (2006) (*https://doi.org/10.1609/aimag.v27i4.1904*).

8 Juergen Schmidhuber, "Annotated History of Modern AI and Deep Learning," *arXiv.org*, December 21, 2022 (*https://arxiv.org/abs/2212.11279*).

9 Shana Lynch, "Andrew Ng: Why AI Is the New Electricity," *Stanford Graduate School of Business*, March 11, 2017 (*https://oreil.ly/5RxyU*).

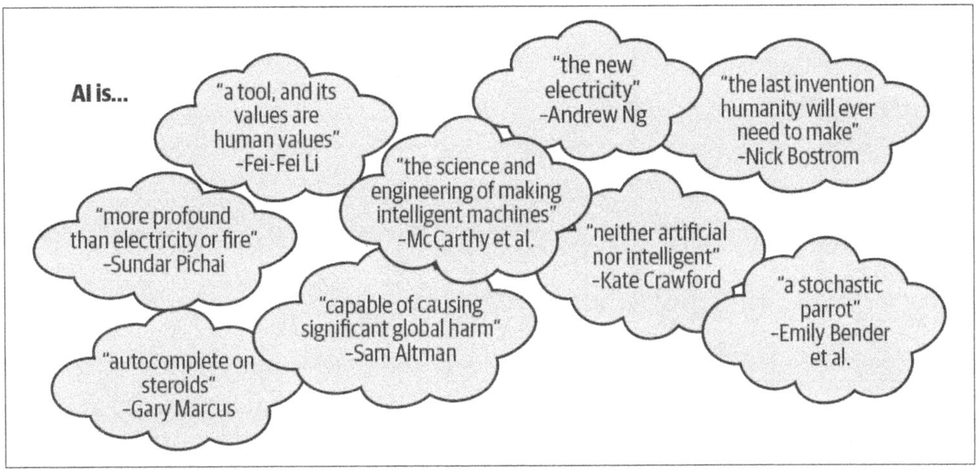

Figure 1-5. What is AI? The responses from the ML/AI community ranges from optimism to doomerism.

That shift raises an important question: what makes AI an infrastructure? And what does that mean for how we understand and build it?

Like all infrastructures, AI is more than just its surface functions. It is not only algorithms or models that learn from data. It is a system deeply entrenched in material resources. Behind the abstractions are the physical components that make it all possible—datacenters, electronic chips, energy grids, network, and the human labor that supports it all. These elements are not just technical necessities; they shape how AI evolves, who it benefits, and who bears its costs.[10] Figure 1-6 captures this notion of AI as infrastructure. While Figure 1-6 doesn't include human labor, I would like to highlight that the pathways between different steps is the flow of human labor, without which this infrastructure would collapse.

This material perspective does not diminish the potential of AI but grounds it. It reminds us that building intelligent systems is also about choices: about what to prioritize and how to allocate resources so that long-term sustainability can be ensured.

10 Matteo Pasquinelli, *The Eye of the Master: A Social History of Artificial Intelligence* (Verso Books, 2023).

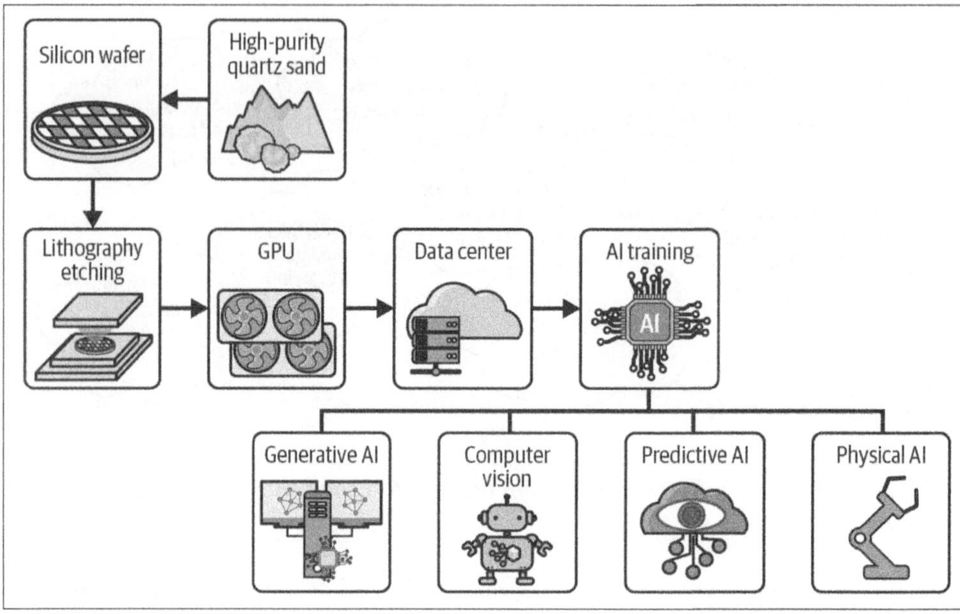

Figure 1-6. AI as infrastructure across its lifecycle, from mining for sand to model deployment. The pathways between steps show the flow of human labor. (Source: adapted from IEA [2025], Energy and AI (https://oreil.ly/qsagl), License: CC BY 4.0.)

Sustainability × AI

We have now outlined what sustainability and AI mean by drawing upon their diverse meanings, historical trajectories, and real-world impacts. Their interaction, marked by the × in this section's title, captures a relationship that is anything but one-directional.[11] At its most immediate, this interplay involves using AI to address sustainability challenges and, in turn, confronting the sustainability challenges created by AI itself. But the implications go further, shaping not only technologies and policies but also the values and systems that will define our future.

The UN Sustainable Development Goals (SDGs) lay out 17 broad ambitions aimed at building a more just and equitable global society. Advancing them will depend in part on how effectively we apply technology, and AI in particular offers real potential across many of them.

Some connections are already well established. AI is making significant progress in healthcare, directly contributing to SDG Goal 3: Good Health and Well-being. In other cases, the connection is less obvious but still worth exploring. SDG Goal 6:

11 Inspired by the Aarhus 2025 conference, Computing × Crisis (*https://aarhus2025.org*).

Clean Water and Sanitation, for instance, might not seem like a natural application of AI at first, yet tools for predictive maintenance, water quality monitoring, and system optimization suggest otherwise.

AI for Sustainability

There is a lot of enthusiasm to tap into the potential of using AI to address climate change. This is captured as the growing interest from research communities. Figure 1-7 shows the rise in the number of research publications on the topic of "AI and sustainability," with almost exponential increase in the past decade.

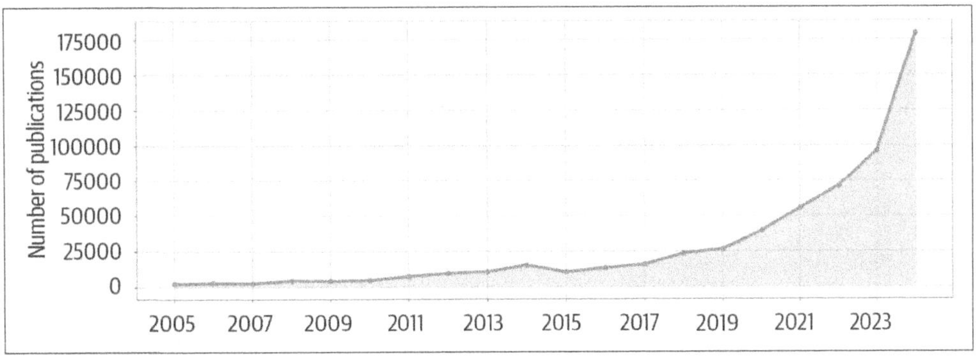

Figure 1-7. Research trend on AI and sustainability over the last two decades. (Source: data from Dimensions.ai (https://app.dimensions.ai) using the search keywords "AI and sustainability.")

AI methods are already being used to address climate change mitigation. One of the recent successful applications has been to manage renewable energy more efficiently. Using predictive models to forecast supply and demand makes it easier to integrate solar and wind into power grids while reducing waste and reliance on fossil fuels.[12]

AI methods have also shown promise in supporting early-warning systems for climate disasters, which is a clear use case for climate change adaptation. In flood-prone areas, predictive models based on real-time data help anticipate extreme weather, improving preparedness and reducing harm, particularly where infrastructure is limited.[13,14]

---

12 Madhumita Murgia and Nathalie Thomas, "DeepMind and National Grid in AI Talks to Balance Energy Supply," *Financial Times*, March 11, 2017 (*https://oreil.ly/p31cd*).

13 Miriam Meister, "AI Predicts Flooding," *DTU*, March 7, 2024 (*https://oreil.ly/D6sDh*).

14 Grey Nearing et al., "Global Prediction of Extreme Floods in Ungauged Watersheds," *Nature* 627 (March 20, 2024): 559–63 (*https://doi.org/10.1038/s41586-024-07145-1*).

Table 1-1 presents a selection of use cases where ML/AI methods have shown promise in advancing the UN SDGs. While one can find a use case that matches all 17 SDGs, the table focuses on a subset of examples that clearly demonstrate the usefulness of AI. Works like "Leveraging Artificial Intelligence to Meet the Sustainable Development Goals" by Ewa Wanda Ziemba et al. (*https://doi.org/10.22367/jem.2024.46.19*) provide a more comprehensive review of methods using AI to advance SDGs.

Table 1-1. A selection of interesting AI use cases that have shown promise in advancing at least one of the UN SDGs

SDG	AI use case	Description
#1: No poverty	Poverty mapping via satellite imagery	DL models analyze satellite images to estimate local wealth levels. For example, an AI model trained on multispectral imagery predicted village asset wealth across ~20,000 African communities, explaining ~70% of the variation in ground-measured wealth and enabling high-resolution poverty maps. Such AI-driven mapping helps identify impoverished areas and inform poverty alleviation efforts.[a]
#3: Good health and well-being	AI for cancer detection from medical images	AI systems in healthcare can greatly enhance early diagnosis. For example, an AI model for breast cancer screening was shown to surpass expert radiologists in accuracy. By catching cancers earlier and more reliably, such AI diagnostic tools improve patient outcomes and overall health system effectiveness.[b]
#7: Affordable and clean energy	Renewable energy forecasting and smart grids	AI methods are accelerating the transition to clean energy by optimizing production and distribution. ML algorithms can analyze vast weather and grid data to forecast solar/wind power output and adjust energy dispatch accordingly. This leads to a more reliable supply of renewables (reducing reliance on fossil fuels) and helps balance supply-demand in smart grids.[c]
#14: Life below water	Satellite AI to combat illegal fishing	AI is aiding ocean conservation by monitoring human impacts. A notable use case is using ML on satellite imagery to detect illegal or unreported fishing ("dark") vessels. A recent global analysis with ESA's Sentinel-1 satellites and AI revealed that about 75% of industrial fishing ships were not appearing in public tracking, and the AI system could identify these previously invisible vessels. By bringing such activities to light, AI helps enforcement agencies curb overfishing and protect marine ecosystems.[d]

[a] Christopher Yeh et al., "Using Publicly Available Satellite Imagery and Deep Learning to Understand Economic Well-Being in Africa," *Nature Communications* 11 (May 22, 2020) (*https://doi.org/10.1038/s41467-020-16185-w*).

[b] Scott Mayer McKinney et al., "International Evaluation of an AI System for Breast Cancer Screening," *Nature* 577, no. 7788 (January 1, 2020): 89–94 (*https://doi.org/10.1038/s41586-019-1799-6*).

[c] Bankole I. Oladapo et al., "Machine Learning for Optimising Renewable Energy and Grid Efficiency," *Atmosphere* 15, no. 10 (October 19, 2024): 1250 (*https://doi.org/10.3390/atmos15101250*).

[d] Fernando S. Paolo et al., "Satellite Mapping Reveals Extensive Industrial Activity at Sea," *Nature* 625, no. 7993 (January 3, 2024): 85–91 (*https://doi.org/10.1038/s41586-023-06825-8*).

Traps of Techno-Solutionism

Be aware of the risks of *techno-solutionism*, which treats technology as the primary or exclusive answer to complex social and environmental problems, often ignoring political, economic, and historical factors.[15] It can be seductive because it offers clear fixes to messy problems. But complex challenges like climate change are not rooted in a deficiency of gadgets; they are rooted in excessive extraction, imbalanced governance, and systems of inequality. Affirming technology's value while remaining clear about its limits, embedded assumptions, and systemic context is crucial. Caution is particularly important whenever dealing with a revolutionary technology such as AI.[16]

Sustainability of AI

Viewing AI as an infrastructure, and not just as a hive of algorithms, allows us to consider the material resources that shape it. This distinction is of critical importance to steer the current AI discourse toward sustainability. While many of the algorithms behind even the most advanced AI methods have been around for several decades,[17] access to vast amounts of data and large-scale compute resources have catalyzed them into action. This approach is now famously dubbed *scale is all you need* in ML/AI communities.[18] All major AI companies have followed the scaling up. They are racing to build hyper-scale datacenters that house thousands of hardware accelerators, powering them with gigawatt datacenters and sucking fresh water sources dry in a global AI arms race.[19] Use of resources at these scales is expensive and simply unsustainable.

Energy consumption of AI

Roughly 1.5% of the world's electricity is currently consumed by datacenters. This may sound modest at first glance, but it masks two crucial facts: the sheer scale of global electricity demand and the steep growth trajectory of digital infrastructure. At

15 E. Morozov, ed., "To Save Everything, Click Here: Technology, Solutionism and the Urge to Fix Problems That Don't Exist," *Information Polity* 18, no. 3 (July 1, 2013): 275–76 (*https://dl.acm.org/doi/10.5555/2659342.2659349*).

16 Benedetta Brevini, "Myths, Techno Solutionism and Artificial Intelligence: Reclaiming AI Materiality and Its Massive Environmental Costs," in *Handbook of Critical Studies of Artificial Intelligence*, ed. Simon Lindgren (Edward Elgar Publishing, 2023), 869–77 (*https://doi.org/10.4337/9781803928562.00086*).

17 For example, all recent AI models are still trained using variations of the gradient descent algorithm, which was used to train the original Perceptron model by Rosenblatt in 1958 (*https://doi.org/10.1037/h0042519*).

18 Jared Kaplan et al., "Scaling Laws for Neural Language Models," *arXiv.org*, January 23, 2020 (*https://arxiv.org/abs/2001.08361*).

19 Pedram Bakhtiarifard et al., "Climate and Resource Awareness Is Imperative to Achieving Sustainable AI (and Preventing a Global AI Arms Race)," *arXiv.org*, February 27, 2025 (*https://arxiv.org/abs/2502.20016*).

today's levels, 1.5% translates to about 465 terrawatt-hours (TWh) per year, and projections from the International Energy Agency (IEA) and others suggest that figure could double by 2030, reaching nearly 1,000TWh if current trends in AI and cloud computing continue unchecked.[20]

To grasp the weight of that number, compare it with the annual electricity consumption of the African continent. Africa, home to nearly one in five people on Earth (about 19% of the global population), uses just 3% of global electricity. That is approximately 960TWh per year as of 2024.

The exact proportion of this energy consumption by AI is not known currently, as datacenters are not required to perform granular reporting of the types of jobs. However, the new demand for more powerful datacenters is clearly driven by the uptake of new frontier AI models.

Figure 1-8 plots two projections using different scenarios of AI uptake. If datacenter consumption continues on the current "base" or "lift-off" trajectory (as modeled by the IEA (*https://oreil.ly/qsagl*)), those facilities alone could surpass 1,100–1,300TWh by 2028. Meanwhile, Africa's electricity demand is currently projected to grow at around 5% annually. Under this scenario, the continent might reach around 970–1,020TWh by the same year.[21] That means that by as early as 2028, the world's datacenters will be using more electricity than the entire African continent.

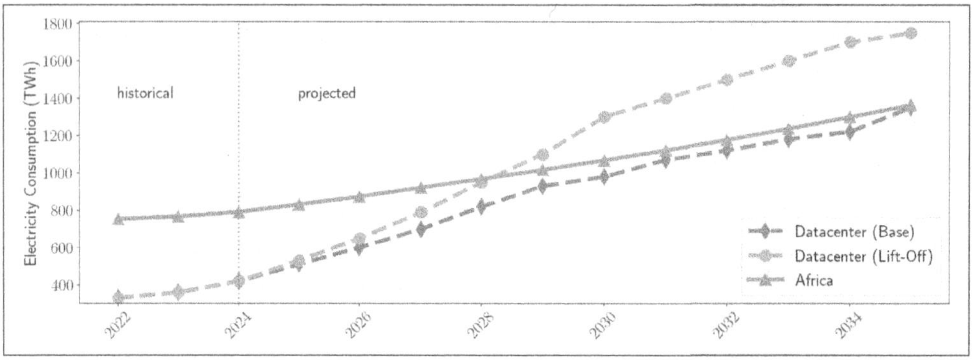

Figure 1-8. Electricity consumption trends for global datacenters and the entire African continent. (Source: for datacenters, the prediction is based on IEA analysis reported in Energy and AI (https://oreil.ly/qsagl), and for Africa, a 5% compounded average annual growth rate is assumed based on the IEA's Electricity 2025 Report (https://oreil.ly/hC8-O).)

20 IEA, *Energy and AI*, (IEA, Paris, 2025) (*https://oreil.ly/qsagl*).

21 IEA, *Electricity 2025*, (IEA, Paris, 2025) (*https://oreil.ly/37dTJ*).

Energy, particularly clean energy, is a constrained and contested resource. As long as basic electricity access remains out of reach for hundreds of millions of people, the unchecked expansion of energy-hungry AI systems must be held to account. The use of shared energy resources must be justified in terms of the social value brought about by any technology, including AI.[22]

Climate impact of AI

The growing energy demands and associated carbon emissions of the new class of frontier AI models are beginning to draw serious attention. But the climate impact of AI extends well beyond electricity use. A broader set of environmental effects is now coming into focus.

One of the less visible impacts is water usage. Large-scale datacenters are remarkably thirsty. The electronic hardware powering AI models generate immense heat, and to keep them running within narrow temperature limits, these facilities rely on intensive cooling. Most often, this is done through *evaporative cooling*, where heat is removed by turning fresh water into vapor in cooling towers. While this method is more energy-efficient than air-based alternatives, it leads to permanent water loss, which is a significant cost, especially in water-stressed regions.

When OpenAI trained GPT-3, estimates suggest it used 5.4 million liters of fresh water, which includes 700,000 liters that was consumed (evaporated) for that single training run.[23] This single event consumed a volume of water comparable to the entire annual domestic demand of 270 people from rural India who consume about 55 liters per day.[24]

The real concern is not just the volume of water use but where this happens. Many datacenters are located in water-stressed areas and often draw from municipal supplies, meaning AI workloads can compete with homes, farms, and hospitals for the same clean water.[25]

---

22 Karen Bickerstaff et al., eds., *Energy Justice in a Changing Climate: Social Equity and Low-Carbon Energy* (Zed Books, 2013).

23 Pengfei Li et al., "Making AI Less *Thirsty*," *Communications of the ACM* 68, no. 7 (2025): 54–61 (*https://doi.org/10.1145/3724499*).

24 *Annual Report 2024-25*, (Ministry of Jal Shakti, 2025) (*https://oreil.ly/yZj6G*).

25 Eli Tan and Dustin Chambers, "Their Water Taps Ran Dry When Meta Built Next Door," *New York Times*, July 14, 2025 (*https://oreil.ly/luB61*).

Heat-Exchange Pumps Can Reuse Surplus Heat for District Heating

Some northern European countries, like Finland, use the surplus heat from datacenters to warm thousands of homes through urban district heating systems. Instead of letting server racks dump heat into the air, the surplus heat is fed into underground pipes that heat buildings. This works well in cold countries with advanced district heating that can support these heat-exchange systems with datacenters.[26] Ideally, this would be the norm, not setting up datacenters in deserts or drought-ridden regions and diverting freshwater from local consumption.[27]

AI's climate footprint runs far deeper than its visible energy use or the invisible water use. The deep supply chains behind AI models are also environmentally expensive at every stage.

Chip manufacturing relies on ultra-pure materials, complex fabrication processes, and a sprawling logistics network. Each NVIDIA graphics processing unit (GPU), commonly used to train large models, embodies at least around 150kgCO_2e, based on lifecycle analyses.[28] A single hyper-scale datacenter may deploy tens of thousands of such chips, turning this into a major source of emissions long before any model is trained.

Furthermore, these chips rely on critical minerals like lithium, cobalt, and other rare earth elements. Extracting them comes at a high environmental cost. Mining in the Democratic Republic of Congo, or *Lithium Triangle* (regions formed between the borders of Argentina, Bolivia, and Chile), has been linked to toxic runoff, groundwater depletion, and deforestation, often in regions already facing ecological and political vulnerability.[29]

The pace of hardware innovation shortens lifespans of electronic chips and accelerates electronic waste (e-waste) accumulation. Retired AI hardware further adds to the e-waste crisis.

---

26 Hanne Kokkegård, "Utilize Waste Heat From Data Centers in District Heating," *Technical University of Denmark*, November 1, 2022 (*https://oreil.ly/U5fj0*).

27 James Temple, "The Data Center Boom in the Desert," *MIT Technology Review*, May 20, 2025 (*https://oreil.ly/n097g*).

28 Alexandra Sasha Luccioni et al., "Estimating the Carbon Footprint of BLOOM, a 176B Parameter Language Model," *Journal of Machine Learning Research* 24, no. 1 (2023): 11990–12004 (*https://oreil.ly/NRBf8*).

29 Elena Giglio, "Extractivism and Its Socio-Environmental Impact in South America. Overview of the 'Lithium Triangle,'" *América Crítica* 5, no. 1 (2021): 47–53 (*https://doi.org/10.13125/americacritica/4926*).

The full climate cost of AI cannot be captured just by the electricity that powers it, but the entire material basis that maintains it. Cleaner energy helps, but it is not enough. Addressing AI's climate impact requires a holistic look at its entire lifecycle.

Sustainability impact of AI

The growing resource consumption (energy, carbon, water, minerals, etc.) needed to develop frontier AI models are negatively impacting the environmental sustainability of AI. As we have seen in "Scope of Sustainability" on page 4 (and visualized in Figure 1-4), sustainability has three facets: environmental, economic, and social. The Samsø experiment ("The Samsø Sustainability Story" on page 4) demonstrated that striving for environmental sustainability can foster economic and social sustainability; the converse can also be true. That is, negatively impacting the environmental sustainability can also affect the economic and social sustainability.

The Fallacy of Green Energy Grids

A common counter-argument to concerns about AI's growing energy consumption is the assertion that future energy grids will be fully renewable. This argument is problematic for several reasons. Let's use Denmark—the poster child of clean energy grids and green datacenters—as an example (see Figure 1-9). In popular destinations for hosting datacenters, like Denmark, electricity consumption of datacenters is projected to reach up to 15% of national consumption by 2030.

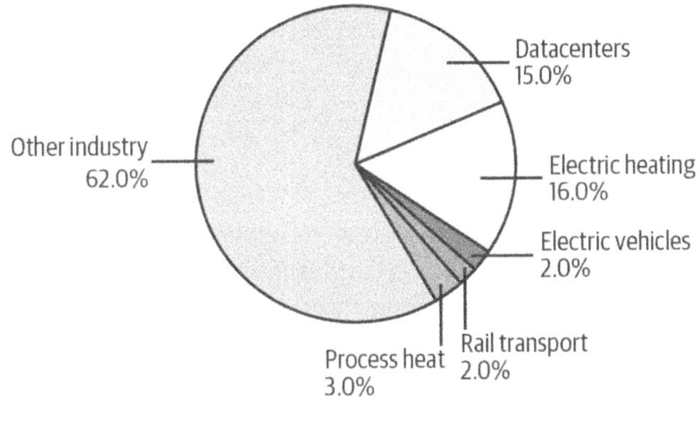

Figure 1-9. Projected electricity consumption of Denmark's datacenters. (Source: adapted from Denmark's Energy and Climate Outlook 2019 [Danish Energy Agency, October, 2019] (https://oreil.ly/y_fbp).)

While Denmark's grid is among the world's greenest, it is also finite. During low-wind periods, datacenters push demand onto imported electricity—often from fossil-based sources like German gas or Swedish biomass. The average carbon intensity may stay low, but the marginal emissions caused by added load increase.

There is also an opportunity cost as the clean electricity that could decarbonize homes, heating, or public transit now powers compute clusters. The resource use is local; the benefits are global and uneven. Meanwhile, public infrastructure absorbs the cost of grid expansions and land use, while profits flow to a handful of firms headquartered elsewhere.

Moving datacenters to greener grids may reduce on-paper emissions, but it does not erase the full climate impact. Upstream emissions from chip fabrication, water use for cooling, and e-waste persist, as does the burden of extractive mining in the Global South. Furthermore, concentrating AI infrastructure in cleaner, wealthier countries risks deepening global inequalities, as those without access to these resources face a double penalty by not only losing access to energy but also a say in how the digital future is built.[30]

A Green Path to Sustainable AI

The algorithms, design recommendations, guidelines, and frameworks presented in this book can be used as a practical guide to improve the sustainability of AI. The primarily focus is on improving the resource efficiency of AI. Improving the energy efficiency, which in turn can reduce the carbon footprint, at each stage of the AI model lifecycle is the key objective. These choices will help us advance toward *green AI*.[31]

Resource efficiency offers a solid platform in the push toward sustainable AI. It offers quantifiable metrics, which can be improved using several off-the-shelf methods. They also scale: an optimization that trims 5% from one training run can save thousands of megawatt hours when applied across a fleet of models and years of inference traffic.

I also argue that efficiency is an indispensable starting point, but it cannot be the destination. History shows that when a technology becomes more efficient, total consumption often rises rather than falls.[32] If a model that once required 100 GPU hours can now be trained in 50, the obvious temptation is to train twice as many models, or bigger ones, or to refresh them more often. Efficiency alone, in other words, can feed the very growth that wipes out its climate gains.

30 Bakhtiarifard et al., "Climate and Resource Awareness Is Imperative to Achieving Sustainable AI (and Preventing a Global AI Arms Race)" (*https://arxiv.org/abs/2502.20016*).

31 Roy Schwartz et al., "Green AI," *Communications of the ACM* 63, no. 12 (2020): 54–63 (*https://doi.org/10.1145/3381831*).

32 J. Daniel Khazzoom, "Economic Implications of Mandated Efficiency in Standards for Household Appliances," *The Energy Journal* 1, no. 4 (1980): 21–40 (*https://doi.org/10.5547/issn0195-6574-ej-vol1-no4-2*).

Efficiency does not also limit the impacts that lie outside the datacenter walls: the carbon and water embedded in chip fabrication, the toxic burdens of mineral extraction, the surge of e-waste when hardware is retired early to chase the next marginal improvement. Even a perfectly run server powered by renewables still sits on a global supply chain of emissions and ecological damage.[33]

The main point to bear in mind for the remainder of the book is that *efficiency is a necessary condition for sustainable AI, but it is not sufficient*. It lowers immediate emissions and proves that smarter practice is possible, but without complementary measures that look beyond resource consumption, efficiency can take us only so far in the journey toward sustainable AI.

TL;DR

So far, I have presented the context for how sustainability and AI intersect to shape our rapidly changing world. This book will explore a wide array of techniques that will help us identify resource bottlenecks in AI systems, improve upon these inefficiencies, and work toward green and ultimately sustainable AI. To do that we have to look closely at each of the complex steps involved in the algorithmic lifecycle of a DL model, as shown in Figure 1-10. I devote a chapter to each of these steps.

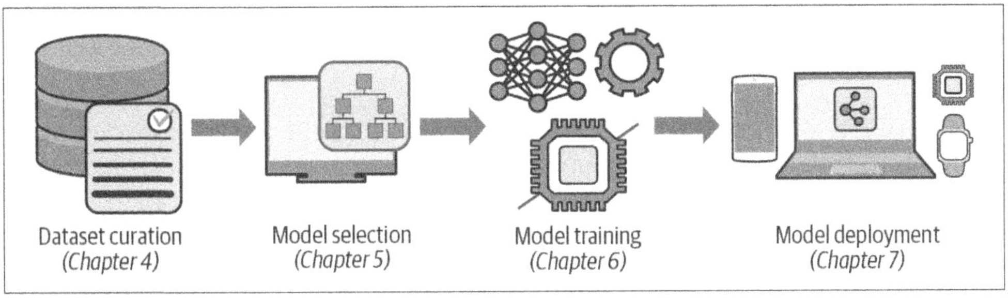

Figure 1-10. A typical AI model lifecycle.

You may already have some questions; I will try to preempt them with short answers and, in doing so, present the book's outline:

Do I have to be a machine learning expert to read the rest of the book?
: *No, but I am assuming you are an ML/AI practitioner with working knowledge and keen interest in these methods.*

  Chapter 2 aims to explore some key ML concepts to look at the foundations of AI. We will use the perspective of *representation learning*, a view of AI where

33 Dustin Wright et al., "Efficiency Is Not Enough: A Critical Perspective of Environmentally Sustainable AI," *Communications of the ACM* 68. no. 7 (2025): 62–9 (*https://doi.org/10.1145/3724500*).

algorithms learn useful features from data. This will be the basis for Chapter 2, which, while intended to be an introduction to key ML concepts, is far from comprehensive. But we will look at the relevant topics with an eye on resource consumption. I have not shied away from using mathematical notations, as they make the presentation of some of the concepts later easier. However, I have tried hard to not lose any readers who might not want to follow the notations with equivalent descriptions everywhere.

How do we know if the tools in this book are actually making AI more sustainable?
Sustainability is difficult to measure. But, we can use proxies that can measure resource efficiency.

Chapter 3 will introduce commonly used measures that give insight into the resource consumption of AI models. We will understand the pros and cons of measuring runtime, energy consumption, and carbon emissions. We will try some easy-to-use tools that can help us better quantify the resource consumption of AI in standardized ways. This chapter will also introduce the key concept of *AI waste*, which we will use to identify wasteful resource usage in different steps of the AI lifecycle. For instance, AI waste can manifest as training a massive model from scratch when using a smaller, pretrained model would have sufficed.

Do we always need big data to build AI models?
Some would say so. However, not all data is equally useful, and knowing this can reduce data-related costs significantly.

Availability of cheap, large-scale data has resulted in the use of more data than what might be needed to solve any given task. This abundance mindset has resulted in a lot of data-related redundancies. The process of dataset curation consists of collecting, cleaning, labeling, and preprocessing data to prepare it for training. Chapter 4 will elaborate on efficient dataset curation practices, show techniques to compress data points, and explain how to distill information in a given dataset into a few data points.

How do we decide if one model is more efficient than another?
Simpler models tend to be more efficient, but they may not perform well compared to a more complex model. Choosing models that offer the right trade-off might be the way to go.

Choosing the right class of model or its configuration is an elaborate procedure. This is dependent on the problem domain, the amount of data that is available, and the resources at our disposal. In Chapter 5 we will formalize the exploration of ML models and configurations, and then use existing techniques to efficiently explore this space so that we can identify the right model and configuration that offers the best trade-off between performance and resource consumption. The notion of Pareto optimality will be a key concept that will drive the discourse in this chapter.

Some recent models are trained for months. Is this always the case?

Yes, for the most recent class of frontier AI models such as the ones behind generative AI (GenAI). However, a broad array of very useful AI models can be trained way faster.

Model training can be one of the most resource-intensive steps. This is by design as the model parameters are updated iteratively until the model captures the desired input-output relations in the training data. Chapter 6 will cover a broad set of methods that can accelerate model training. This can be done either by "mimicking" knowledge from already trained models or by reducing the number of computations performed by modulating the number of bits being used. Recent AI models require more specialized ways to accelerate their training, which will also be discussed.

Using a model at inference does not seem expensive, compared to training it. How is model use contributing to AI being resource-intensive?

Training is done once, but models can be used millions of times. Depending on how successful a model is, its usage cost can outweigh development costs.

AI models are developed with the hope they will be used, and used widely. Once this happens, even if the energy consumption and carbon emission for a single use is small, this can become significant at scale. Chapter 7 will aim to model when the training and inference costs cross over for models. The chapter will also build upon the efficient training techniques in Chapter 6 and specialize them for deployment or inference scenarios. We'll also answer questions about how to adapt models across programming languages and hardware platforms.

As an ML/AI practitioner, I can tweak algorithms. How can this influence the resource efficiency of the AI hardware?

Underutilization of hardware is a chronic issue in AI. Many algorithmic tweaks can improve the resource efficiency of hardware.

Most recent AI models require specialized hardware for faster development. These come at huge costs (monetary and environmental) but are underutilized due to several factors. Chapter 8 will explore some easy-to-implement strategies to better utilize hardware, ranging from single computers to datacenters. That being said, there are challenges that cannot be fixed by algorithms alone. For example, e-waste is not something that can be optimized away. We will discuss these hardware-related points in depth in Chapter 8.

Building AI models involves many tedious steps. Is there a cascading effect of resource inefficiency that could percolate between steps?

Yes, certainly. AI models are developed in a long sequence of steps; poor choices in one step can blow up the resource consumption down the line.

Figures 1-6 and 1-10 show the elaborate lifecycle of recent AI models. Each of these steps requires considerable resources, and one of the main arguments of this book is that there are wasteful resource allocations everywhere. Chapter 9 points out that choices made at one step can have a huge impact down the line. Using concepts derived from systems engineering and ML operations, this chapter introduces frameworks that can be used to holistically manage and improve the resource consumption of AI models.

Let's say we do all this. Can we achieve sustainable AI?

This question lies at the heart of the matter, and the answer is necessarily complex.

CHAPTER 2
Under the Hood of Generative AI

In the 2004 science-fiction movie *I, Robot*, there is a memorable scene where the human protagonist derisively asks a humanoid robot, "Can a robot write a symphony? Can a robot turn a canvas into a beautiful masterpiece?" The robot responds, "Can you?" and the protagonist's face turns pale in response.

We have considered the arts such as creative writing, painting, and composing music as the highest feats of human intelligence. We have ascribed machines to be good at more "mechanical" tasks like crunching big numbers or doing repetitive tasks. That is, until the recent revolution of generative AI (GenAI), which has brought us to fundamentally question what it means to create. Models like ChatGPT can generate text,[1] Stable Diffusion can generate images in artistic styles,[2] and MusicLM can generate songs.[3] Whether the output of these GenAI models is comparable to human creativity is being disputed from both technical and philosophical standpoints, as it should be.[4] In this book we're concerned with the material resources necessary to develop AI models like the ones behind GenAI, and their impact on sustainability.[5]

1 Tom B. Brown et al., "Language Models Are Few-Shot Learners," *arXiv.org*, May 28, 2020 (*https://arxiv.org/abs/2005.14165*).

2 Robin Rombach et al., "High-Resolution Image Synthesis With Latent Diffusion Models," *arXiv.org*, December 20, 2021 (*https://arxiv.org/abs/2112.10752*).

3 Andrea Agostinelli et al., "MusicLM: Generating Music From Text," *arXiv.org*, January 26, 2023 (*https://arxiv.org/abs/2301.11325*).

4 Emily M. Bender, "Resisting Dehumanization in the Age of 'AI,'" *Current Directions in Psychological Science* 33, no. 2 (2024): 114–20 (*https://doi.org/10.1177/09637214231217286*).

5 Bakhtiarifard et al., "Climate and Resource Awareness Is Imperative to Achieving Sustainable AI (and Preventing a Global AI Arms Race)" (*https://arxiv.org/abs/2502.20016*).

To assess the environmental sustainability of AI models, including GenAI, we first need to understand these models. And fundamental concepts from ML are essential to do this. Furthermore, improving the resource efficiency of AI models requires a careful analysis of several underlying technical phenomena. The objective of this chapter is to present a high-level overview of some relevant fundamental ML concepts. Specifically, this chapter will introduce core concepts, key terminologies, and common notations. Equipped with this background, we can delve deeper into the wide range of methods presented in the remaining chapters.

There are plenty of introductory resources offering a thorough overview of ML concepts. We'll attempt to take the shortest path to understanding the core principles behind GenAI models. This can be achieved in many ways; however, I will take up the view of *representation learning*, which broadly means learning useful and, in most cases, compact features of data, as the path to understanding recent developments in GenAI.[6] To understand why training these models consumes so much energy, we first need to look at how they learn to process information.

Representation Learning

Consider how colors—a property of the physical world—are represented in computers. Inspired by the human color perception, they are represented as different extents of red (R), green (G), and blue (B), in the common RGB format. The standard representation uses 256 levels to represent each of the colors so that the vector [255,0,0] represents pure red, [0,0,255] represents blue, and other combinations capture different colors, as shown in the color map in Figure 2-1.[7] Each color is mapped to a unique encoding represented in different predefined formats, either as a combination of red-green-blue (RGB) values or as a single value (HEX). While Figure 2-1 works best in color, the grayscaled version also captures the inherent usefulness of such a space, wherein instead of different colors we can traverse the intensity of all the shades of gray.

Formulating numerical representations of physical properties, in a way that also makes semantic sense, is quintessential to using algorithms in the real world.

6 Yoshua Bengio et al., "Representation Learning: A Review and New Perspectives," *arXiv.org*, June 24, 2012 (*https://arxiv.org/abs/1206.5538*).

7 Using unsigned 8 bits results in $2^8 = 256$ levels.

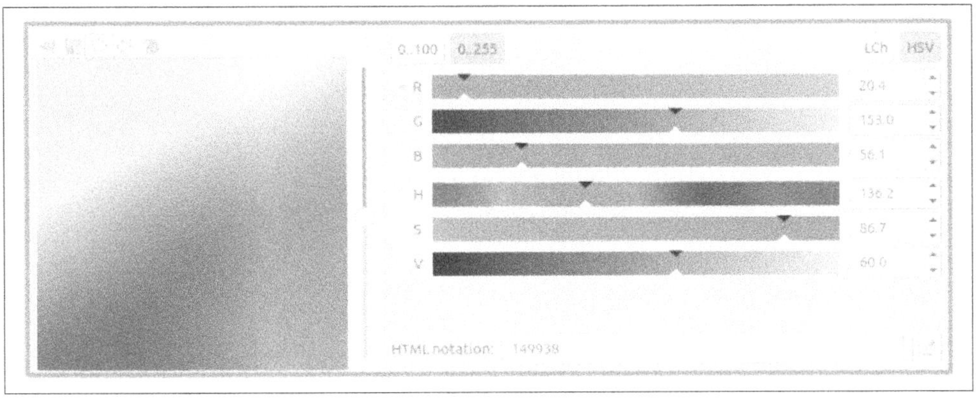

Figure 2-1. A color palette showing the encoding for different colors. Color palettes like this are designed by standards organizations such as World Wide Web Consortium (W3C). (See the full-color version online) (https://oreil.ly/figure_0201).

Overview of Representation Spaces

Figure 2-1 maps a physical property like color into a numerical space. These representations were *designed* by standards organizations and are used widely. In machine learning terminology, these would be called *hand-crafted features*, wherein domain experts come up with mappings that best capture the property of interest.

Representation Spaces and Their Properties

Figure 2-1 is an example of *representation spaces*.[8] For these representation spaces to be meaningful, they should satisfy some basic properties.

First, the points that are close in this space should have similar properties compared to distant points. For example, the points within the red region are more similar than the points in the blue region. This translates into the representation space having a notion of *distance*. Two points with small Euclidean distance are more similar than two points with larger Euclidean distance.

Furthermore, there is a smooth transition between any two points in the space. Consider any two points in this space; if you were to draw a straight line between these two points, the colors along the line would change smoothly.

8 Representation spaces are also known as *embedding spaces* or *latent spaces*. I will try to stick to using representation spaces as it is close to the idea of representation learning we are after.

These properties endow the representation space with a metric so that arithmetic manipulation of the points of the space is possible, which makes the space extremely useful.

But, how far can these representation spaces be expanded? Can we *design* spaces that represent more complex data like human faces, language, or molecules, as shown in Figure 2-2?

Designing hand-crafted features for complex data, such as the types shown in Figure 2-2, is not straightforward. For example, the bulk of early research in computer vision focused on developing expressive representations for images. These ranged from using well-thought-out filters for edge detection, operators for texture enhancement, or sophisticated filters like the wavelets.[9] ML methods, particularly the ones based on DL, offer flexible ways to *learn representations from data* instead of features designed by hand.

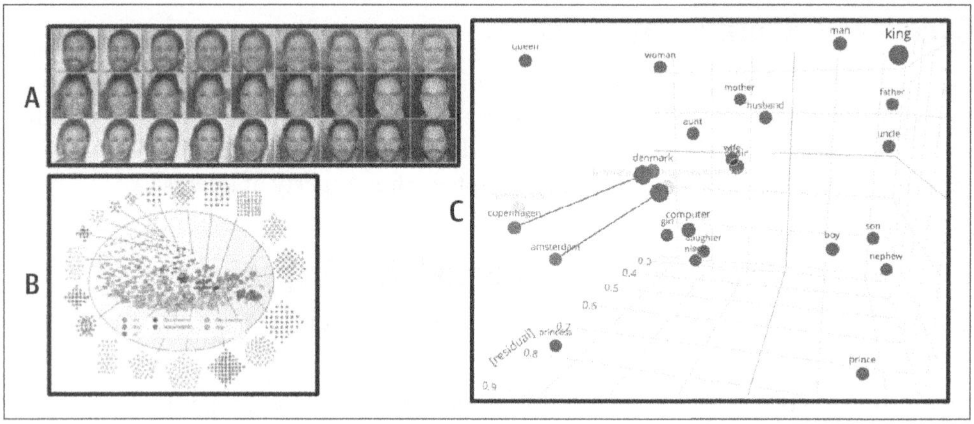

Figure 2-2. Some learned representations using DL methods. (Source: A. Human face interpolation from SpaceSheet (https://oreil.ly/q8RHy); B. Embedding of nanomolecules from DeepStruc (https://doi.org/10.1039/D2DD00086E); C. Vector representation of words using Word Embedding (https://oreil.ly/2CJQn).)

Learning Representation Spaces

Domain experts designed the RGB color space for it to be generally useful. Designing similar expressive spaces for other types of data can be cumbersome, if not impossible. Instead, *learned* representation spaces turn this idea on its head. Rather than defining the axes of the space manually, we let a trainable model discover them based on the structure of the data using representation learning. The goal of representation

9 Rafael C. Gonzalez and Richard E. Woods, *Digital Image Processing*, 3rd ed. (Prentice-Hall, 2006).

learning is to capture the essence of each data point in a way that is useful for some downstream task like classification, generation, clustering, etc.

There are many approaches to perform representation learning. However, the most commonly used method, which is quite powerful, uses a class of DL models known as *autoencoders*; these models can be interpreted as nonlinear versions of principal component analysis (PCA; see "Principal component analysis" on page 99 for more).[10] Figure 2-3 depicts an autoencoder implemented as a cascade of two neural networks: encoder and decoder. The *encoder* network compresses the input data into a lower-dimensional vector (also known as latent code), which is akin to mapping colors to RGB values. The *decoder* network, on the other hand, maps the learned latent code back to the original data.

Encoder and decoder blocks are typically implemented using deep neural networks (see "Tour of Neural Architectures" on page 31). The autoencoder learns to map the high-dimensional input data into lower-dimensional representation spaces as shown in the center. The spaces are constrained so that they can capture essential properties of the data that correspond to useful features like the RGB color map for colors.

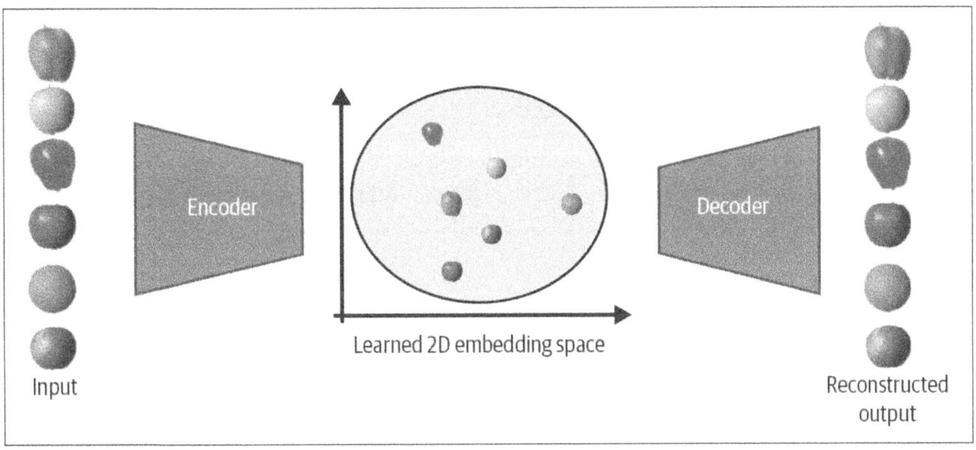

Figure 2-3. Schematic of an autoencoder shown here with the encoder and decoder blocks.

To illustrate, the autoencoder in Figure 2-3 is tasked to learn compact representations of a bunch of images of apples and oranges. Suppose we constrain the representation space to just two dimensions, i.e., we have asked the model to map every apple and orange image as a point in a 2D space. As the input data is in higher dimensions

10 Mark A. Kramer, "Nonlinear Principal Component Analysis Using Autoassociative Neural Networks," *AIChE Journal* 37, no. 2 (1991): 233–43 (*https://doi.org/10.1002/aic.690370209*).

compared to the 2D latent dimension, these methods are known as *undercomplete autoencoders*.[11]

By training the encoder-decoder pair to reconstruct images of apples and oranges from the latent code, we force the encoder to learn a compact 2D representation that can be used to map images of apples and oranges to vectors. If the training set includes many varied images of apples and oranges, consisting of different colors, shapes, and lighting conditions, the model *could* learn:

Dimension 1
: Something akin to color hue, spanning from redder apples to more orange-like hues. This dimension is not "red" or "orange" per se but a direction in the representation space that correlates with the dominant color needed to reconstruct the image.

Dimension 2
: Shape, capturing smooth roundness versus slightly irregular contours.

Note that the autoencoder can't attach any semantic labels to these dimensions that align with human concepts, such as "appleness" or "orangeness." But we might observe that apple images cluster in one part of the space and oranges in another, not because the model was told to separate them, but because it *had to* to represent them effectively with only two degrees of freedom.[12]

Now returning to the examples of human faces, words, and molecules, in Figure 2-2, autoencoders can also be used to learn representations for more complex data by choosing appropriate encoder and decoder networks.

Learning Representations to GenAI

Building on the intuition from "Learning Representation Spaces" on page 24, we will next take a closer look at autoencoders. This will be essential to appreciate how the recent class of GenAI models function.

Autoencoders

Autoencoders embed complex, high-dimensional data into a low-dimensional representation space. Choosing the appropriate design and structure of the low-dimensional space decides the usefulness of the learned representations. Central to

11 Ian Goodfellow et al., "Autoencoders," in *Deep Learning* (MIT Press, 2015) (*https://oreil.ly/AAruB*).

12 Works like Voynov et al. (2020) (*https://oreil.ly/hRRUm*) and Schön et al. (2022) (*https://doi.org/10.1007/978-3-031-18576-2_3*) provide ways to explore latent spaces of autoencoders and discover concepts that make sense.

this is the question of *regularization*:[13] should the latent space be left unconstrained, or should it be forced to adhere to some constraints (like shape or to match a known probability distribution)? The difference between either not regularizing or regularizing the representation space decides what types of applications the autoencoder can be used for.

Unregularized autoencoders

As the name suggests, unregularized autoencoders are trained primarily with no constraints on the representation space itself. Their main objective is to map input data into a low-dimensional space and then reconstruct the input data with high fidelity, i.e., to minimize the reconstruction error. An image of an apple could be mapped to some fixed point, say *(1.7, -3.2)*; an orange might be mapped to *(4.1, 2.0)*. The encoding of each image in the latent space is optimized for that image alone. The model becomes adept at remembering where the input data was mapped to in the representation space so that the decoder can reverse the mapping. The encoding in these autoencoders is deterministic, like in a code book.

You could think of this deterministic mapping as throwing of darts into the representation space, wherein each data point is likely to be mapped to a unique point in the low-dimensional embedding space. If we continue with this dart-throwing analogy, darts are inherently isolated; they do not influence the regions in the neighboring space. This means the representation space in an unregularized autoencoder often becomes arbitrary and unstructured. Two points may lie close together in Euclidean terms but could represent semantically distant objects. Worse, most of the latent space is effectively empty. This is of particular importance if we try to decode (or generate new data) from these unused regions, as the decoder is likely to produce garbage.

Figure 2-4 (left) illustrates this where decoding the interpolated latent code between the oval and the spherical apples might not result in reasonable data. In an unregularized autoencoder, each input data point is mapped, deterministically, to a single point the representation space. This effectively leaves empty regions that, when decoded using the decoder, can result in infeasible data. Regularized autoencoders, Figure 2-4 (right), cover the representation space with probability distributions instead of point maps and fill the empty regions. Regularized autoencoders are better suited for generative tasks.

This form of point-wise embedding of data in the embedding space has its utility: if the task is compression or reconstruction without generative intent, dart-like

13 Loosely speaking, regularization controls how regular or irregular the representation space will be. Higher regularization should typically yield more regular or smoother spaces.

embeddings suffice. They allow for tight, dense encoding of individual inputs. However, they offer little in terms of generalization or semantic continuity.

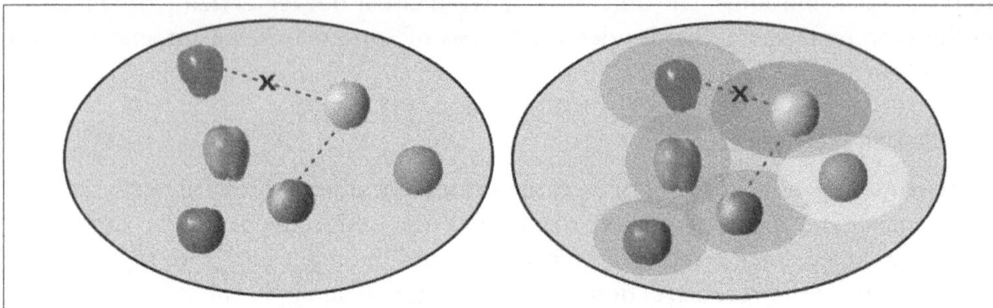

Figure 2-4. Unregularized and regularized autoencoders.

Regularized autoencoders

Regularized autoencoders try to induce regular structure to the representation space. They typically don't map each input data point to a single point in the representation space, but they map each point to a region of the latent space centered around a point with a certain spread. This can be thought of as throwing a paintball instead of a dart. Instead of landing in a sharp point, the mapping splashes and smears across the space. Specifically, in regularized autoencoders like *variational autoencoders* (VAEs) the latent space is constrained to be a spherical Gaussian, and each point is embedded using a Gaussian density with a certain mean and variance. The additional penalty term known as the *regularization loss* ensures that the embedding space is constrained to a regular structure.[14] Figure 2-4 (right) illustrates this "smeared" representation space for the apples and oranges example.

What does this smearing of the representation space achieve? First, it forces the space to be continuous (with no "holes"). Nearby points in the space are likely to decode into semantically similar images. The smearing effect of the paintball-like mapping ensures that the decoder sees a neighborhood of latent codes for each input, not just a single dart point. This builds interpolation capacity and generative potential into the very geometry of the representation space.

Imagine now interpolating between an apple paintball and an orange paintball, shown in Figure 2-4 (right). The transition can be smoother, and the decoder responds with plausible intermediate forms. This is possible only because the latent space has been filled in, by regularization.

14 Diederik P. Kingma and Max Welling, "Auto-Encoding Variational Bayes," *arXiv.org*, December 20, 2013 (*https://arxiv.org/abs/1312.6114*).

Large Language Models

Autoencoders like the VAEs we just discussed cover (or regularize) the representation space by mapping each data point to a probability distribution. The recent class of large language models (LLMs) and foundation models take a slightly different route to achieve a similar outcome. Rather than smoothing the space through explicit regularization, LLMs are trained on such vast corpora that the sheer density of training examples effectively saturates the representation space. To return to the dartboard analogy, an LLM trained on astronomical volumes of data floods the board with so many darts that gaps mostly cease to exist.[15]

This is not smoothing by design but smoothing by *coverage*. Large-scale models like LLMs, under the pressure to generalize across millions of subtly different contexts, must place even rare or ambiguous inputs in densely populated semantic neighborhoods. The result is a *quasi-continuous representation space*, where interpolation, analogy, and compositional reasoning are not just plausible but statistically reinforced. Figure 2-5 depicts the representation space that is densely covered for the apples and oranges example. The space is filled by sheer volume of the data, unlike in VAEs where each data point is mapped to a probability distribution. While some regions are better covered, others not as well. Decoding from regions that are not covered results in "hallucinations" in GenAI models.

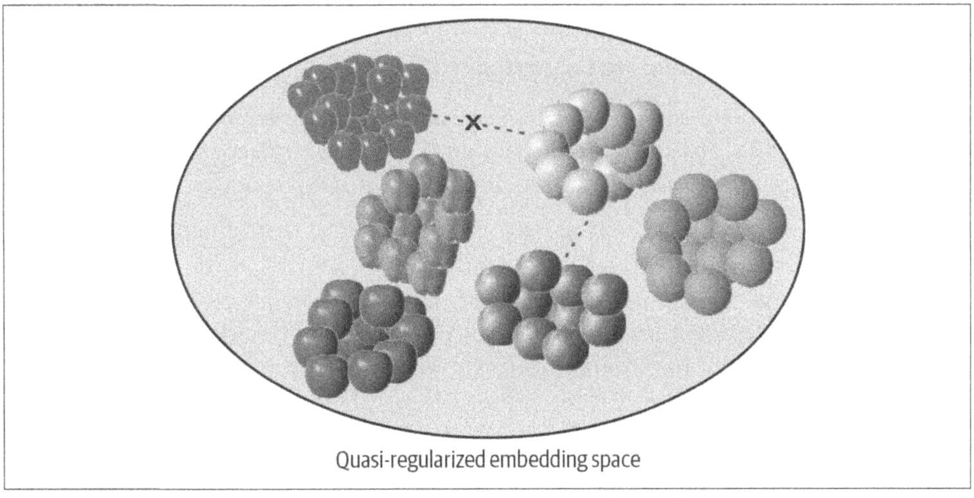

Figure 2-5. A quasi-continuous representation space achieved by mapping vast amounts of training data.

15 Brown et al., "Language Models Are Few-Shot Learners" (*https://arxiv.org/abs/2005.14165*).

In this view, the scale (of data) becomes its own form of regularization. It fills the space not by spreading out each point but by making sure everywhere is somewhere and that there are enough darts to make the entire representation space habitable, navigable, and semantically meaningful.

Multimodal Generative Models

In the previous sections we have seen how different concepts like images and text can be embedded into representation spaces using autoencoder-like models. However, in our examples we have primarily focused on single modality autoencoders, i.e., either models that map images or text that maps images into representation spaces. *Multimodal generative models*, on the other hand, try to map data from different modalities (see "Data Modalities" on page 32 for details on data modalities) into a common representation space.

Multimodal generative models are trained on combinations of text, images, audio, video, and so on. Now, not only is the representation space filled with embeddings from a single modality, but mappings from different modalities are fused in the same common representation space.[16] Figure 2-6 illustrates this idea, wherein data from different modalities are encoded using modality-specific encoders into the same representation space. Additional constraints during training *align* these representations so that the concept from one modality can match the same concept in another modality. As an example, the word *apple* should align with the image of an apple or the speech recording of someone saying *apple*.

Modality-specific encoders are used to map raw data into vectors that are further aligned across modalities using additional constraints. The decoder can map from one modality to another, resulting in capabilities like text-to-image or image-to-video generation.

The fused space becomes smooth and continuous due to the scale of multimodal training data. As with training LLMs, recent multimodal generative models require vast training datasets consisting of paired examples between modalities. This results in the quasi-continuous representation space, now fused with representations from different modalities.

This is the key reason why multimodal models can generate a caption for a novel image or infer the next action in a video from text, or ground language in vision. The fused multimodal representation space is entangled across modalities and makes the generation of data based on input from one modality to another feasible.

16 Alec Radford et al., "Learning Transferable Visual Models From Natural Language Supervision," *arXiv.org*, February 26, 2021 (*https://arxiv.org/abs/2103.00020*).

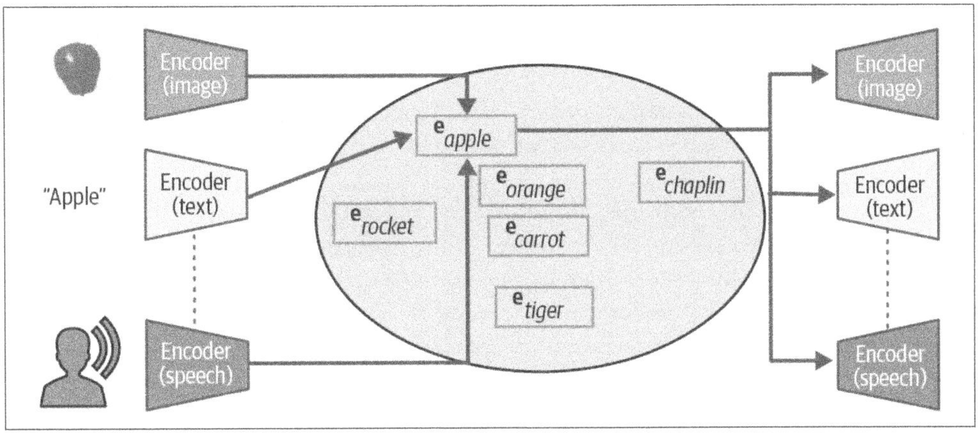

Figure 2-6. A multimodal representation space showing how the representations for similar concepts align to the same vector in the common representation space.

Tour of Neural Architectures

Complex DL models like autoencoders (see "Autoencoders" on page 26) learn compact and useful representations of the data. Depending on the type of data, different neural network architectures can be used to build the autoencoders. For example, a DL model that can handle images might not be well-suited to encode text, or vice versa. Figure 2-7 shows an overview of commonly encountered data modalities mapped to categories of ML methods. The suggestions for which methods are useful is based on the historical development of these methods. While almost all methods can be applied to all modalities with modifications, only some offer appropriate inductive biases that are better suited for any given modality.

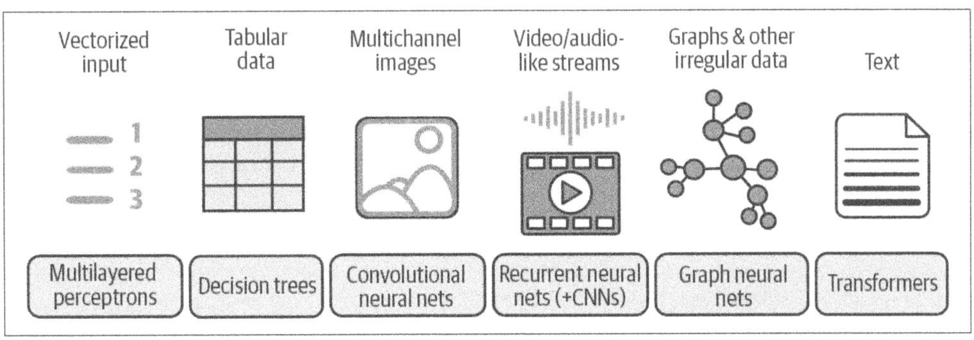

Figure 2-7. Commonly encountered data modalities in ML, loosely ordered based on the complexity of modeling them using ML methods.

Data Modalities

The simplest way to describe a data point is as a vector consisting of descriptive numerical features. For example, a color input to an ML model can be provided as a vector with three elements (for RGB values). For more complex objects, additional features can be enumerated resulting in *feature vectors* that describe any given data point. These were, and still are, some of the easiest types of data to obtain. And almost any other data type can be converted into feature vectors. For example, when dealing with images, properties such as average intensity, contrast, histogram, and so on, can be enumerated into long feature vectors. Or as is more common in deep learning, the pixel information itself can be enumerated as a long feature vector by flattening images. Say we are dealing with an image of resolution 32 × 32; then all 1,024 pixels can become the feature vector. Figure 2-7 depicts other common forms of data that are ubiquitous, ranging from tabular data, images comprising multiple channels of information, data streams that include audios and videos, irregular or unstructured data that are represented as graphs, and text documents.

Inductive Bias Based on Data Modality

Each data modality has structural characteristics that certain models are naturally better suited to exploit (as indicated in Figure 2-7). Choosing a model based on data modality is effectively a form of inductive bias where practitioners are injecting assumptions about the structure of the data into the learning process. This bias helps constrain the hypothesis space, often making learning more efficient and generalization more reliable, but it can also limit flexibility if the assumptions do not hold.

Neural Network Zoo

Using the lens of data modality, we will next take a look at some of the widely used classes of neural networks. This will follow a similar flow as shown in Figure 2-7 as neural network design has progressed with the hurdles posed by each new commonly encountered data modality. Every time a major type of data dominated the research agenda, the ML research community has tried to embed these requirements into a novel architecture.

Multilayer perceptrons ("Everything is just a vector")

The early successes of supervised learning in applications like credit scoring, handwritten-digit recognition, and basic speech features came from data that could be flattened into rows of numbers with no inherent order among dimensions. Multilayer perceptrons (MLPs) are ideal for such vectorized data and are one of the fundamental artificial neural networks.

The development of MLPs has its origins in the pioneering work on artificial neural networks from the late 1950s. Frank Rosenblatt's groundbreaking paper from the late 1950s introduced the perceptron model, which represented an early form of a single-layer neural network capable of binary classification.[17] Rosenblatt's perceptron was a significant milestone, demonstrating a rudimentary form of learning through supervised training and thereby establishing a foundational framework for subsequent neural network research. The conceptual leap to what we now recognize as MLPs was driven by the introduction of the backpropagation algorithm, discussed in "How to Train Your Model" on page 43. This advancement was detailed in the seminal 1986 paper.[18]

An MLP typically consists of an input layer, one or more hidden layers, and an output layer. Figure 2-8 illustrates an MLP with two hidden layers.

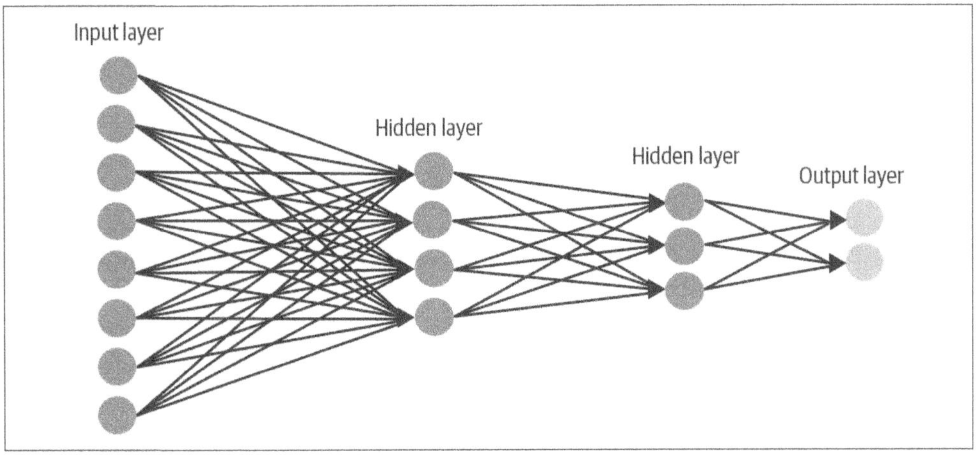

Figure 2-8. A simple MLP with two hidden layers consisting of four neurons and three neurons, acting on an input of size eight to predict two output classes. Each edge weight corresponds to a trainable weight.

If the input is D-dimensional and the MLP has L hidden layers with N_ℓ neurons at each hidden layer ℓ, as well as an output layer with N_{out} neurons, corresponding to the output of the network, the total number of trainable weight parameters is obtained based on the number of connections between successive layers.

17 Frank Rosenblatt, "The Perceptron: A Probabilistic Model for Information Storage and Organization in the Brain," *Psychological Review* 65, no. 6 (1958): 386–408 (*https://oreil.ly/qWmNy*).

18 David E. Rumelhart et al., "Learning Representations by Back-Propagating Errors," *Nature* 323, (October 9, 1986): 533–36 (*https://doi.org/10.1038/323533a0*).

This results in the following:

$$N_{params} = \sum_{\ell=1}^{L+1} (N_\ell \times N_{\ell-1} + N_\ell)$$

The additive term N_ℓ arises due to the bias parameter per layer.

For the MLP in Figure 2-8, the input dimension $D = 8$, it has two hidden layers with $N_1 = 4$ and $N_2 = 3$ neurons, and the output dimension $N_{out} = 2$. Using these values, the number of parameters can be estimated as:

- Weights: $(8 \times 4) + (4 \times 3) + (3 \times 2) = 32 + 12 + 6 = 51$
- Biases: $8 + 4 + 3 = 15$
- Total number of parameters: $51 + 15 = 66$

Convolutional neural networks ("Local patterns repeat everywhere")

Even a modest-resolution image contains tens of thousands of pixels. If we flatten an image into a vector and feed it directly to an MLP, the input layer alone would require an enormous number of parameters. This is because in MLPs the layers are fully connected (see Figure 2-8), and the number of parameters scales linearly with the input dimension (i.e., the number of pixels). For high-dimensional data-like images, this quickly becomes inefficient and computationally expensive.

The development of convolutional neural networks (CNNs) marked a pivotal advancement in the field of computer vision and pattern recognition from image modality. The key innovation of CNNs lies in their use of convolutional layers, pooling layers, and hierarchical feature extraction, which enable the network to learn translation-invariant features.

Convolutional layers typically use small learnable filters that slide across the whole height and width of the image, which is sharing its weights at every location. This *weight sharing* injects two biases. First, *spatial locality*: the network mixes only the information that is near each pixel in the early layers and then gradually builds larger contexts by stacking layers or downsampling intermediate representations with pooling. Second, *translation equivariance*: if input is shifted to the right, the feature map also shifts by the same amount, so the network no longer has to relearn concepts like "cat ears" for every possible location in the image.

The conceptual foundation of CNNs can be traced back to in the late 1980s and early 1990s. The work by LeCun et al.[19] demonstrated the power of convolutional layers to automatically and hierarchically extract spatial hierarchies of features, such as edges, textures, and shapes, directly from raw image data. The LeNet-5 architecture laid the groundwork for more sophisticated CNN models like VGGNet (shown in Figure 2-9) and has had a profound influence on the design and development of modern DL systems.

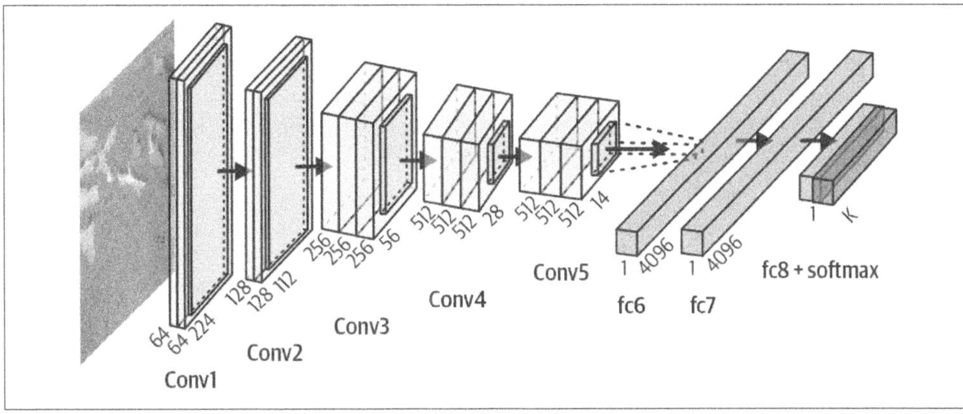

Figure 2-9. A typical CNN like VGGNet downsamples the image (and corresponding feature maps) between layers, while increasing the number of features at each level. The last layer usually is a fully connected layer. (Source: created using code from PlotNeuralNet (https://oreil.ly/PYGx2).)

> **CNN Kernels as MLPs**
>
> Each CNN kernel can be viewed as a small MLP applied to a local patch of the input image, typically called the *receptive field*. Instead of treating the entire image as input like a full MLP would, the CNN slides this localized MLP across spatial positions, sharing the same weights at each step. At each location, the kernel takes the neighborhood pixels, flattens them, and computes a dot product followed by a nonlinearity—just like a single-layer MLP.

Recurrent neural networks ("Yesterday affects today")

Modeling sequential data with temporal ordering such as speech, text, audio waveforms, and sensor read-outs requires a memory of what came before. MLPs and CNNs typically cannot capture these temporal relationships. *Recurrent neural networks* (RNNs) grant that memory by cycling information from the previous time step into the calculation of the next. In the vanilla form of RNN, shown in Figure 2-10, that recurrence multiplies a hidden representation by a single weight matrix again and again, unfolding the loop into a deep chain when viewed across time.[20] Note how at each time step, the input $\mathbf{x}^{(t)}$ is combined with the intermediate

---

20 Jeffrey L. Elman, "Finding Structure in Time," *Cognitive Science* 14, no. 2 (1990): 179–211 (*https://doi.org/10.1207/s15516709cog1402_1*).

representations ($\mathbf{a}^{(t-1)}$) from the previous time step. Also note that the same weight w is used at each time step.

This design mirrors the structure of time-dependent data, where each observation is influenced by past events. The use of shared parameters across time steps gives RNNs the ability to generalize across positions in the sequence, making them efficient and flexible for tasks like language modeling, speech recognition, and time-series prediction, where the temporal order of inputs is essential.

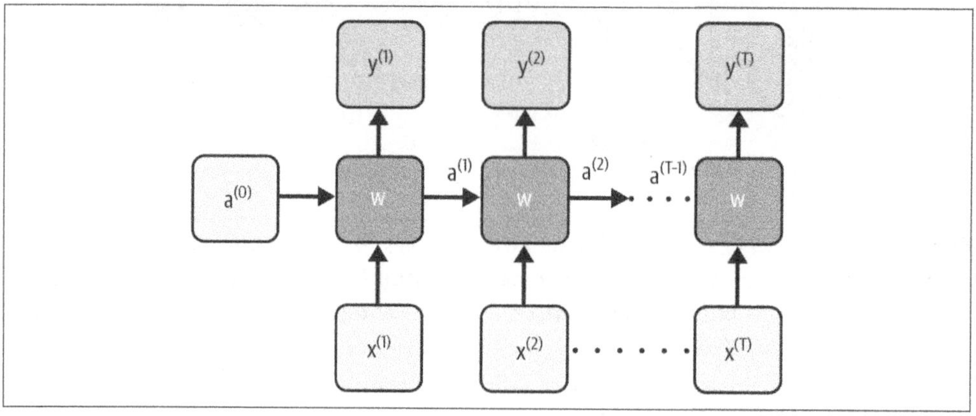

Figure 2-10. A simple RNN unrolled into T time steps.

Unfortunately, updating the model parameters through successive multiplications forces gradients toward zero (vanishing gradients) or toward infinity (exploding gradients). The long short-term memory (LSTM) variant fixes the problem by introducing gates that modulate information flow, letting the network decide what to keep, what to forget, and when to expose its internal "cell" to the outside.[21]

21 Sepp Hochreiter and Jürgen Schmidhuber, "Long Short-Term Memory," *Neural Computation* 9, no. 8 (1997): 1735–80 (*https://doi.org/10.1162/neco.1997.9.8.1735*).

> **RNNs as MLPs**
>
> Consider the vanilla RNN in Figure 2-10, which is unrolled into T steps. We can find an MLP of depth $T + 1$, except that all the hidden layers happen to share weights. At each step, the cell concatenates the current input with the previous hidden state and passes that vector through a linear map plus nonlinearity, which is exactly what a single MLP layer does. The twist is that the same parameters are reused at every time index, injecting a rigid prior: whatever transformation you apply to the first time step you must also apply at time step T or any intermediate ones. In other words, an RNN can also be viewed as an MLP wrapped in a recurrence that ties its layers together, trading parameter efficiency and temporal generalization.

Graph neural networks ("Relationships, not grids")

Social networks, transportation maps, molecules, and several other data sources lack a natural grid or sequence structure. So, the use of CNNs or RNNs might not be straightforward on this graph-structured data. In such cases, the relationship between the different entities is more informative than the ordering of these entities.

Graph neural networks (GNNs) embrace this invariance to ordering (permutation invariance) by passing learnable "messages" along the edges of the graph.[22] In each round of message passing, every node gathers a small vector from its neighbors, aggregates those vectors with an appropriate function such as summation or maximization, and then updates its own state before the next round begins.

Figure 2-11 illustrates one round of message passing and aggregation in a GNN. The change in number of features is shown as the difference in the size of the vectors (rectangles adjacent to each node). Note how different nodes have different aggregate features—depending on the number of neighbors. Repeating the cycle a handful of times allows information from increasingly distant nodes to permeate the graph. Nodes in an L-layered GNN can access information from nodes that are L hops away.

As the same update rule is shared across every edge, the model automatically respects any relabelling or reordering of the nodes. This is an essential symmetry when dealing with graphs such as in chemistry, where swapping two hydrogen atoms should not alter the predicted solubility of a molecule.

22 Thomas N. Kipf and Max Welling, "Semi-Supervised Classification with Graph Convolutional Networks," *arXiv.org*, September 9, 2016 (*https://arxiv.org/abs/1609.02907*).

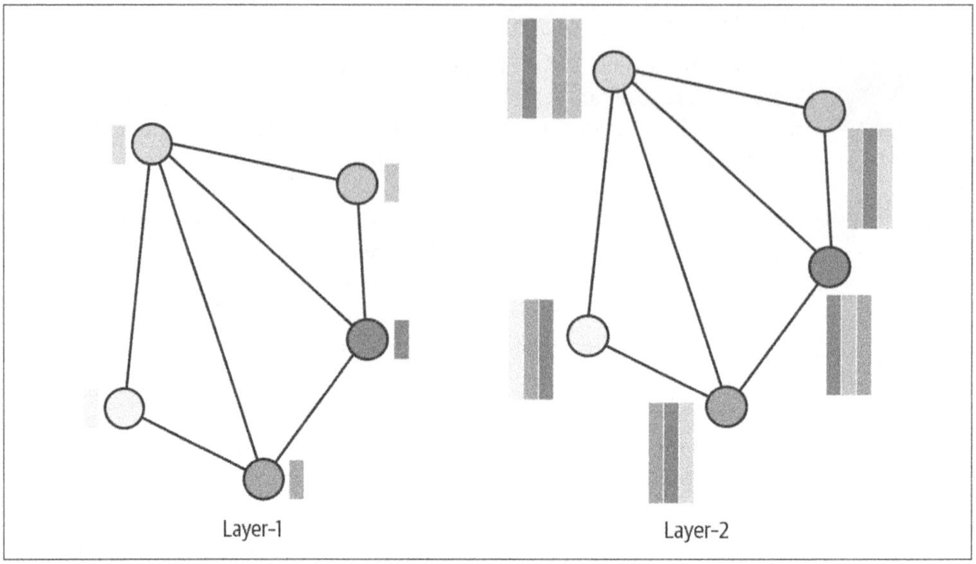

Figure 2-11. The message passing or neighborhood aggregation in GNNs. Features of each node at layer 1 are nonlinearly transformed into a different number of features before aggregation.

Transformers ("Let every token talk to every other token")

Consider the sentence "I decided to duck when I saw the duck flying at my head." The word *duck* appears twice with different meanings, but resolving either one depends on the context found elsewhere in the sentence. As RNNs rely on local temporal interactions (memory of one hidden state), it might guess the first *duck* refers to a bird before seeing the second use, and that early interpretation might persist. GNNs, on the other hand, rely on local structural interactions (localized to neighborhoods in a graph). As a result, a GNN that links each word to only its immediate neighbors would let *duck* talk to *to* and *when*, but not to the more informative *flying* or *head* without deeper layers to propagate signals. Both methods rely on local interactions and require stacked (deep) layers or repeated steps for information to travel across longer ranges.

Transformers take a different approach to accessing such contexts. Instead of restricting updates to adjacent time steps, as in RNNs, or to neighboring nodes, as in GNNs, transformers assume from the outset that any given state (or *token*) might be relevant to any other. Every token is connected to every other through a mechanism called *attention*, which computes learned relevance scores between tokens based on their content.

Each token then updates itself by aggregating information from the rest of the sequence, weighted by these scores. It's like an RNN where each time step has immediate access to the entire sequence, or a GNN operating on a complete graph where the connections adapt to the data at every layer. Figure 2-12 shows this view of transformers, which allows them to model long-range dependencies and subtle contextual relationships from the very first layer, without the bottlenecks of recurrence or local neighborhood propagation. There are additional complexities in how transformers learn, but the high-level abstraction in Figure 2-12 can be a useful intuition to carry forward.

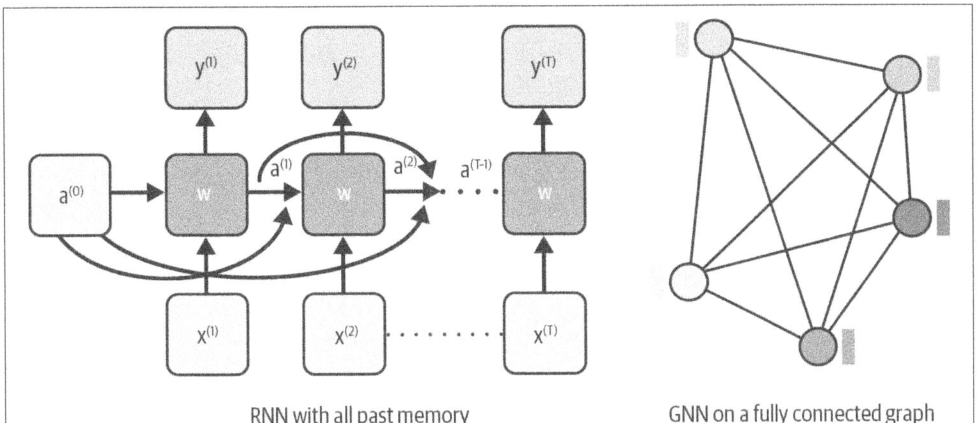

Figure 2-12. A high-level view of transformers as RNNs, where each token is connected to all its previous states, and as a GNN, operating on a fully connected graph.

The introduction of the Transformer architecture truly revolutionized the field of natural language processing and extended its impact to various domains requiring sequential data modeling. Vaswani et al. introduced the Transformer architecture, which departed from traditional CNNs or RNNs by leveraging self-attention mechanisms.[23] Coupled with a robust engineering of the architecture that uses multiple attention heads, layer normalization, and fully connected layers for additional nonlinearities, transformers have proven to be effective in capturing long-range dependencies.

Tokenization makes transformers versatile

Tokenization is the process of breaking down raw input data into a sequence of discrete units or *tokens* that can be mapped into vectors and fed into a model.[24] In language modeling, this usually means splitting text into words or subword units; in

23 Ashish Vaswani et al., "Attention Is All You Need," *arXiv.org*, (June 12, 2017): 5998–6008 (*https://arxiv.org/pdf/1706.03762v5*).

24 Gregory Grefenstette, "Tokenization," in *Syntactic Wordclass Tagging*, ed. H. van Halteren (Springer, 1999), 117–133 (*https://doi.org/10.1007/978-94-015-9273-4_9*).

images, it often involves dividing the image into fixed-size patches; in audio, one might extract short overlapping frames. The goal is to convert structured, often high-dimensional data into a uniform sequence of vectors, making it suitable for models like transformers that expect tokenized inputs.

Importantly, tokenization does not always mean literal chunking of raw data. In images, for instance, a CNN can be used to map a high-resolution input into a grid of patch-level embeddings, effectively producing tokens. Similarly, an MLP can process local regions of an image to generate token-like representations. These CNNs or MLPs act as learnable tokenizers: they don't just extract chunks; they learn to encode local structure into compact, meaningful vectors.

This abstraction of treating all information as vectorized tokens is what makes transformers so versatile. Once inputs are tokenized, a transformer-based model does not need to know whether a token came from language, vision, or speech. It simply operates over the set of tokens using attention. This allows the same transformer architecture to be applied across modalities, and even to combine them. In multimodal tasks like image captioning, visual question answering, or speech-to-text, tokens from different sources can be embedded and fed jointly into a transformer, which then models interactions across them in a unified way. Tokenization, in this sense, is what bridges raw data and the transformer's domain-agnostic attention mechanism. See "Tokenization and Data Efficiency in Modern AI Models" on page 93 for additional details on tokenization schemes.

Quadratic Complexity and Transformers

Transformers scale poorly (in memory and compute) with the number of tokens. The quadratic compute complexity in transformers arises from the attention mechanism, which compares every token in the input with every other token to compute pairwise interactions. If there are N tokens, this means computing scores across all $N \times N$ pairs, which is analogous to operating on a fully connected graph with N^2 edges. Each edge represents a potential flow of information between two tokens, and the model must compute and apply a weight for each one. This dense, all-to-all interaction is what gives transformers their expressive power, but it also leads to quadratic scaling in both compute and memory with respect to sequence length.[25]

25 Feyza Duman Keles et al., "On the Computational Complexity of Self-Attention," *Proceedings of Machine Learning Research* 201 (February 13, 2023): 597–619 (*https://oreil.ly/Ou_nF*).

Formalizing Machine Learning

Before we build on the concepts from "Learning Representations to GenAI" on page 26 and "Tour of Neural Architectures" on page 31 to understand how the new frontier GenAI models are made in "Building GenAI" on page 46, a few more ML concepts warrant a brief discussion. Consider the task of transforming temperature reading from Celsius to Fahrenheit. This conversion is a simple transformation; one way of mathematically representing this is using a model, f_θ:

$$y = f_\theta(x) = 32 + 1.8 \times x$$

where x is the input temperature in Celsius, y is the output temperature in Fahrenheit, and the two model parameters are $\theta = [32,1.8]$. As the relation between the input and output are described linearly, this model belongs to the widely used class of linear models. This can be written more succinctly as the inner product:

$$y = f_\theta(\mathbf{x}) = \ = 1 \cdot \theta_0 + \theta_1 x = \mathbf{x}^T \theta$$

where we have collected the scalars $x_0 = 1, x_1 = x$ into the vector notation $\mathbf{x}$. More generally, linear models that operate any D-dimensional data can be written as:

$$\widehat{\mathbf{y}} = f_\theta(\mathbf{x}) = \sigma\left(\sum_{i=0}^{D} x_i \cdot w_i\right) = \sigma\left(\mathbf{x}^T \theta\right)$$

where the input data is *(D+1)*-dimensional, consisting of D real-valued features and an additional feature, $x_0 = 1$. As a result, the model has (D+1) dimensional trainable parameters including one bias parameter. σ is a nonlinear activation function,[26] the real-valued output $\widehat{\mathbf{y}}$ is obtained by propagating the inner product of the input features and the parameters into the activation function.

Nonlinear Models and Deep Learning

The linear models like $\widehat{\mathbf{y}} = \sigma\left(\mathbf{x}^T \theta\right)$ are the backbone of classical ML. They model the relationship between input and output as a linear relationship. These models work well when that assumption holds. But once the data shows curvature or more complex structure, a linear model falls short.

26 In linear regression, no nonlinear activation is used. However, in logistic regression, the sigmoid function is used as the nonlinear activation.

This is where nonlinear models can be useful. Figure 2-13 shows the linear- and nonlinear-decision boundaries for a complex dataset, and we see that the nonlinear model is able to classify the data correctly. DL offers a rich family of expressive nonlinear models. You can think of DL models as a stack of continuous, nonlinear transformations. Each layer in a deep network applies a function like:

$$f^{(i)}(x) = \sigma\left(\mathbf{x}^T\theta^{(i)}\right)$$

and the network composes these:

$$\hat{\mathbf{y}} = f^{(n)}\left(f^{(n-1)}\left(\cdots f^{(1)}(\mathbf{x})\right)\right)$$

Each layer transforms the data into a new intermediate representation, and as we stack them, the model learns to capture increasingly abstract features. These networks do not rely on predefined features, but they learn them directly from the data.

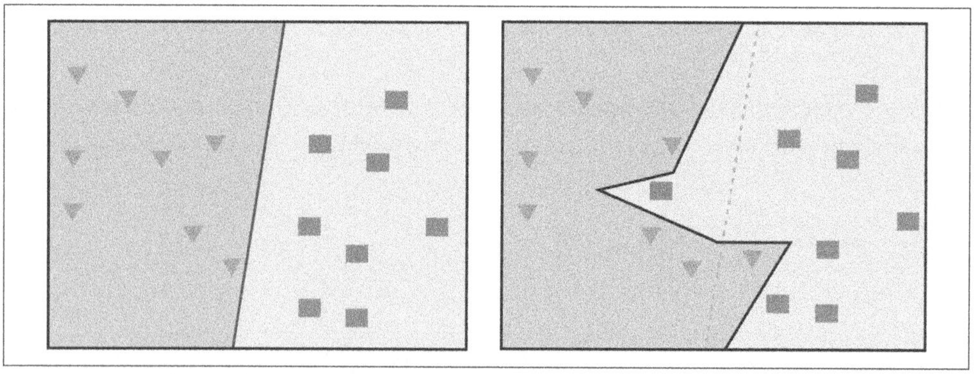

Figure 2-13. A linear boundary between the two classes if the data were linearly separable in a two-dimensional feature space (left). A nonlinear decision boundary (solid, jagged line) as the data here can't be resolved by a linear model (dashed, straight line) in two dimensions (right).

DL models like the ones presented in "Tour of Neural Architectures" on page 31 are generally overparameterized. That is, they often use more parameters than number of training examples, which at first seems like a recipe for overfitting.[27] But when trained on large enough datasets, they have shown to generalize remarkably well.

27 Overfitting is the phenomenon when any ML model learns the noise or random fluctuations in the training data instead of the underlying pattern, making it perform well on that data but poorly on unseen data. It's like memorizing answers for an exam rather than understanding the material.

How to Train Your Model

We have looked at simple linear models to more complex DL models, all without explicitly discussing how these models learn, or conversely, how to train them. So, how does one go about adjusting or training these parameters so that the input-output relations can be captured from the data? How does one train the autoencoder described in "Learning Representation Spaces" on page 24 to perform representation learning? How are GenAI models like Llama and GPT trained?

Surprisingly, the answer to all these questions is some variant of the *gradient descent* algorithm, which is a widely used optimization method in ML and beyond.

Gradient descent

Let's return to our running example of the temperature conversion model. We already know the true relationship between x and y:

$$y = 32 + 1.8x$$

But imagine we don't know this relation and would like to estimate a model based on N noisy measurements that we have collected in the dataset $\mathscr{D}:\{x_i,y_i\}_{i=1}^{N}$. We can model this using a simple linear model:

$$\hat{y} = \theta_0 + \theta_1 x$$

where θ_0 and θ_1 are the parameters (intercept and slope of the linear model) that we want to learn. To do this, we define a loss function $\mathscr{L}$ that measures how far off our predictions $\hat{y}$ are from the true values y. A common choice is mean squared error (MSE):

$$\mathscr{L}(\theta) = \frac{1}{N}\sum_{i=1}^{N}(\hat{y}_i - y_i)^2 = \frac{1}{N}\sum_{i=1}^{N}\left((\theta_0 + \theta_1 x) - y_i\right)^2$$

The goal of optimization is to obtain the parameters θ_0,θ_1 that minimize the loss function:

$$\hat{\theta} = \arg\min_{\theta} \mathscr{L}(\theta)$$

Gradient descent, as the name suggests, starts from a random set of θ parameters and adjusts them so that it descends by following the gradient of the loss landscape. In Figure 2-14, the loss landscape over a broad range of parameters is shown along with the trajectory taken by the optimization algorithm to reach the optimum. The optimization descends along the negative gradient to reach the optimum.

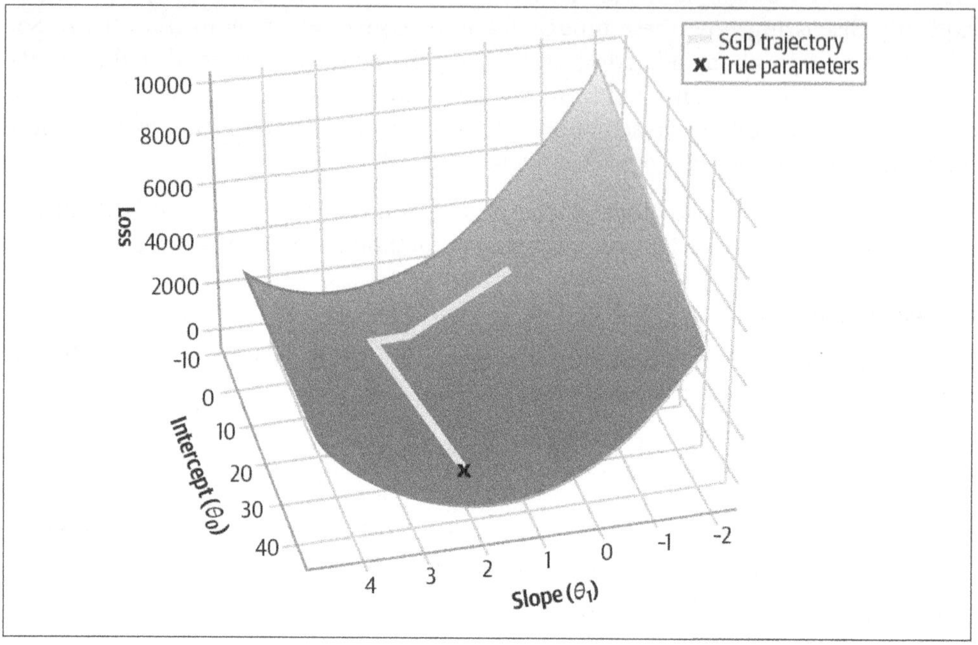

Figure 2-14. Stochastic gradient descent for the temperature conversion model.

Technically, at each iteration, we compute the partial derivatives of $\mathscr{L}$ with respect to θ_0 and θ_1:

$$\frac{\partial \mathscr{L}}{\partial \theta_0} = \frac{2}{N}\sum_{i=1}^{N}((\theta_0 + \theta_1 x) - y_i); \quad \frac{\partial \mathscr{L}}{\partial \theta_1} = \frac{2}{N}\sum_{i=1}^{N}(\theta_1(\theta_0 + \theta_1 x) - y_i)$$

Then we update θ_0 and θ_1 in the *negative* direction of the gradients (to minimize the loss):

$$\theta_0 \leftarrow \theta_0 - \alpha\frac{\partial \mathscr{L}}{\partial \theta_0}; \quad \theta_1 \leftarrow \theta_1 - \alpha\frac{\partial \mathscr{L}}{\partial \theta_1}$$

Here, α is the *learning rate*, usually a small number that controls how big each step is when descending in the loss landscape.

Over many iterations, these updates guide the model parameters θ_0 and θ_1 toward values that make our predicted temperatures $\hat{y}$ closely match the actual Fahrenheit values. In this case, at convergence, gradient descent should steer θ_0 toward 32 and θ_1

toward 1.8—recovering the true conversion formula from data. This is demonstrated in Figure 2-14 and Example 2-1.

Example 2-1. Python code illustrating gradient descent algorithm for the temperature conversion model

```
import numpy as np

# Ground truth parameters
true_w = 1.8
true_b = 32

# Generate data
np.random.seed(42)
celsius = np.random.uniform(-20, 40, size=100)
noise = np.random.normal(0, 2.0, size=100)
fahrenheit = true_w * celsius + true_b + noise

# Initialize model parameters
theta0 = np.random.randn()
theta1 = np.random.randn()

# Training config
lr = 0.001
epochs = 10000
trajectory = [(theta0, theta1)]

# Training loop
for _ in range(epochs):
    y_pred = theta0 + theta1 * celsius
    grad_theta0 = np.mean(2 * (y_pred - fahrenheit))
    grad_theta1 = np.mean(2 * (y_pred - fahrenheit) * celsius)
    theta0 -= lr * grad_theta0
    theta1 -= lr * grad_theta1
    trajectory.append((theta1, theta0))

print("At convergence: theta_0 = %.2f, theta_1 = %.2f"%(theta0,theta1))
```

Depending on the random initialization, the model should converge to a value close to the ground truth values with output similar to:

```
At convergence: theta_0 = 32.12, theta_1 = 1.78
```

Stochastic gradient descent

The gradient descent algorithm we just discussed is more commonly known as the *batch gradient descent* algorithm, where the model parameters are updated using the gradient of the loss function using the *entire* training dataset. This can be computationally expensive, especially for large datasets, because it requires processing all data points before making any updates.

Stochastic gradient descent (SGD), on the other hand, uses one random data point (or a small random subset, called *mini-batch gradient descent*) at a time to compute the gradient. This means that instead of waiting to compute the gradient over the entire dataset, parameter updates are much faster. For each data point (or mini-batch), the model parameters θ are updated based on a noisy estimate of the gradient:

$$\theta \leftarrow \theta - \eta \cdot \nabla_\theta \mathscr{L}(x_i, y_i)$$

where $\nabla_\theta \mathscr{L}(x_i, y_i)$ is the gradient of the loss function $\mathscr{L}$ with respect to the parameters θ, computed using a single training example (x_i, y_i).

Note that each update to model parameters happens after processing just one data point, rather than the entire dataset in SGD with the batch size equal to 1. Depending on how and how often the parameters of a model are updated, there are several advanced SGD algorithms in use, with improved convergence properties.[28]

Automatic Differentiation: The Secret Sauce of Deep Learning

SGD or its variants are used to optimize most ML models. It's worth stepping back for a second and asking: how did we get to a place where we can train millions or billions of parameters reliably, across networks with complex architectures, in a relatively painless way? It's not just faster hardware or clever architectures. The real enabler is that we can compute gradients for SGD automatically, accurately, and efficiently, no matter how messy the model becomes. That's what automatic differentiation (autodiff) gives us. Autodiff is the unsung hero or the "secret sauce" of DL, and it deserves that reputation.

Autodiff applies the chain rule programmatically, letting us compute exact gradients through arbitrarily complex networks without symbolic math or approximation.[29]

Building GenAI

In "Learning Representations to GenAI" on page 26, we looked at how to conceptually build GenAI, starting from representation learning. Figure 2-6 showed us how we can fuse representations from different modalities into a common representation

28 Sebastian Ruder, "An Overview of Gradient Descent Optimization Algorithms," *arXiv.org*, September 15, 2016 (*https://arxiv.org/abs/1609.04747*).

29 Atilim Gunes Baydin et al., "Automatic Differentiation in Machine Learning: A Survey," *arXiv.org*, February 20, 2015 (*https://arxiv.org/abs/1502.05767*).

space. Once this is done and the representations inform each other, the modality-specific decoders could output predictions in one modality when provided input from another. This principle at a high level reflects how the current class of GenAI models work, resulting in predictions that can go from text-to-text, text-to-image, or image-to-video. We have also discussed different neural network architectures (see "Neural Network Zoo" on page 32), including transformers, and we have seen how DL models are trained (see "Gradient descent" on page 43). Given all these concepts, we can see how these frontier GenAI models are built.

GenAI Ingredients

Modern GenAI systems consist of three key components, as shown in Figure 2-6. First, modality-specific encoders operate on raw data and convert them into a shared token space. Images arrive as grids of pixels that a CNN encodes into a sequence of patch embeddings; audio streams are sliced into frames that a small RNN or 1D CNN maps to vectors; graphs are summarized into vectors using message passing in GNNs; and tabular data passes through a shallow MLP. Each encoder therefore speaks its native dialect but outputs a single, language-agnostic representation: fixed-width tokens.

Once the data is mapped into this common representation space, a transformer takes over. Its self-attention layers let every token, regardless of modality, consult every other, so an image patch can borrow context from a caption token, and an audio frame can query both. Training is usually unsupervised: the system predicts masked or future tokens, forcing it to model the joint distribution of all modalities at once.

The final stage is the modality-specific decoders. A stack of deconvolution layers turns latent tokens back into pixels; an autoregressive RNN or transposed convolution reconstructs waveforms; and a small MLP or graph decoder regenerates structured outputs. In each case, the transformer provides a rich latent representation, and the decoder translates these tokens into the desired output modality.

Throughout, the learning algorithm is plain SGD (or Adam,[30] its adaptive cousin). Gradients flow from the decoders through the transformer into the encoders, aligning every component under a single objective. The pipeline looks heterogeneous (with learnable encoders, transformers, and decoders), but the optimization process is unified.

30 Diederik P. Kingma and Jimmy Ba, "Adam: A Method for Stochastic Optimization," *arXiv.org*, December 22, 2014 (*https://arxiv.org/abs/1412.6980*).

Resources and Engineering at Scale

These frontier GenAI models, comprising encoders, decoders, and attention-using transformers, are viable only because data, compute, and parallelism have been scaled accordingly. The curated dataset for some of these models is basically the internet itself consisting of trillions of text tokens, millions of hours of speech, and petabytes of images and video. Parsing that volume through SGD would be impossible without hardware that can execute billions of floating-point operations per second.

Transformers fit into this ecosystem almost perfectly. Their core operations are matrix multiplications, which map cleanly to the dense linear algebra units of modern GPUs. Because attention in transformers treats every token independently until the final reduction, entire sequences can be processed in parallel, and the computation can be split across devices. Furthermore, residual connections and layer normalization that are used in transformers keep the optimization landscape smooth enough. This has the implication that the same training procedure works whether the model has a million or a trillion parameters, so the software stack can ramp capacity simply by adding more hardware, not by redesigning the model architecture.[31] The net effect is that adding eight times the hardware often gives close to an eight-fold speedup in training.

Pushing generative models to ever larger scales has turned each training run into an engineering moonshot requiring large-scale resources. Some recent training runs have drawn as much electricity as a small town for weeks, consuming petabytes of storage while using thousands of high-end GPUs whose global supply is already strained.[32] The scientific payoff is undeniable as these models can translate between data modalities and tackle open-ended tasks. However, every incremental gain now demands exponentially more hardware, capital, energy, and carbon emissions, raising hard questions about who can afford to participate and what the sustainability of AI will look like in the future.

Additional Resources

We have already used some basic notations in this chapter. In this section, we will elaborate on them and introduce two datasets used in the exercises.

---

31 Lex Clips, "Transformers: The Best Idea in AI | Andrej Karpathy and Lex Fridman," November 1, 2022 (*https://youtu.be/9uw3F6rndnA?t=393*).

32 Jaime Sevilla et al., "Compute Trends Across Three Eras of Machine Learning," *2022 International Joint Conference on Neural Networks (IJCNN)*, July 18, 2022, 1–8 (*https://doi.org/10.1109/ijcnn55064.2022.9891914*).

Common Notations

There are no universally agreed upon notations within ML. For the sake of clarity in this book, all the commonly used notations are described in Table 2-1. I will also reintroduce these notations when used in subsequent chapters.

Table 2-1. Common mathematical notations

Mathematical notation	Definition
$\mathcal{X}$	Input domain
$\mathcal{Y}$	Output domain
$\mathbf{x}_i \in \mathbb{R}^F$	The i-th data point with *F* features
$\mathbf{y}_i \in \mathbb{R}^K$	The i-th target label with *K* classes
$(\mathbf{x}_i, \mathbf{y}_i)$	The i-th training example
$\mathbb{D} = \{(\mathbf{x}_i, \mathbf{y}_i)\}$	Set of labeled data
$\lvert\mathbb{D}\rvert = \mathrm{N}$	Size of labeled data
$\mathbb{X} = \{\mathbf{x}_j\}$	Set of unlabeled data
$P(\mathbf{x}, \mathbf{y})$	Data generating distribution
$\mathcal{F}$	Hypothesis space of functions/models to be learned
$f_\theta : \mathcal{X} \rightarrow \mathcal{Y}$	Learnable function with parameters θ to map input-output domains
$\hat{\mathbf{y}} = f_\theta(\mathbf{x}) \in \mathbb{R}^K$	Target prediction by a model
$\mathcal{L}(\cdot) : \mathcal{X} \times \mathcal{Y} \rightarrow \mathbb{R}_{\geq 0}$	Loss objective

Datasets

Toy datasets for benchmarking ML models have been widely used. Exercises in this book will use two new datasets that are relevant to demonstrate the different techniques presented along the way.

AerialNIST dataset

An existing dataset used for crop monitoring from airborne images (SAT-4 dataset) has been adapted as the AerialNIST dataset to stay closer to the overall themes of this book that focus on AI and climate impact.[33] The original consisted of 500,000 image patches of size 28 × 28 extracted from larger airborne images. The AerialNIST dataset

33 This dataset is adapted from the "SAT-4 and SAT-6 Airborne Datasets" (*https://csc.lsu.edu/~saikat/deepsat*). See Saikat Basu et al., "DeepSat: A Learning Framework for Satellite Imagery," *SIGSPATIAL '15* (2015): 1–10 (*https://dl.acm.org/doi/10.1145/2820783.2820816*).

presented as part of this book's dataset consists of randomly selected 60,000 images (to match `MNIST` statistics) from the original SAT-4 dataset. Of the total 60,000 image patches, 40,000 will be used for training, 10,000 for validation, and 10,000 for testing purposes. Each patch consists of three channels (RBG) with intensity values between `[0-255]`. Each patch has a label corresponding to four classes that could be of interest for airborne image classification for crop monitoring: *{grassland, trees, barren, none}*. The final *none* class contains all other types of terrain that cannot be categorized into the first three categories.

Figure 2-15 shows some sample images sorted by their class labels. The dataset contains four classes: *{grassland, trees, barren, none}*. Blocks of four columns consisting of 32 images belong to the four classes. The four classes can be simplified further by aggregating them as *{vegetation, others}* for binary tasks.

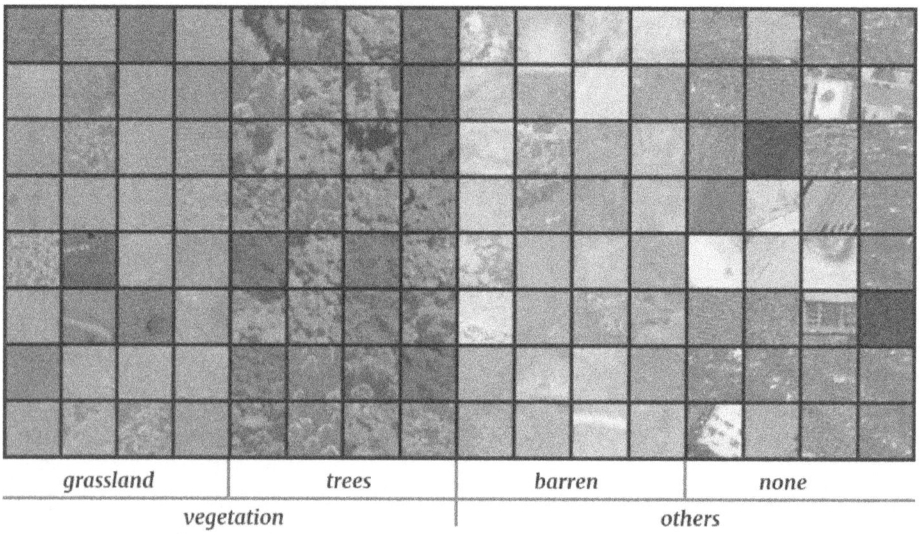

Figure 2-15. Samples from the AerialNIST dataset used in this book.

FAIRYTALES dataset

For language modeling tasks, we will use another toy dataset, FAIRYTALES, in this book. This has been curated from all the fairy tales written by Hans Christian Anderson. This resulted in a text file with 388,803 characters (see Figure 2-16). This will serve as a simple dataset that can be used in the text processing exercises.

```
THE LITTLE MERMAID


Far out in the wide sea,--where the water is blue as the loveliest
cornflower, and clear as the purest crystal, where it is so deep that
very, very many church-towers must be heaped one upon another in order
to reach from the lowest depth to the surface above,--dwell the
Mer-people.

Now you must not imagine that there is nothing but sand below the water:
no, indeed, far from it! Trees and plants of wondrous beauty grow there,
whose stems and leaves are so light, that they are waved to and fro by
the slightest motion of the water, almost as if they were living beings.
Fishes, great and small, glide in and out among the branches, just as
birds fly about among our trees.
```

Figure 2-16. Samples from the FAIRYTALES dataset consisting of about 388,000 characters, which can be used for training language models.

From ML Basics to Sustainable AI

In this chapter, we have seen how the recent class of GenAI models are built from a high level. The ML basics and concepts of representation learning interleaved throughout this chapter should be treated as intuitive pointers to more technical concepts.

We will be drawing upon these concepts in the rest of the book to discuss more detailed technicalities and to focus on AI methods through a resource consumption lens. Many of the arguments in the rest of the book are applicable to all AI models, but some might be better suited for the frontier AI models that include GenAI.

CHAPTER 3

Quantifying the Efficiency of Deep Learning

Recent advancements in ML/AI methods have enabled remarkable progress in multiple application domains such as computer vision, natural language processing, drug discovery, and entertainment. In particular, these advancements are due to the accelerated progress in DL that, in turn, has coincided with access to big data and large-scale compute. In this chapter, we will formalize redundancies in DL pipelines at the algorithmic and behavioral levels using the concept of AI waste, explore the compute-energy-carbon efficiency of DL, and present tools to quantify the resource efficiency of DL pipelines.

AI Waste

ML in its simplest formulation is the process of learning from data. Modern DL methods take this to another level, in terms of the volume of data and the size of models used to learn from data.[1] The data-driven approach necessitates training of overparameterized models on large datasets using some variation of the stochastic gradient descent algorithm (see "How to Train Your Model" on page 43 for more details). The combination of overparameterized models, large datasets, and iterative optimization results in large-scale computations during the development and deployment of DL models. While most of these computations are necessary, there are redundant computations we can identify in DL models that do not significantly influence the downstream performance. We will refer to such redundant computations in the development and deployment of AI models as *AI waste*.

1 Jaime Sevilla et al., "Compute Trends Across Three Eras of Machine Learning," *2022 International Joint Conference on Neural Networks (IJCNN)*, July 18, 2022, 1–8 (*https://doi.org/10.1109/ijcnn55064.2022.9891914*).

At a high level, any DL model lifecycle consists of several steps: dataset curation, model selection, model training, and finally model deployment, as illustrated in Figure 1-10. We can identify AI waste in each of these steps if we look at them more closely. For instance, using large datasets that are not sufficiently curated can deteriorate the learning efficiency of DL models (see Chapter 4 for recommendations on dataset efficiency). Further, exploring the space of hyperparameters to obtain a DL model in an unsystematic manner can also amount to AI waste (see Chapter 5 for recommendations on efficient model selection). In the remainder of the book, we will explore methods and tools to measure and improve the resource efficiency of DL, at both the algorithmic and behavioral levels.

Resource Consumption of Deep Learning

Measuring the resource consumption of DL is the first step toward improving its overall efficiency. In Chapter 1, we reviewed how energy consumption and carbon footprint are more relevant measures than focusing on only algorithmic efficiency when talking about the sustainability of AI. This is not to say that algorithmic efficiency is inconsequential, but having a sole focus on improving algorithmic efficiency alone is not enough.[2]

Developing efficient algorithms is certainly not a new topic of research. Charles Babbage and Ada Lovelace grappled with the notions of "correctness in the results, united with economy of time" as early as in 1842.[3] Basic algorithmic research has continued to focus on reducing the space-time complexity of the computational solutions. Popular measures of such algorithmic efficiency include memory consumed (space) and latency (time) when running algorithms.

Of late, the efficiency of DL models, or rather their complexity, is measured by reporting the number of trainable parameters, memory required, and number of computations required. These measures of DL model complexity continue to be the predominant method of measuring the resource efficiency of AI methods.

From the perspective of sustainable AI, a more holistic view of the resource efficiency of DL should include energy consumption and carbon footprint. As discussed in Chapter 1, the energy consumption and carbon footprint of AI methods are growing considerably and will continue to do so in the coming years. Including energy consumption and carbon footprint as additional resources will provide a more comprehensive view of resource consumption. Therefore, in this book, the Resource Pyramid

2 Dustin Wright et al., "Efficiency Is Not Enough: A Critical Perspective on Environmentally Sustainable AI," *Communications of the ACM* 68, no. 7 (2025): 62–69 (*https://doi.org/10.1145/3724500*).

3 L. F. Menabrea, "Sketch of the Analytical Engine invented by Charles Babbage," *Bibliothèque Universelle de Genève*, (October 1842), *http://psychclassics.yorku.ca/Lovelace/menabrea.htm*.

(Figure 3-1) illustrates how different resources relate to the sustainability of AI. The most commonly reported measure is the number of trainable parameters. This is followed by the more informative computation time, which is also reported as the number of GPU hours. Energy consumption is more encompassing, which is followed by the carbon footprint.

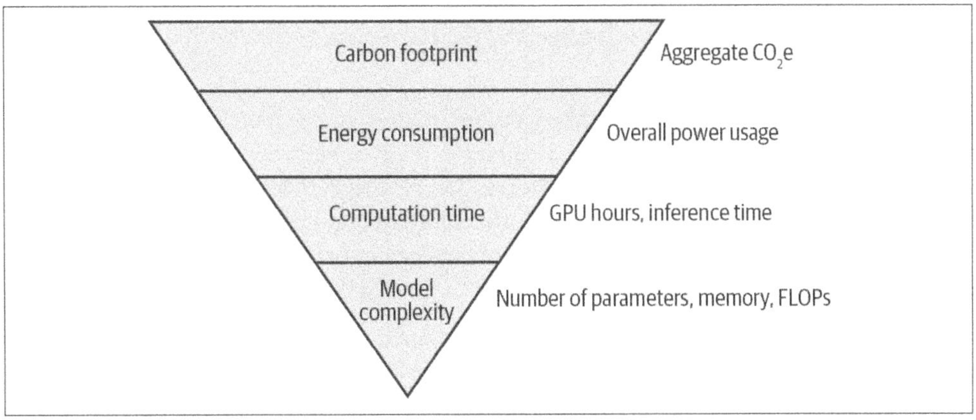

Figure 3-1. The Resource Pyramid of a DL model, visualizing the resource consumption granularity in increasing order of informativeness.

At the base of this Resource Pyramid is the concept of *model complexity*, which includes the standard metrics such as the number of parameters, the memory required, and the number of computations needed. Above model complexity is the computation time for DL models, which accounts for data processing and optimization, providing a more complete picture than model-specific measures alone. To advance sustainable AI, this book argues that, in addition to model complexity and computation time, the energy consumption of DL model development should also be measured.

Energy consumption due to CPUs, GPUs, and memory power usage, along with any overhead from cooling or distribution costs, should be measured and reported. When comparing different AI methods, model complexity and computation time may not sufficiently represent their overall resource requirements.

Ultimately, the most informative resource for improving the environmental sustainability of AI is the carbon footprint, which occupies the topmost level in the Resource Pyramid. While the energy consumption for a given model for a given task remains fixed, the corresponding carbon footprint can be optimized by adjusting the temporal and spatial aspects of when and where the computation is performed (see "Green scheduling" on page 207). Additionally, the carbon footprint can account for the environmental costs of the material infrastructure.

Resource Efficiency and Climate Awareness

Most work on improving the efficiency of AI methods has focused on model complexity and computation time. The efficiency gains made by improving these aspects might not always have a positive climate impact, however. Reducing the resource consumption of DL models can inadvertently lead to a negative climate impact due to the rebound effect (see "Rebound Effects and AI" on page 248).[4]

For example, suppose a new algorithm reduces the energy required to train a DL model by 50%. This efficiency improvement makes it cheaper and faster to train models, encouraging more frequent and larger-scale deployments. As a result, while each individual training session consumes less energy, the aggregate energy consumption may rise significantly due to the increased number of training sessions. This higher total usage can lead to a greater energy consumption, counteracting the benefits of the initial efficiency improvements.

Energy production continues to be the largest source of anthropogenic GHG emissions, estimated at about 35% of total GHG emissions.[5] The carbon footprint of the information and communication (ICT) sector is estimated to be somewhere between 2.1 and 3.9% of total GHG emissions, making it larger than that of the global aviation sector.[6]

The methods discussed in this book strive to improve the overall resource efficiency of AI methods, with an explicit focus on energy consumption and the corresponding carbon footprint of AI methods.

Actual Carbon Footprint of AI

The datacenter industry and ICT sector as a whole have massive electricity demands. In several datacenter-friendly countries (such as Denmark and Ireland),[7,8] they are estimated to be more than 15% of national electricity consumption. This has a proportional impact on the carbon footprint of these sectors. It is unclear, however,

4 The *rebound effect*, also known as the Jevons paradox, states that "as technological improvements increase the efficiency with which a resource is used, total consumption of that resource may increase rather than decrease." See *The Myth of Resource Efficiency: The Jevons Paradox* by John M. Polimeni et al. (Routledge, 2009).

5 Thomas Bruckner et al., "Energy Systems," in *Climate Change 2014: Mitigation of Climate Change, Contribution of Working Group III to the Fifth Assessment Report of the Intergovernmental Panel on Climate Change*, (Cambridge University Press, 2014) (*https://www.ipcc.ch/report/ar5/wg3*).

6 Charlotte Freitag et al., "The Real Climate and Transformative Impact of ICT: A Critique of Estimates, Trends, and Regulations," *Patterns* 2, no. 9 (2021): 100340 (*https://doi.org/10.1016/j.patter.2021.100340*).

7 The estimate for Denmark (*https://oreil.ly/rBeuB*) is 15% by 2030.

8 The estimate for Ireland (*https://oreil.ly/uEyFU*) is 18% in 2022.

what portion of this datacenter energy and carbon consumption is due to AI model development and deployment. The general trends in AI point to incessant growth, but the precise numbers for AI as a field are currently difficult to estimate.

Resource Efficiency and Sustainable AI

Sustainability is a multifaceted concept (see "Scope of Sustainability" on page 4).[9] This book is mainly concerned with the environmental sustainability of AI models. Even this focus on environmental sustainability is limited to the reduction of carbon footprints of AI models due to their energy consumption. The methods and practices in this book can advance toward sustainable AI only in this specific context.

That being said, focusing on reducing the carbon footprint of AI models is important and will play an important role in reducing their negative climate impact given their ever-increasing energy consumption. A more comprehensive outlook about sustainable AI is also presented in Chapter 10.

Quantifying Resource Consumption of AI

The Resource Pyramid (Figure 3-1) can be a useful framework to assess and improve the resource efficiency of AI methods. As the idiom goes, "You can't improve what you don't measure,"[10] so in this section we will look at a variety of tools that can measure different quantities corresponding to each level in the Resource Pyramid. This section covers tools to quantify the bottom three levels: model complexity, computation time, and energy consumption. The topmost level (carbon footprint) will be discussed in more detail in "Carbon Footprint of AI Models" on page 68.

Model Complexity

The model complexity aims to measure the hardware resources required to perform a certain computation. The number of CPU cores, CPU utilization, number of GPUs, GPU utilization, and memory consumption are all some aspects of the model complexity and are often reported. These measures, however, are device specific and can be difficult to compare across devices. We next present two measures of model complexity that are striving toward more standardization for meaningful comparisons across devices.

---

9 Common definitions consider three aspects: social, economic, and environmental sustainability. See Ben Purvis et al., "Three Pillars of Sustainability: In Search of Conceptual Origins," *Sustainability Science* 14, no. 3 (2019): 681–95 (*https://doi.org/10.1007/s11625-018-0627-5*).

10 Often attributed to Peter Drucker.

Number of parameters

For any DL model, $f_{\theta}: \mathscr{X} \rightarrow \mathscr{Y}$, as described in Chapter 2, the number of parameters is simply estimated by counting the number of trainable model weights, i.e., $|\theta|$.

Consider a simple MLP with two hidden layers (with four and three hidden units, respectively) that operates on vector of size eight and predicts two classes as output, shown in Figure 2-8. The total number of trainable weights in this simple MLP is 66, as discussed in "Multilayer perceptrons ("Everything is just a vector")" on page 32.

Estimating the number of parameters for even slightly more complicated MLPs or CNNs can be cumbersome and can be even more so when using specialized operations such as Dropout or Layer Normalization. Several open source tools exist that can be used to count the number of trainable parameters. When using PyTorch this can be obtained as shown in Example 3-1.

Example 3-1. Obtaining the number of trainable parameters for a model defined in PyTorch

```
# For any trainable neural network defined in the variable "model" in PyTorch:
num_param = sum(p.numel() for p in model.parameters() if p.requires_grad)
```

Multiply-accumulate

Multiply-accumulate (MAC) is a basic operation underlying many common computations such as convolution and dot products. MAC is a simple arithmetic operation involving element-wise multiplications followed by summations:

```
accumulator = accumulator + (multiplicand x multiplier)
```

The use of MAC as a measure of model complexity arises mainly from embedded devices because most processors have multiplication and addition implemented in hardware.

In DL models, MAC operations are prevalent in neural network operations such as fully connected layers, convolutional layers, pooling, and normalizations. Counting the number of MAC operations in these operations is also a common practice to compare the complexity of different models. For the simple MLP in Figure 2-8, the number of MAC operations is the same as the number of edges, since each edge corresponds to one MAC operation, resulting in MAC=66. For more complex models, we resort to other utilities.

Frameworks like PyTorch don't have built-in methods to estimate the MAC operations for a given neural network. External packages can be used for this. One such external package and its usage, along with sample output, is shown in Example 3-2. This tool can be used for different models in the Jupyter notebooks (*https://github.com/raghavian/sustainable_ai*) for this chapter. Other packages like PyTorch model summary (*https://oreil.ly/KbHQV*) can also be used to obtain the number of parameters and MACs.

Example 3-2. Obtaining MACs for a model defined in PyTorch using THOP: PyTorch-OpCounter (https://oreil.ly/2ICzC)

```
# Import the profile function from THOP
from thop import profile

# If the input size for the model is 3x32x32 (something like CIFAR10)
# MAC for the model can be retrieved using
input = torch.randn(1, 3, 32, 32)

macs_dn, params_dn = profile(densenet_model, inputs=(input, ))
macs_vt, params_vt = profile(vit_model, inputs=(input, ))

print('MAC for DenseNet  =%.2f'%(macs_dn/1e6))
print('MAC for ViT model =%.2f'%(macs_vt/1e6))
```

It should print the following output for the DenseNet and ViT provided:

```
MAC for DenseNet  =74.39 M
MAC for ViT model = 7.34 M
```

Floating-point operations

In general, all the computations in DL are performed on real numbers, which are stored on computers by quantizing them into floating-point data up to a certain numerical precision. The most common quantization is `FP32`, where real numbers are stored as floating points using 32 bits (see "Quantization" on page 161 for more details). Furthermore, all the computations are composed of the same basic arithmetic operations $(+, -, \times, /)$. These factors are combined to arrive at a notion of computational complexity measured as the number of *floating-point operations* (FLOPs).

FLOP, as the name suggests, estimates the number of floating-point operations required to train or deploy a DL model and is a measure of the quantity of computations. Here are the FLOP counts for basic operations:

Vector operations

For any two vectors of length N: $\mathbf{x},\mathbf{y} \in \mathbb{R}^N$

- Addition $\mathbf{x} + \mathbf{y}$ has a FLOP count of N for the N element-wise additions.
- Multiplication $\mathbf{x} \cdot \mathbf{y}$ has a FLOP count of N for the N element-wise multiplications
- Inner product $\mathbf{x}^T\mathbf{y}$ has a FLOP count of 2N-1 for the N element-wise multiplications and N-1 additions

Matrix operations

For any square matrices of order M: $\mathbf{X},\mathbf{Y} \in \mathbb{R}^{M \times M}$

- Matrix trace $Tr(\mathbf{X})$ has a FLOP count of M, as computing the trace requires M additions because the main diagonal has the same number of elements as the matrix order.
- Matrix product **XY**: Each element of the resulting matrix is computed by performing M multiplications and M – 1 additions (same as the inner product from above). Since there are M × M elements in the resulting matrix, the total FLOP count is M × M × (2M – 1), indicating a complexity of $O(M^3)$.

By definition, both FLOP and MAC are related to each other. Remember that a MAC is composed of a multiply and accumulate (or add) operation. This implies that $FLOP = 2 \times MAC$.

As with estimating MAC, even for simple arithmetic operations involving vectors or matrices, obtaining the exact FLOP count can be cumbersome, and even more so for DL algorithms. Tools that can be used to obtain the FLOP count are demonstrated in Example 3-3. fvcore (*https://oreil.ly/xeOR_*) can be used for different models in the this chapter's Jupyter notebooks (*https://github.com/raghavian/sustainable_ai*). Tools like flopth (*https://github.com/vra/flopth*) and pthflops (*https://oreil.ly/3vhfp*) can also be used to estimate the FLOP counts.

FLOP, FLOPs, FLOP/s

Several variations of the term related to FLOPs are used in practice, which can be confusing in many instances. Be warned that FLOP is a quantity that measures the number of floating point operations. While some would write FLOPs to indicate a plural form of FLOP, this can be confused with the number of FLOPs per second, which is a measure of performance of a processor. This is more precisely denoted FLOP/s. In this book we will adhere to FLOP (and FLOPs) when talking about the *quantity* of computations and FLOP/s when describing *performance* with respect to time.[11]

Example 3-3. Obtaining FLOP count for a model defined in PyTorch using fvcore maintained by the computer vision team at META AI Research

```
# Import the FlopCountAnalysis function from fvcore
from fvcore.nn import FlopCountAnalysis

# If the input size for the model is 3x32x32 (something like CIFAR10)
```

11 Lennart Heim makes additional clarifications in "FLOP for Quantity, FLOP/s for Performance" (*https://oreil.ly/jDb9J*).

```
# FLOPs for the model can be retrieved using
input = torch.randn(1, 3, 32, 32)

flop_dn = FlopCountAnalysis(densenet_model, input)
flop_vt = FlopCountAnalysis(vit_model, input)

print('FLOP count for DenseNet  = %.2fM'%(flop_dn.total()/1e6))
print('FLOP count for ViT model = %.2fM'%(flop_vt.total()/1e6))
```

It should print the following output for the DenseNet and ViT provided:

```
FLOP count for DenseNet  = 77.42M
FLOP count for ViT model =  9.08M
```

Efficient matrix multiplications

For large matrices there exist efficient matrix multiplication algorithms that can reduce the FLOP count considerably, notably when using algorithms such as the Strassen algorithm with the naive algorithm,[12] which has an asymptotic complexity of $O\left(M^{\log_2(7)}\right)$ instead of $O\left(M^3\right)$. Research into faster matrix multiplication algorithms is ongoing with some advancements reported using reinforcement learning.[13]

Further, square matrices of orders $M = 2^N$ have properties that are better exploited for efficiency. This is one of the reasons that input image sizes, neural network weights, and embeddings in transformers are commonly represented in factors of 2, i.e., $[2,4,8,16,\cdots]$.

As transformers perform large matrix multiplications, it's common to pad context windows to be power of 2 to get considerable speedups.[14]

Computation Time

Time complexity of algorithms, conventionally, has been measured using the growth rate of its runtime as the input size increases. This is usually expressed as the upper bound on the growth rate using the *Big O* notation. This would involve enumerating different classes of operations within the algorithm. The AI community has moved away from these theoretical bounds to more practical measures such as runtime and latency, and reporting aggregate computational time as GPU hours.

12 Volker Strassen, "Gaussian Elimination Is Not Optimal," *Numerische Mathematik* 13, no. 4 (August 1, 1969): 354–56 (*https://doi.org/10.1007/bf02165411*).

13 Alhussein Fawzi et al., "Discovering Faster Matrix Multiplication Algorithms With Reinforcement Learning," *Nature* 610, no. 7930 (October 5, 2022): 47–53 (*https://doi.org/10.1038/s41586-022-05172-4*).

14 Karpathy notes this behavior in a social media post (*https://oreil.ly/2SpMM*).

Runtime and latency

For a given hardware device and a computational task, the most common measure of time complexity is the runtime, which is the wall clock time elapsed between the start and finish of the task. For more granular reporting, in *nix systems, the runtime can further be partitioned into user and system time. User time is the time spent by the CPU/GPU performing the computations for the user in user space, whereas system time is the time spent on operating system tasks. For DL models, the runtime is the most useful notion of time complexity, which takes the CPU, GPU, and other overheads into account.

In some time-critical applications, the total runtime at inference from the initiation of a request to execution can be interpreted as latency. In addition to the runtime, latency also accounts for the network delays:

```
latency = runtime+transport_delay
```

This can be important when AI models are served from cloud services. Both runtime and latency are measured in units of time such as seconds (s) or milliseconds (ms).

The simplest way to measure the runtime or latency of AI methods is by wrapping the code between the Python `time` module, as shown in Example 3-4.

Example 3-4. Runtime and latency can be measured by wrapping the built-in time module in Python

```
# Import the time module
import time

latency_start_time = time.time() # Get the time at the start of code

# Initial code that is used to setup data, models

runtime_start_time = time.time() # Get time at start of model computations

# Prediction code on new data

runtime_end_time = time.time() # Get time at end of model computations
runtime = runtime_end_time - runtime_start_time

# Postprocessing, visualisation, garbage collection

latency_end_time = time.time() # Get time (almost) at end of code
latency = latency_start_time - latency_end_time

print('Runtime = %.4f s'%(runtime))
print('Latency = %.4f s'%(latency))
```

GPU hours

The concept of *GPU hours* has emerged as a common measure for quantifying the computational resources required for training models and running experiments. This offers a practical and intuitive measure of resource utilization, reflecting the actual time a GPU is actively engaged in processing tasks.

A GPU hour is defined as the usage of one GPU for one hour. For instance, if a model is trained for 10 hours using a single GPU, it consumes 10 GPU hours. Alternatively, if another model is trained for five hours but utilizes two GPUs simultaneously, it also accumulates 10 GPU hours. Despite the differences in training duration and the number of GPUs used, both models in this example require the same total computational effort in terms of GPU resources.

> **Computation Time for Llama-3 Models in GPU Hours**
>
> The total compute used to train the Llama-3.1 family of models was reported to be about 39.3 million GPU hours using H100-80GB GPUs (*https://oreil.ly/qE3o_*). This number will differ if the hardware used was different.

However, it's important to recognize the limitations of using GPU hours as a measure. The performance of GPUs can vary significantly depending on their type and capabilities. For example, a GPU hour on a high-end model like the NVIDIA A100 is not directly comparable to a GPU hour on a mid-range GPU like the NVIDIA GTX 1080. Furthermore, GPU hours do not account for other factors such as CPU usage, memory bandwidth, or input/output operations, all of which can influence overall performance and efficiency.

Role of Efficiency in Democratization of AI

The discussions on resource efficiency in this book are primarily focused on the environmental sustainability of AI. However, these resource efficiency methods can also influence the social sustainability of AI methods. Access to large-scale resources that are expensive is evolving to become a barrier for ML practitioners. By improving the resource efficiency, these methods can be democratized to some extent. The question of improving equitable AI by improving access is something researchers are grappling with.[15]

15 Nur Ahmed and Muntasir Wahed, "The De-democratization of AI: Deep Learning and the Compute Divide in Artificial Intelligence Research," *arXiv.org*, October 22, 2020 (*https://arxiv.org/abs/2010.15581*).

Energy Consumption

Model complexity and computation time depicted as the bottom two levels in the Pyramid of Resource Consumption in Figure 3-1 have been used to assess the complexity of algorithms. *Energy consumption* as the third level is crucial for the AI era. In this section, we will look at what the energy consumption of AI entails, tools to measure it, and the larger implications of focusing on energy consumption in AI.

Energy consumption of AI

The design, development, and deployment of AI models are energy-intensive processes due to their reliance on large datasets, exploration of massive hypothesis spaces, and long training regimes. These processes can be accelerated by parallel computations on hardware accelerators such as GPUs, tensor processing units (TPUs), intelligence processing units (IPUs), or other AI-specific hardware. In addition to these devices, the base CPU, memory usage, networking, and cooling costs amount to the increasing energy consumption of AI models (see Chapter 1 for additional statistics on the growing energy consumption of AI). Although TPUs and IPUs are being used to develop DL models, the bulk of the development is carried out on GPUs. In the remainder of this book, the discussions will be focused on GPUs but can be easily extended to other AI hardware accelerators.

Estimating the individual contributions of the various components tied to the energy consumption of AI models is not straightforward. One important factor is the nature of the hardware used: a standalone workstation with dedicated GPU and supporting infrastructure would have different contributions than a cloud instance with shared resources. For a single GPU cloud instance or workstation, GPUs are estimated to account for about 74%, CPUs for 13%, and dynamic random-access memory (DRAM) for 13% of the total dynamic power consumed.[16] Although not exact, similar estimations could be made for cloud instances with multiple GPUs. Furthermore, the energy consumption due to idling of devices, networking/distribution, and cooling of infrastructure should also be accounted for but is much harder to estimate.

Estimating energy consumption

The total energy consumption of AI models consists of measuring the *average* power consumption of different devices over a certain period of time. The power consumption itself consists of two components: dynamic and static. Dynamic power consumption is due to the active computations performed on behalf of the AI models, whereas

16 Jesse Dodge et al., "Measuring the Carbon Intensity of AI in Cloud Instances," *2022 ACM Conference on Fairness, Accountability, and Transparency*, June 20, 2022, 1877–94 (*https://doi.org/10.1145/3531146.3533234*).

static power consumption is mainly due to the idling costs of the devices independent of the computations.

Energy is generally measured in joules (J); however, electrical energy is more commonly measured using kilowatt-hour (kWh), and 1kWh = 3600 kJ. If a workstation rated to consume 500W is operated for 2 hours, it would consume 500 × 2 = 1,000 Wh, or 1kWh of energy.

> **Converting Between Joule and kWh**
>
> Tools like pyJoules estimate the energy consumption in micro joule, i.e., $\left(10^{-6}J\right)$. Energy estimations in joule can be converted to kWh using the following conversion: $1J = \frac{10^{-6}}{3.6}kWh$.

Total electrical energy consumed, E, in time, T, is measured in watt-hour (Wh) and obtained as:

$$E = PUE \times \left(P_{dynamic} + P_{static}\right) \times T \qquad (Wh)$$

where $P_{dynamic}$ considers the set of all measured devices D, most common of which are CPUs, GPUs, and DRAM:

$$P_{dynamic} = \sum_{d \in D} P_d \qquad (W)$$

Finally, the additional power consumption due to infrastructure involved in dissipation, cooling, and networking, for example, is calculated using an overhead factor known as *power usage effectiveness* (PUE). It is defined as the ratio of the total energy used in a datacenter to the energy used by the devices for compute, storage, and networking:

$$PUE = \frac{\text{Total Facility Energy}}{\text{IT Equipment Energy}}$$

In a datacenter, PUE = 2.0 indicates that for every watt spent on compute, another watt is spent as overhead. Ideally, PUE should be 1.0, which is mostly unattainable. The annual average datacenter PUE has steadily improved over the years and was at

1.54 in 2025, as shown in Figure 3-2. Some cloud service providers, however, claim better values with PUE = 1.1.[17]

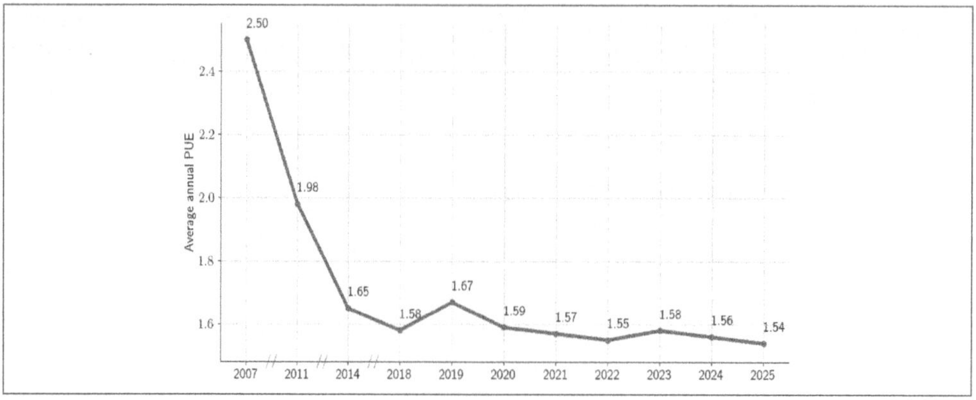

Figure 3-2. Average annual PUE for datacenters. (Source: Uptime Institute Global Data Center Survey Results 2025 (https://oreil.ly/V1oe2).)

Measuring the power consumption of CPUs, GPUs, and DRAM relies on the tools provided by the hardware manufacturers. Most existing tools primarily support measuring the power consumption of Intel CPUs and Nvidia GPUs running Linux-based operating systems, due to their widespread usage. Nvidia GPUs, for instance, have dominated the AI market with estimations to be more than 70% in 2018 and more than 90% in 2024.[18] Example 3-5 demonstrates a simple Python tool to measure this energy consumption.

Root Privileges to Read CPU Power Consumption

Most software energy measurement tools, such as pyJoules, rely on the intel-rapl library for querying the instantaneous power consumption of Intel CPUs and DRAM. In Linux machines, as a security measure, reading these values requires root privileges. See possible solutions on GitHub (*https://oreil.ly/jfpbW*).

Example 3-5. Obtaining the total energy consumption due to CPU, GPU, and DRAM costs for training a `model` defined in PyTorch using pyJoules (https://oreil.ly/v0Rls)

```
# Import the relevant functions from pyJoules
from pyJoules.energy_meter import measure_energy
from pyJoules.handler.pandas_handler import PandasHandler
```

17 Google Data Centers claimed a PUE of 1.1 in 2022 (*https://oreil.ly/hMLuB*).

18 Tim Hwang, "Computational Power and the Social Impact of Artificial Intelligence," *arXiv.org*, March 23, 2018 (*https://arxiv.org/abs/1803.08971*).

```
# Instantiate output handler to be Pandas dataframe
pandas_handler = PandasHandler()

@measure_energy(handler=pandas_handler) # decorate main() with energy meter
def main():
    # Main function code goes here...

if __name__ == "__main__":
    main()
    df = pandas_handler.get_dataframe() # Get the measured energy as a dataframe

    print('Total time elapsed: %.4f s'%(df['duration'].values[0]))
    for c in df.columns[4:]: # Loop over detected devices
        print('Energy consumption of '+c+' : %.4f J'%(df[c].values[0]/1e6))
```

Depending on the devices detected and the task run, it should print an output similar to this:

```
Total time elapsed: 40.8244 s
Energy consumption of dram_0 : 60.1534 J
Energy consumption of core_0 : 1068.9771 J
Energy consumption of nvidia_gpu_0 : 5.0297 J
```

Energy Efficiency, Sustainable AI, and the Jevons Paradox

The current discourse on sustainable AI has primarily focused on the energy consumption related to the development and deployment of AI.[19] Improving energy efficiency, by improving model complexity or computation time, cannot help us make AI more sustainable. Historically, energy efficiency has always been at odds with environmental sustainability, which is a key topic of debate using the framework of the Jevons paradox that argues that improving energy efficiency can increase overall consumption and have a net negative effect on sustainability.[20] To achieve sustainable AI, the focus has to be beyond only the energy consumption and must take the associated carbon footprint into consideration. This is the fourth level in the Resource Pyramid in Figure 3-1, which is the most encompassing of resources when talking AI and sustainability.

19 Emma Strubell et al., "Energy and Policy Considerations for Deep Learning in NLP," *arXiv.org*, June 5, 2019 (*https://arxiv.org/abs/1906.02243*).

20 Polimeni et al., *The Myth of Resource Efficiency: The Jevons Paradox*.

Carbon Footprint of AI Models

Estimating the energy consumption of AI models provides a meaningful way to compare classes of models that are trained on different hardware. The bottom three levels of the Resource Pyramid (model complexity, computation time, and energy consumption), however, do not immediately translate into assessing the climate impact of developing and deploying AI models. In this section we will take a look at the carbon emissions resulting from the electricity production of the energy consumed during the development and deployment of AI models. Assessing the carbon footprint of AI is the top level of the Resource Pyramid in Figure 3-1 as it also allows the inclusion of additional environmental impacts such as those due to the manufacturing of hardware.

GHG Emissions and Carbon Footprint

Carbon footprint is an umbrella term that refers to the total amount of GHGs released into the atmosphere as a result of human activities. The key contributors in the US (*https://oreil.ly/2-472*) are consumption of fossil fuels for transportation (28%), energy production (24%), and various industrial processes (12%).

Carbon dioxide (CO_2) is the primary GHG, whereas other GHGs such as methane, nitrous oxide, hydroflourocarbons, perflourocarbons, sulfur hexaflouride, and nitrogen triflouride are also considered to be GHGs contributing to climate change. To facilitate comparisons and calculations, the global warming potential (GWP) (*https://oreil.ly/yKCfM*) of various GHGs relative to CO_2 are expressed as CO_2e, which stands for carbon dioxide equivalent, usually measured in kilograms (kg). For instance, the GWP for methane is 28, meaning it is 28 times more efficient than CO_2 at trapping radiation in the atmosphere over a 100-year period. In terms of CO_2e, emitting 1kg of methane into the atmosphere is equal to 28kgCO_2e.

As energy production is a key contributor of GHGs worldwide, the amount of GHGs (CO_2e) produced per unit of electricity generated is measured using the concept of carbon intensity of electricity production. The carbon intensity of electricity is measured in grams of CO_2e emitted per kWh, in units of gCO_2e/kWh. Lower carbon intensity indicates cleaner and more environmentally friendly electricity production with a smaller fraction of fossil fuel sources and more contribution by renewable energy sources such as solar and wind.

Figure 3-3 shows the carbon intensity variations across the globe for countries where the data are available. Within the European Union (EU), where data is more consistently available (*https://oreil.ly/WvO8Q*), the carbon intensity fluctuates quite drastically between the 27 member states. In 2022, Sweden had the lowest annual average carbon intensity (8gCO_2e/kWh), compared with Estonia, which had the highest (693gCO_2e/kWh). An overview of the carbon intensity for different regions in the world, where the data is available, is shown in Figure 3-3; paler regions have lower carbon intensity compared to the darker regions. Regions without data are unshaded.

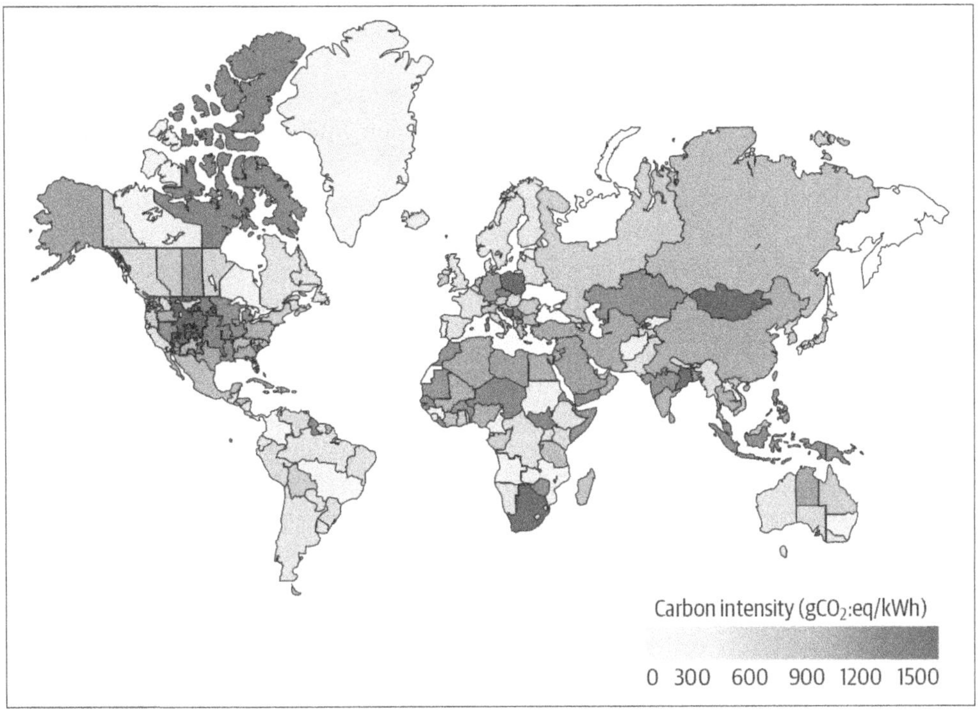

Figure 3-3. Carbon intensity variations across the globe for the countries with available information. Paler regions have lower carbon intensity than the darker regions. Based on the data at electricitymaps.com at the time of this writing.

The units to quantify power usage, energy consumption, and carbon footprint are specific and have been standardized by now. Table 3-1 summarizes them.

Table 3-1. Energy- and carbon footprint–related quantities along with their commonly used measurement units

Quantity	Unit	Notation
Power (*P*)	watt	W
Energy (*E*)	joule or kilo watt-hour	J or kWh
CO_2 emissions	kilogram	kg
Carbon footprint (CO_2e)	kilogram	$kgCO_2e$
Carbon intensity	gram CO_2e per kWh	gCO_2e/kWh

Relating Carbon Footprint to Energy Consumption

A linear relationship exists between energy consumption and carbon footprint, which is simply the product of the energy consumed and the average carbon intensity for that duration of energy production:

$$\text{Carbon Footprint} = \text{Energy Consumption} \times \text{Carbon Intensity}$$

For a given DL model that is run on the same hardware, the energy consumed is the same irrespective of the location. However, the carbon footprint corresponding to this energy consumption could vary depending on the location. This is due to the difference in carbon intensities for different countries, and even regions within the same country, as shown in Figure 3-3.

Further, the carbon intensity of the power grid fluctuates during the course of a day and across days of the week. Depending on the availability of renewable energy, or the demand on the power grid, the mixture of fossil fuel and renewable energy can vary. The instantaneous carbon intensity can increase as much as 10 times during the day, and a similar fluctuation can be noticed between weekdays and weekends. As with the variations in the carbon footprint due to location, there can also be fluctuations in the estimated carbon footprint when using real-time data. Figure 3-4 shows such fluctuations in instantaneous carbon intensity for UK and Denmark.

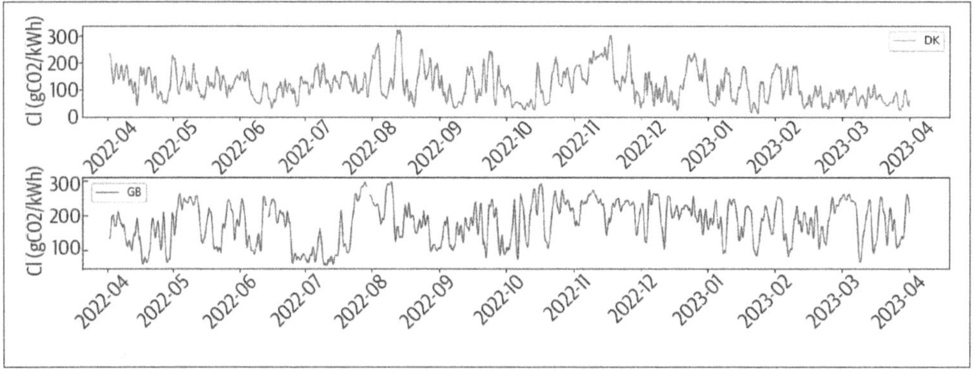

Figure 3-4. Carbon intensity fluctuations for Denmark (DK) and Great Britain (GB) over a period of one year, shown as daily averages. (Source: DK (https://energidataservice.dk), GB (https://carbonintensity.org.uk).)

Carbon Intensity Variations and Green Scheduling

The spatial variations (Figure 3-3) and temporal fluctuations (Figure 3-4) in the carbon intensity of electricity production can be used to reduce the carbon footprint of computations. By scheduling computations in regions with lower carbon intensity or during periods of low carbon intensity, large reductions in carbon footprint of computations are achievable. This is commonly known as *green scheduling* and is an active area of research.[21] Green scheduling specific to AI is discussed in more detail in "Green scheduling" on page 207.

Estimating the Carbon Footprint of AI Models

Measuring energy consumption helps provide a more holistic view of the resource consumption and efficiency of a given DL model. However, energy consumption does not directly capture the climate impact of AI models. Relating the energy costs to their underlying GHG emissions and estimating the carbon footprint is a useful way to assess the environmental sustainability of AI models due to their growing electricity consumption. To act on reducing the carbon footprint of AI models, systematic measurement and standardized reporting are essential. In the remainder of this section we will take a look at the landscape of carbon footprint reporting methods and tools that have evolved in recent years with a particular focus on AI models.

Carbon footprint is generally measured and reported in $kgCO_2e$, which can be somewhat abstract as it's not a common unit used in our daily jargon. Within the ML community, several attempts have been made to present the carbon footprint estimation using other quantities that are perhaps easier to parse. For example:

- The carbon footprint of training the BERT model on a GPU was estimated to be roughly equivalent to a trans-Atlantic flight.[22]
- The carbon footprint of training the GPT-3 model on a GPU was estimated to be roughly equivalent to traveling 703,808km by a newly registered car in the EU.[23]

With the increasing awareness and interest in the estimation of the carbon footprint of AI models, several methods have been recently developed. Most of these methods focus on estimating the carbon footprint due to the energy consumption during the development/deployment of AI models. These tools are built on software energy measurement tools and use the carbon intensity information of the power grid to estimate the carbon footprint. The limited availability of software tools implies that the energy costs due to the electricity consumption of CPUs, DRAM, GPUs, and the overhead accounted in PUEs are the main factors considered. The energy/carbon

21 Ana Radovanovic et al., "Carbon-Aware Computing for Datacenters," *arXiv.org*, June 11, 2021 (*https://arxiv.org/abs/2106.11750*).

22 Strubell et al., "Energy and Policy Considerations for Deep Learning in NLP" (*https://arxiv.org/abs/1906.02243*).

23 Lasse F. Wolff Anthony et al., "Carbontracker: Tracking and Predicting the Carbon Footprint of Training Deep Learning Models," *arXiv.org*, July 6, 2020 (*https://arxiv.org/abs/2007.03051*).

costs due to the manufacture of devices, for instance, is not accounted for with these tools.

Table 3-2 presents a high-level overview of some of the tools currently available to track the carbon footprint of AI models.[24] Example 3-6 demonstrates how to use one of the tools for tracking the carbon footprint of model training. This tool can be used for different scenarios, such as training or inference in this chapter's Jupyter notebooks (*https://github.com/raghavian/sustainable_ai*).

Table 3-2. High-level comparison of different tools available for tracking the carbon footprint of DL methods

Tool	Track	Predict	Report	Plot	Pip	API	CPU	DRAM	GPU	Comments
ML Emissions Calculator (MLEC) (*https://oreil.ly/KkmSN*)	✗	✗	✓	✗	✗	✗	✗	✗	✓	Online calculator where users can self-report. Does not take datacenter PUE into account.
experiment-impact-tracker (EIT) (*https://oreil.ly/sgTO8*)	✓	✗	✓	✗	✓	✗	✓	✓	✓	First Python tool published with a focus on tracking the carbon footprint of DL models. Not actively maintained.
Carbontracker (*https://carbontracker.info*)	✓	✓	✓	✗	✓	✗	✓	✓	✓	Predicts energy consumption based on a single epoch. Using data from Electricity Maps (*https://app.electricitymaps.com*) supports real-time carbon intensity for several global regions.
CodeCarbon (*https://oreil.ly/gTE6R*)	✓	✗	✓	✓	✓	✓	✓	✓	✓	Actively maintained tool with growing user base. Similar to EIT, Carbontracker. No real-time carbon intensity.
Eco2AI (*https://oreil.ly/4E1n5*)	✓	✗	✓	✗	✓	✗	✓	✓	✓	Most recent among the tools. Similar to EIT, Carbontracker. No real-time carbon intensity.

24 For a more comprehensive survey of carbon-tracking tools, see Lucía Bouza et al., "How to Estimate Carbon Footprint When Training Deep Learning Models? A Guide and Review" (*https://doi.org/10.1088/2515-7620/acf81b*).

Example 3-6. Obtaining the carbon footprint due to the energy consumption of CPU, GPU, and DRAM when training a model defined in PyTorch using Carbontracker (https://carbontracker.info)

```
from carbontracker.tracker
import Carbontracker

tracker = Carbontracker(epochs=<your epochs>)

for epoch in range(<your epochs>):
    tracker.epoch_start()

    # Your model training.

    tracker.epoch_end()

tracker.stop()
```

Sample output from Carbontracker, depending on the hardware detected, could look like this:

```
CarbonTracker: The following components were found:
GPU with device(s) NVIDIA GeForce RTX 3090.
CPU with device(s) cpu:0.
YYYY-MM-DD 15:42:49 - CarbonTracker:
Predicted consumption for 50 epoch(s):
        Time:   0:24:12
        Energy: 0.125254 kWh
        CO2eq:  33.213131 g
        This is equivalent to:
        0.275857 km travelled by car
YYYY-MM-DD 16:02:35 - CarbonTracker:
Actual consumption for 50 epoch(s):
        Time:   0:20:15
        Energy: 0.124411 kWh
        CO2eq:  33.528735 g
        This is equivalent to:
        0.278478 km travelled by car
YYYY-MM-DD 16:02:35 - CarbonTracker: Finished monitoring.
```

Carbontracker also supports a command-line interface that can be useful to measure the carbon footprint of jobs in a nonintrusive way in any shell environment:

```
carbontracker python train_model.py --log_dir=./carbontracker-logs
```

It will print the same output as shown previously and log the output into the *carbontracker-logs* directory.

> ### Operational Carbon Emissions and Sustainable AI
>
> The tools presented here and the discussions about carbon footprints are quite specific to carbon emissions, due to the energy production for the electricity consumed when developing/deploying AI models. These carbon emissions are commonly known as *operational emissions*. This should not be conflated with the overall carbon emissions, which also include embodied emissions and take into account the carbon emissions due to the hardware manufacturing, transportation, electronic waste, and other factors. Focusing on the operational emissions and improving resource efficiency should be viewed as a starting point for ML/AI practitioners in their journey toward greener AI.

Efficiency Quantified: What Comes Next?

The classical view of algorithmic complexity using space-time analysis is limited when analyzing the efficiency of DL models. This book introduced the more holistic view on resource consumption of AI models using the Resource Pyramid (Figure 3-1). The carbon footprint of AI models sits on the top level of this pyramid and is the most important resource when it comes to improving the environmental sustainability of AI. Now that we have the methods, metrics, and tools to quantify the overall resource efficiency of AI models, a few questions can help guide us through the remainder of this book and in our pursuit of sustainable AI:

What to do with the resource measurements?

First, measure; then, improve.

Measuring the various resources consumed by AI models is the first step toward improving them. The exorbitant resource costs of DL models is not always reported. Improving the awareness within the community about these large resource costs can spawn actions that can help tackle these issues. Systematic reporting of the space-time-energy complexity along with the carbon footprint is an essential step toward reducing the climate impact of AI models.

From a technical standpoint, these measures can be integrated into the optimization criteria when designing or deploying AI models to obtain models that are less resource-intensive. In the remaining chapters, practical ways of using these measurements to improve some aspect of resource efficiency of AI models to reduce the climate impact will be presented.

Why focus on resource efficiency?

Because technology cannot be decoupled from its resource consumption.

The widespread adoption of AI models in our daily lives is already in progress. Any small improvements in their efficiency can percolate system wide and yield large benefits. Another obvious benefit that is directly correlated with efficiency is monetary savings. In Figure 3-4, the fluctuations in carbon intensity during the course of a day were demonstrated. High carbon intensity times are representative of high demand regimes. Some electricity markets regulate demand by modulating price with demand (higher price during high demand times). As a result, reducing the carbon footprint by optimizing for low demand times can also yield direct monetary gains.

Further, and more importantly, AI models are already being used to help us tackle climate change in many shapes and forms. AI models are highly valuable tools in tasks such as large-scale remote-sensing, climate modeling, and optimizing renewable energy by modulating the energy grids. Given these potential applications that can have a positive impact on climate, it would be counterproductive (and ironic) if the AI models themselves are resource hungry and have massive carbon footprints.

Does efficiency come at no cost?

There is always a trade-off. There is still no free lunch.[25]

The resource consumption metrics and tools presented in this chapter will focus on reducing AI waste and hence improve their overall resource efficiency. However, many of the underlying principles driving the current success of AI models are not fully understood. As a result, these models appear to possess redundancies that can be reduced. In many instances, as we will see in the upcoming chapters, these efficiency gains have to be balanced with small deterioration in performance or an increase of some other resource. Depending on the tasks, these trade-offs can be meaningfully balanced.

25 In the same spirit as D.H. Wolpert and W.G. Macready, "No Free Lunch Theorems for Optimization," *IEEE Transactions on Evolutionary Computation* 1, no. 1 (1997): 67–82 (*https://doi.org/10.1109/4235.585893*).

Resource Pyramid for a ChatGPT Class AI Model

The first released version of ChatGPT in November 2022 was a conversational engine based on the GPT family of LLMs, with 175B trainable parameters and trained using 3.14×10^{23} FLOPs. The training energy consumption of GPT-3 was estimated to be 188,701.92kWh, or 84,738.48kgCO_2e, or about the same carbon footprint as traveling for 703,808km in a newly registered car in the EU.[26]

There have been subsequent updates to this model, and not all the resources consumed are publicly known. The arguments in this book are to publish the resource costs, following the Resource Pyramid framework. For a similar open source model, Llama, the data is available and is visualized in the Resource Pyramid in Figure 3-5 based on the following calculations.

In the model card for LLama-3.1 405B, it was reported that the total computation time for training was 30.84M GPU hours. The models were trained on the H100-80GB models with a 700W rating. Given these, we estimate the total energy consumption according to the method used by Meta.[27]

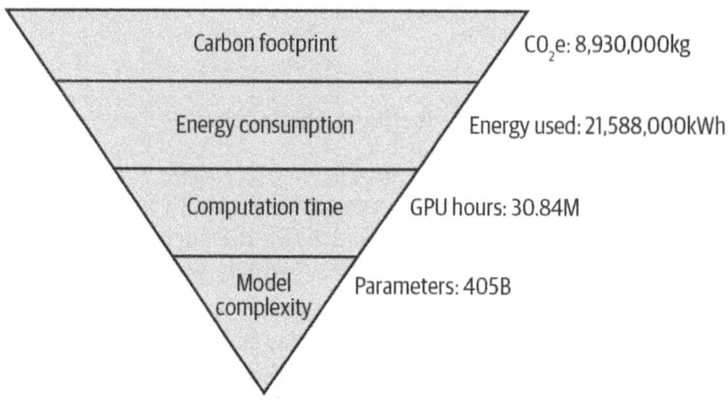

Figure 3-5. Resource costs at each level of the Resource Pyramid for Llama-3.1 405B model. (Source: Model Card for Llama-3.1 [2024] (https://oreil.ly/Copu0).)

26 Anthony et al., "Carbontracker: Tracking and Predicting the Carbon Footprint of Training Deep Learning Models" (*https://arxiv.org/abs/2007.03051*).

27 David Patterson et al., "The Carbon Footprint of Machine Learning Training Will Plateau, Then Shrink," *arXiv.org*, April 11, 2022 (*https://arxiv.org/abs/2204.05149*).

CHAPTER 4
Data Parsimony

Data is the new oil was a common idiom in the early 2010s, used in the context of generating value via digital data. It also unintentionally captures the increasing carbon footprint of storing and processing vast amounts of data. Lifecycle emissions for each terabyte of data on hard drive storage are estimated to be anywhere between 2 and 20kgCO_2e per year, as Figure 4-1 illustrates for commonly used storage devices.

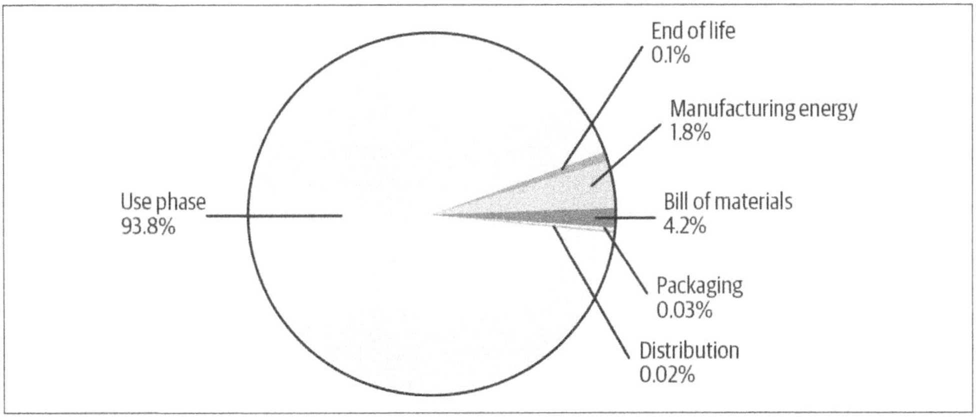

Figure 4-1. Typical GHG emissions across the lifecycle of storage devices. (Source: Seagate Sustainability Report (https://oreil.ly/z1XEL).)

Large-scale computations on massive amounts of data have been essential to the progress in AI model development, with the most recent LLMs being trained on datasets that consist of more than 15 trillion data points (tokens).[1] Not all of the data used for

1 Aaron Grattafiori et al., "The Llama 3 Herd of Models," *arXiv.org*, July 31, 2024 (*https://arxiv.org/abs/2407.21783*).

training ML models is informative, however. Uninformative or duplicative data can also contribute to the notion of AI waste that was presented in Chapter 3. Reducing the amount of data used can have a considerable impact on reducing the energy consumption and carbon footprint of selecting and developing AI models.

In this chapter we introduce methods of identifying informative data points and extracting useful information from them. This chapter offers a paradigm of developing DL models while reducing AI waste from a data perspective, which we refer to as *data parsimony.* It also discusses the performance trade-off between using data frugally and using data parsimoniously. The goal of achieving sustainable AI using data efficiently will be the key focus of this chapter.

The Cost of Data

Chapter 2 presented some of the fundamentals of DL. The key insight to bear in mind is that ML models learn from data, and the recent class of DL models learn from even more data.

Consider the task of discerning *vegetation* from *others* images in the AerialNIST dataset, visualized in Figure 2-15. A rule-based method to distinguish the two classes could be designed in simple steps. One approach can be to use the fact that images of vegetation have more green content in them. This can be converted into a rule that estimates the average intensities in the RGB channels of the image, and then applies an appropriate threshold on the green channel. This is a simple enough rule, requiring few MAC operations.

A DL model such as an MLP or CNN needs to learn the color threshold rule solely from training data. This can increase the data processing costs. The feature design described in the previous paragraph underlines the implicit knowledge users have about the data—in this case about images consisting of RGB channels and that average intensity could be useful to discern *vegetation* from *others.* Such knowledge or useful assumptions about the data that users have is related to the notion of inductive bias introduced in Chapter 2. When DL models are tasked with learning from data, the gap in knowledge due to a lack of inductive bias should be compensated for by learning from the data. This requires additional data when compared to a rule-based method that has relatively more inductive bias encoded in its design rules. The strength in ML models, and more so with DL models, lies in the fact that they can learn arbitrarily complex rules that would be difficult for practitioners to design.

Carbon Footprint of Data Storage

Storage in datacenters is energy-intensive due to the underlying storage infrastructure, computation, networking, and cooling requirements. Storing 1TB of data for one year can cost about 60kWh with a carbon footprint of up to 44kgCO_2e (see the next sidebar). The massive amounts of data being generated and stored in datacenters consume about 2% of global electricity.[2] The corresponding GHG emissions are also considerable, reaching up to 3.9% of global GHG emissions.[3] And in datacenter-friendly countries like Denmark, energy usage of datacenters is projected to grow 3% annually and by 2030 will account for around 15% of the country's electricity use (see Figure 1-9).

These massive energy costs of large-scale datasets also influence the efficiency of developing AI models as training DL models requires iterative optimization over large datasets. With growing dataset scale, the computational resources required to train DL models also grow almost linearly.

Energy Consumption and Carbon Footprint of Storing 1TB Data

Enterprise hard disk drive (HDD) with 1TB capacity has an idle average power consumption of 4.5W (operational power consumption can be higher, about 6W).[4]

The total energy consumption of storing 1TB for data then can be estimated as:

- 4.5W × 24 (h/day) × 365 (d/year) ≈ 40kWh/year
- Assuming a PUE (see "Estimating energy consumption" on page 64 for details on PUE) of 1.5, the total energy consumption = 1.5 × 40 = 60kWh

Therefore, only *storing* 1TB of data for 1 year can cost about 60kWh.

Depending on the carbon intensity of energy production in a region, the corresponding carbon footprint can be different. For instance, according to Carbontracker (*https://carbontracker.info*), the carbon intensity of energy production for Sweden, the US, and Estonia in 2020 was as follows:

- Sweden: $12gCO_2e/kWh$, resulting in 60 × 12 = $0.72kgCO_2e$
- US: $357.2gCO_2e/kWh$, resulting in 60 × 357 = $21.42kgCO_2e$
- Estonia: $739gCO_2e/kWh$, resulting in 60 × 739 = $44.34kgCO_2e$

Depending on where the datacenter is located, the carbon footprint of storing 1TB of data can vary anywhere between 0.75 and $44.34kgCO_2e$.

2 "Data Centres and Data Transmission Networks," IEA, accessed September 21, 2025 (*https://oreil.ly/pxl2E*).

3 Charlotte Freitag et al., "The Climate Impact of ICT: A Review of Estimates, Trends and Regulations," *arXiv.org*, February 3, 2021 (*https://arxiv.org/abs/2102.02622*).

4 Seagate Technology LLC, "Enterprise Capacity 3.5 HDD: v5.1 Product Manual," September 2017 (*https://oreil.ly/9SUny*).

Scale of Datasets in AI

Until recently a common rule of thumb when developing ML models was to have at least an order of magnitude more training examples than the number of trainable parameters in the model. This rule was a heuristic to avoid overfitting to the training data.

Recent large-scale models appear to violate this rule. Models like GPT-3 and LaMDA were trained using about the same amount of training data or tokens (see Chapter 2 for details on transformers) as the number of trainable parameters in them. Some models like MT-NLG were even trained with fewer data points than the number of trainable parameters.[5] New analyses that could be specific to large-scale DL models are being developed within the community for improved utilization of existing data, as useful data is finite. For instance, the approach currently dubbed the *Chinchilla Effect* recommends scaling model size and training data equally. Specifically, for every doubling of model size, the number of training examples should also double.[6] This was put to practice with the Llama-3 class of models (*https://oreil.ly/ODZqt*) where a dataset comprising 15 trillion tokens was used to train models with 7 billion and 70 billion parameters. A dataset at this scale, such as the FineWeb dataset (*https://oreil.ly/ahX2M*), would require about 43TB of disk space for storage.

The past decade has seen several benchmarking datasets that have steered the development of ML/AI models, particularly for image analysis and natural language processing. As shown in Figure 4-2, the scales of these datasets have grown tremendously by about 0.23 orders of magnitudes per year (OOM/y). A similar estimation was carried out for vision datasets, indicating a growth of about 0.09 OOM/y.[7]

5 Shaden Smith et al., "Using DeepSpeed and Megatron to Train Megatron-Turing NLG 530B, a Large-Scale Generative Language Model," *arXiv.org*, January 28, 2022 (*https://arxiv.org/abs/2201.11990*).

6 Jordan Hoffman et al.'s observations in "Training Compute-Optimal Large Language Models" (2022) (*https://arxiv.org/abs/2203.15556*) are dubbed the *Chinchilla Effect*.

7 Pablo Villalobos and Anson Ho, *Trends in Training Dataset Sizes* (Epoch AI, 2022) (*https://oreil.ly/_efRj*).

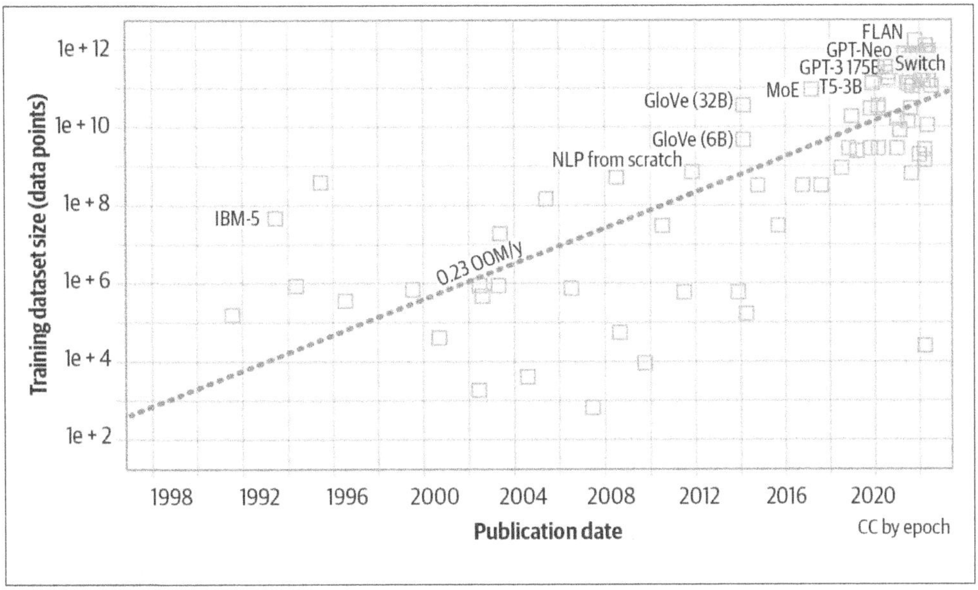

Figure 4-2. Trends in training dataset sizes for language models. (Source: Epoch AI) (https://oreil.ly/_efRj).

Carbon Footprint of Processing Data

The carbon footprint of storing large datasets is primarily due to the electricity consumed in datacenters and the embodied emissions of manufacturing the hardware. The carbon emissions of data storage have been the focus in this chapter this far, as illustrated in Figure 4-1 and in "Energy Consumption and Carbon Footprint of Storing 1TB Data" on page 79.

From the perspective of AI methods, the carbon footprint of data is not only due to the storage but also due to the processing of the data. AI model development at all stages involves processing the data using large models.[8]

What Is 1 Watt Worth?

How many images can we process with 1W on a standard GPU? Consider one of the commonly used GPUs for developing AI models, which is the A100GPU. It has a maximum rating of 48.75GFLOP/W, which we can round up to 50GFLOP/W.[9]

8 Anthony et al., "CarbonTracker: Tracking and Predicting the Carbon Footprint of Training Deep Learning Models" (*https://arxiv.org/abs/2007.03051*).

9 Radosvet Desislavov et al., "Compute and Energy Consumption Trends in Deep Learning Inference," *arxiv.org*, March 29, 2023 (*https://arxiv.org/abs/2109.05472*).

Let's simplify the processing to the simplest case: of computing the mean over the entire image. For an image of size 1,000 × 1,000, computing the mean incurs a FLOP count of 999,999 + 1 = 1 million where the final 1 is for the division operation. That is, computing the mean over this image has a FLOP count of 1 million. Using the rating of 50GFLOP/W, then we are able to compute the mean of 50,000 images.

For more complex operations, such as inference using a model like ResNet-50, which uses about 8GFLOP, only about six such images can be processed with 1W of power.

Dataset Curation

Developing DL models for real-world applications involves several processes. The most important of these, which does not always get sufficient attention, is the process of dataset curation. Dataset curation is the process of collecting, preparing, and organizing a dataset so that it is in a form that makes ML feasible.

The principle of *garbage in, garbage out* sometimes refers to the reliance on the quality of the datasets used to train DL models. Because these models are overparameterized function approximators, they have the capacity to learn arbitrarily complex patterns in the data. Sometimes these patterns can be trivial, irrelevant, or outright problematic. For example, see the cases in Figure 4-3, where the model focuses on features that are not exactly relevant for the corresponding label prediction. In other cases these learned patterns can be problematic and may point to ethical issues such as models not performing as expected on underrepresented groups.[10] Carefully curated data can alleviate some of these challenges in ML.

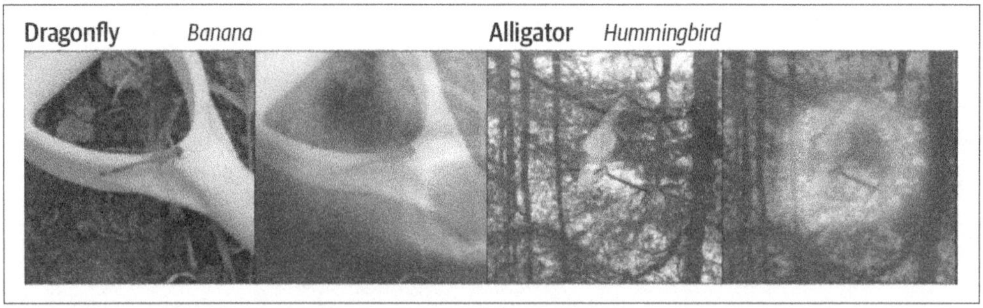

Figure 4-3. Two instances where the model prediction (label in italics) is incorrect compared to the ground truth (label in ***boldface****). In the first case, the color is the key feature that appears to be used to predict Banana. (Source: Hendrycks et al. "Natural Adversarial Examples" [2021] (https://arxiv.org/abs/1907.07174).)*

10 María Agustina Ricci Lara et al., "Addressing Fairness in Artificial Intelligence for Medical Imaging," *Nature Communications* 13, no. 1 (August 6, 2022) (*https://doi.org/10.1038/s41467-022-32186-3*).

Some of the key steps involved in dataset curation are:

Data collection
: Gathering sufficient data from appropriate sources, keeping the downstream tasks in mind. If sensitive data is involved, obtaining adequate permissions for usage is essential.

Data cleaning
: When large-scale data is collected for developing ML models, basic quality control to handle noisy samples, outliers, or missing data that could bias the ML models should be considered.

Data preprocessing
: Data collected from multiple sources might not be stored in the same format or be in the same numerical ranges. Transforming such diverse data into suitable formats for ML could include normalizing or standardizing features, encoding categorical variables, and performing other transformations to make the data compatible.

Domain-specific considerations
: Depending on the application, domain-specific knowledge might be needed to properly curate the dataset. For instance, when using data generated in hospitals, encoding information about the equipment (such as scanners used) can be useful.

Effective dataset curation can significantly contribute to the success of ML models by ensuring that the models are trained on accurate, diverse, and representative data. This could lead to better performance on the downstream tasks and alleviate the risks posed by the *garbage in, garbage out* phenomenon.

As ML practitioners, we are also generating a lot of data that when shared with others should adhere to the FAIR principles (*https://oreil.ly/CJuaq*), which recommends that data be Findable, Accessible, Interoperable, and Reusable (see Figure 4-4). Processing FAIR data can reduce the overhead in tedious preprocessing or regeneration of already existing data. One way to reduce the number of copies of existing data is if the data is shared with FAIR principles, which can directly reduce the overall environmental impact of data storage.

Most ML model development happens with already curated datasets that also consist of labels. In real application scenarios, this is seldom the case; however, as labeling is often costly. We next look at one of the common ML approaches to efficiently curating a labeled dataset with user interaction and iterative model refinement.

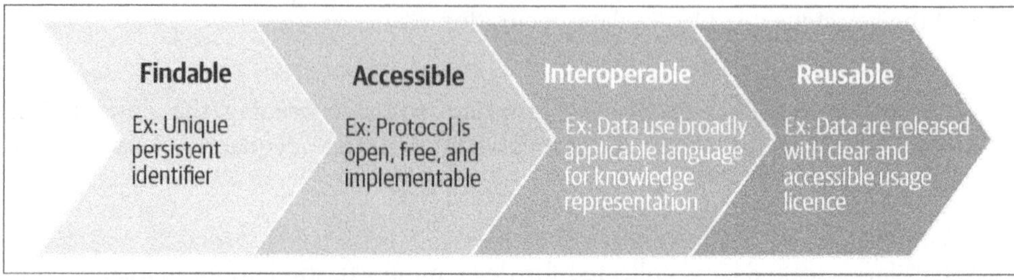

Figure 4-4. Overview of FAIR principles for data sharing.

Curating Datasets Frugally for Global Tree Identification

Automatically identifying trees from satellite images can be a useful way to measure the extent of carbon captured in them, as shown in Figure 4-5.[11] And doing this over time becomes a highly important tool toward climate change adaptation. Further, monitoring deforestation and reforestation could be beneficial in building ecological models to better inform climate action.

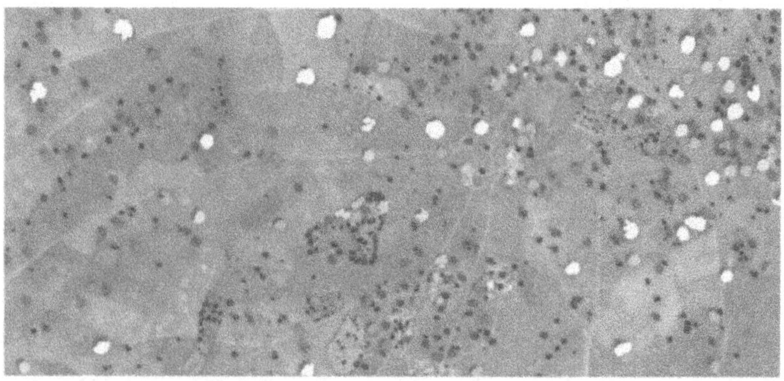

Figure 4-5. Carbon stock in individual trees in African drylands. Paler tree crowns store more carbon compared to darker ones. (Source: NASA's Scientific Visualization Studio (https://svs.gsfc.nasa.gov/5031).)

To detect trees meaningfully from these images, one must choose high-resolution satellite images, where each pixel could be about 10m × 10m. Under these assumptions and using the standard value of 5.2×10^{14} m^2 as the surface area of Earth, it would result in a dataset comprising about 5.2 million images of size 100 × 100 pixels.

11 We will use this task of global tree identification as a running example for discussing the different methods in this chapter.

Within supervised learning settings, obtaining the labels for a subset of these images is essential.

One way of labeling this data could be to choose a random subset of images. However, this random subset might not be useful, as not all images could contain regions of interest, i.e., trees (imagine all the image patches over oceans!). To choose a representative subset of images that is most informative for the task of tree detection, an interactive process has to be considered. This could involve a simple tree detection model and a domain expert who interactively chooses a subset of data for labeling. This can be formalized using principles of active learning, which are described next.[12]

Active Learning for Dataset Creation

Supervised ML requires labeled datasets. In cases where no labeled data is available, informed decisions on which of the data should be labeled can reduce the effort required in labeling. *Active learning* is one such ML approach that involves iteratively selecting the most informative instances from an unlabeled dataset and requesting their labels from an oracle (such as a human annotator). The goal of active learning is to maximize the performance of the ML model while minimizing the number of labeled instances needed for training. It is particularly useful when labeling instances is expensive, time-consuming, or resource-intensive.[13]

Figure 4-6 shows how active learning can be used to create a new labeled dataset $\mathbb{D} = \{(\mathbf{x}_1,\mathbf{y}_1),\cdots,(\mathbf{x}_L,\mathbf{y}_L)\}$ from an unlabeled dataset $\mathbb{X} = \{\mathbf{x}_1,\cdots,\mathbf{x}_N\}$:

1. *Initial labeled pool*

   Start with a small initial labeled dataset. This can be a random subset of the entire dataset, a domain-knowledge-based selection, or even a set of easy-to-label instances. Let $\mathbb{D} = \{(\mathbf{x}_1,\mathbf{y}_1),\cdots,(\mathbf{x}_N,\mathbf{y}_N)\}$ with L instances be the initial labeled dataset labeled by the oracle.

2. *Model training*

   Train an ML model f_θ (such as a classifier) using the initial labeled dataset $\mathbb{D}$. This model serves as the starting point for active learning.

3. *Uncertainty measurement*

   Apply the trained model f_θ to the remaining unlabeled instances $\mathbb{X}' = \mathbb{X} \setminus \mathbb{D}$ and calculate a measure of uncertainty for each instance. A common uncertainty

12 Maurice Mugabowindekwe et al., "Nation-wide Mapping of Tree-level Aboveground Carbon Stocks in Rwanda," *Nature Climate Change* 13, no. 1 (2023): 91–97 (*https://doi.org/10.1038/s41558-022-01544-w*).

13 Burr Settles, *Active Learning Literature Survey*, (University of Wisconsin-Madison CS Technical Reports, 2009) (*https://oreil.ly/Gnkra*).

measure is entropy H, where $H\left(f_\theta(\mathbf{x})\right)$ represents the entropy of the predicted probabilities for the possible labels.

4. *Instance selection*

   Select the instance with high uncertainty as the candidates for labeling. This is the instance for which the model is uncertain:

   $$\mathbf{x}_k = \operatorname{argmax}_{\mathbf{x}_i \in \mathbb{X}'} H\left(f_\theta(\mathbf{x}_i)\right)$$

5. *Oracle labeling*

   Request label $\mathbf{y}_k$ for the selected instance $\mathbf{x}_k$ from an oracle (human annotator or labeling process). Add the newly labeled instances to the labeled pool:

   $$\mathbb{D} = \mathbb{D} \cup \left\{\left(\mathbf{x}_k, \mathbf{y}_k\right)\right\}$$

6. *Model update*

   Retrain the model f_θ using the expanded labeled dataset $\mathbb{D}$. The new model benefits from the additional labeled instances.

7. *Iteration*

   Repeat steps 3 to 6 for a predefined number of iterations or until a stopping criterion is met, such as obtaining a labeled dataset of a predetermined size K. In each iteration, the active learning process selects instances that provide the most informative value for model improvement.

> **Active Learning Tools**
>
> Creating labeled datasets by harvesting labels for image analysis can be tedious. The process of labeling data with the primary purpose of using them for training ML models is known as *annotation*. Open source tools like Napari (*https://napari.org/stable*) offer utilities that can be used to build annotation pipelines. Other tools, such as Rootpainter (*https://oreil.ly/tyTG6*) for image analysis and DeepLabCut (*https://oreil.ly/Meyq9*) for video analysis, enable the rapid training of DL models.

The active learning process aims to optimize the balance between model performance and labeled instances by focusing on instances that provide the most informative value for model improvement. It allows the model to learn more effectively from the data, especially when labeling new instances is costly or resource-intensive.

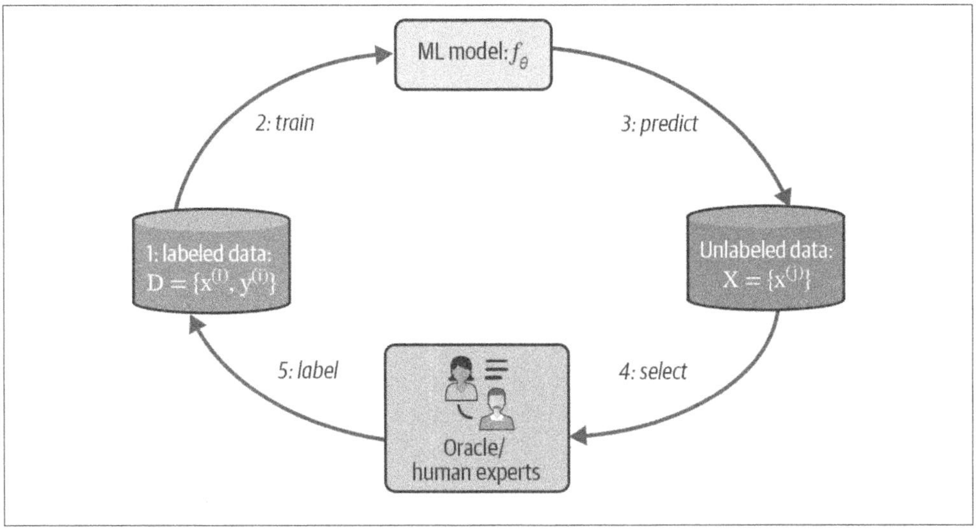

Figure 4-6. Overview of the active learning setting, in which a labeled dataset is curated from an unlabeled dataset based on the interaction between human experts and the ML model.

Active Learning Can Reduce AI Waste

Active learning can significantly enhance the resource efficiency of the global tree identification task.

By targeting the most informative samples, active learning reduces the need to process and train on large volumes of data. For instance, achieving similar model performance might require only 100,000 strategically selected images instead of 5 million. This reduction in data volume translates directly into decreased computational load and substantial energy savings.

Further, the data curated with active learning could also improve the model performance with fewer computational resources as it can be designed to focus on difficult or uncertain samples, such as mixed vegetation types or overlapping canopies. Studies show that active learning can reach comparable accuracy to traditional methods with only 10% to 20% of the labeled data, which translates into a reduction of the carbon footprint of model training.[14]

14 Jason Baldridge and Miles Osborne, "Active Learning and the Total Cost of Annotation," *Proceedings of the 2004 Conference on Empirical Methods in Natural Language Processing* (July 2004): 9–16 (*https://oreil.ly/X_eMT*).

Further, the efficient handling of class imbalance further optimizes resource use. Active learning ensures underrepresented classes, such as rare tree species or trees in arid regions, are adequately sampled, reducing the need for extensive retraining and fine-tuning, which saves computational resources and energy.

Learning with Pruned Datasets

It is difficult to quantify the information content of individual data points in a large dataset. As a result, some data points may contain repetitive information. Identifying the most informative data points can reduce the size of the training dataset. In this section we look at two classes of methods—instance selection and coreset selection—that yield smaller subsets while retaining the overall characteristics of the original dataset.

Instance Selection

Instance selection involves choosing a subset of instances (data points) from a given dataset while aiming to preserve the overall distribution and characteristics of the data. Instance selection methods often involve heuristics, clustering, or other similarity measures to determine which instances to keep. Some common methods for instance selection include random sampling, K-means clustering, and K-center selection.

Random sampling

Random sampling is the simplest of the instance selection strategies. For a given budget K, it randomly selects a subset of data from the original dataset. It gives equal preference to all the data points in the original dataset.

More formally, given a dataset $\mathbb{X} = \left\{\mathbf{x}^{(j)}\right\}$ with N data points, random sampling selects a smaller subset, $\mathbb{S} = \{\mathbf{s}_1, \cdots, \mathbf{s}_K\}$, of a predetermined size K by the following steps:

1. Obtain random indices: generate K random integers from $[1, \cdots, N]$, each representing index of an instance in the original dataset.
2. Select subset: update $\mathbb{S}$ with the K instances corresponding to the K random indices from the original dataset $\mathbb{X}$.

Using random sampling for instance selection comes with trade-offs. The algorithm is particularly useful when dealing with exploratory data analysis, when quick prototyping, or when the datasets are too large to fit into memory for further processing. Depending on the budget K, it can improve computational efficiency. However, when $K < < N$ (K is very small compared to N), random sampling might lead to information loss or biased samples, and it may pose additional challenges in maintaining class balance. Note that in the setting when $K = N$, a randomly sampled dataset converges to the original dataset.

In its simplest formulation, random sampling does not take the label information into account. This could result in a scenario where the class distribution in $\mathbb{S}$ could become skewed compared to the original class distribution in $\mathbb{D}$. This can be overcome by taking the number of classes into consideration. For a labeled dataset $\mathbb{D}$ with N samples and M classes, random sampling can be performed by distributing the budget of K data points equally between the M classes. This results in an approximate budget of $\frac{K}{M}$ instances per class.

> **Stratified Sampling**
>
> In most applications, the class distribution in the dataset is not uniform. That is, the number of data points per class can vary in the original dataset. Uniform random sampling that allocates equal sampling budget to every class can result in over- or underrepresentation of instances. To alleviate this problem, use stratified sampling. The main goal of stratified sampling is to ensure that the selected subset retains the same class distribution as the original dataset. This is important to prevent introducing bias and to maintain the representation of rare classes or attributes that might be critical for model training and evaluation.

Example 4-1 demonstrates the use of random sampling with different data budgets for the AerialNIST classification task.

Example 4-1. Random sampling to assess the trade-off between performance and resource costs

```
import numpy as np

# Generate random dataset (replace with your own dataset)
np.random.seed(42)
num_instances = 100
num_features = 10
dataset = AerialNIST()
train_dataset, valid_dataset = random_split(dataset)

# Specify the desired sample sizes
sample_sizes = [1,2,4,16,256,1024]

for sample_size in sample_sizes:
    # Perform random sampling
    indices = np.random.choice(num_instances, size=sample_size, replace=False)
    train_dataset = train_dataset[indices]
```

```
print("Original Dataset Shape:", dataset.shape)
print("Sampled Dataset Shape:", sampled_dataset.shape)
val_acc, train_acc, resource_metrics = \
  trainer.fit(model,train_loader,valid_loader)
print("Validation Performance:",val_acc)
print("Resource costs:",resource_metrics)
```

It should output the following:

```
N=1, E=0.003kWh, val_acc = 0.50
N=2, E=0.005kWh, val_acc = 0.55
N=4, E=0.007kWh, val_acc = 0.59
N=16, E=0.03kWh, val_acc = 0.54
N=256, E=0.08kWh, val_acc = 0.78
N=1024, E=0.23kWh, val_acc = 0.81
N=48000, E=1.02kWh, val_acc = 0.89
```

Is Random Sampling Sustainable?

Random sampling can also enhance the resource efficiency of the global tree identification task. Assuming a labeled dataset is obtained through active learning, random sampling can be used to further optimize the computational resources, energy consumption, and carbon emissions.

Random sampling maintains model accuracy by ensuring the randomly chosen subset represents the overall dataset, including different geographical regions, tree species, and environmental conditions. Studies show that models can achieve comparable performance with random sampling if the subset is diverse enough.

Scalability is a key advantage, enabling the management of large, diverse datasets with fewer computing resources. This is crucial for applications requiring high precision, such as tracking deforestation or assessing urban tree health globally.

Figure 4-7 depicts random sampling for the AerialNIST dataset. The overall budget is $K = 16$, which is distributed equally among the $M = 4$ classes, resulting in four samples per class.

Figure 4-7. Random sampling of AerialNIST dataset with M = 4 classes with a sampling budget of K = 16.

K-means clustering

K-means clustering is an unsupervised ML algorithm used for partitioning a dataset into a specified number of clusters. The algorithm aims to group similar data points together based on their features. It can also be used to reduce the dataset size, as the cluster centroids can be viewed as representative data points for the members within a cluster.

Given a dataset $\mathbb{X} = \{\mathbf{x}_1,\cdots,\mathbf{x}_N\}$ with N data points, a smaller dataset $\mathbb{S} = \{\mathbf{s}_1,\cdots,\mathbf{s}_K\}$ of predetermined size K can be obtained using K-means clustering by the following steps:

1. *Initialize cluster centers*
   Select K initial cluster centers, $\mathbb{S} = \{\mathbf{s}_1,\cdots,\mathbf{s}_K\}$.

2. *Assign points to clusters*
   Assign each data point, $\mathbf{x}_i$, to the nearest cluster center:

$$\mathbf{s}_\mathbf{j}\text{:}\operatorname{argmin}_{\mathbf{s}_j \in \mathbb{S}}||\mathbf{x}_i - \mathbf{s}_j||^2$$

3. *Update cluster centers*
   Recalculate the cluster centers by taking the mean of the data points assigned to each cluster:

$$\mathbf{s}_j = \frac{1}{|\mathbb{X}_j|}\sum_{\mathbf{x}_i \in \mathbb{X}_j}\mathbf{x}_i$$

4. *Repeat until convergence*
   Repeat steps 2 and 3 until cluster assigns no longer change.

The final output of K-means clustering algorithm is the set of cluster centroids $\mathbb{S} = \{\mathbf{s}_1, \cdots, \mathbf{s}_K\}$.

The centroids obtained by performing K-means clustering on the original dataset are not guaranteed to yield instances that correspond to the original dataset. The centroids could correspond to points in the data space where no observed data is present. This is illustrated in Figure 4-8 (left) where the centroids obtained using K-means clustering do not coincide with data points in the original dataset.

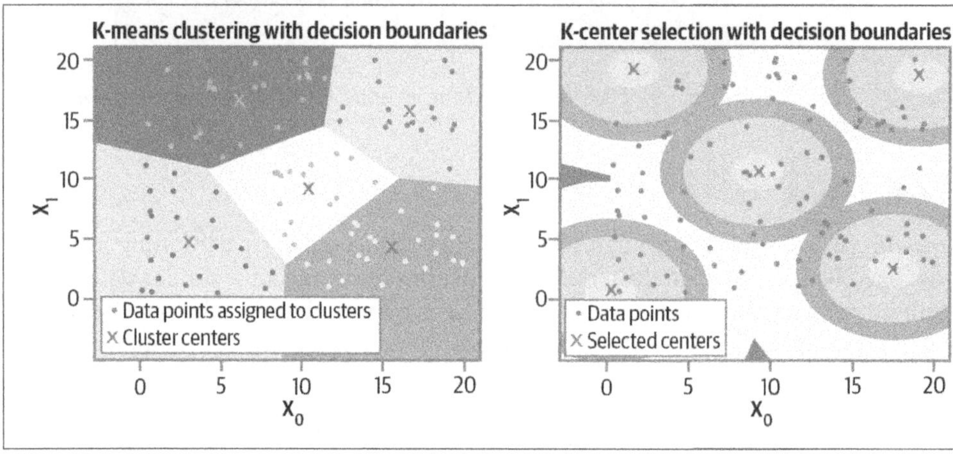

Figure 4-8. K-means clustering and K-center selection for instance selection.

K-center selection

The objective of *K-center selection* method is to select a subset of k points (centers) from a larger set of points in a way that minimizes the maximum distance between any point and its nearest selected center. The selected points represent the "center" of each cluster or region in the data. K-center selection can be seen as a clustering problem where the goal is to choose the most representative points as cluster centers.

Given a dataset $\mathbb{X} = \{\mathbf{x}_1, \cdots, \mathbf{x}_N\}$ with N data points, a predetermined smaller dataset $\mathbb{S} = \{\mathbf{x}_1, \cdots, \mathbf{x}_K\}$ of size K can be obtained using K-center selection by the following steps:

1. *Initialize cluster centers*
   Select K initial cluster centers, $\mathbb{S} = \{\mathbf{x}_1, \cdots, \mathbf{x}_K\}$.

2. *Assign points to clusters*
   Assign each data point, $\mathbf{x}_i$ to the nearest cluster center:

$$\mathbf{x}_{\mathrm{j}}: \operatorname{argmin}_{\mathbf{x}_j \in \mathbb{S}} ||\mathbf{x}_i - \mathbf{x}_j||^2$$

3. *Update cluster centers*
   Recalculate the cluster centers by selecting the farthest data point from each cluster center:

$$\mathbf{x}_{\mathrm{j}}: \operatorname{argmin}_{\mathbf{x}_j \in \mathbb{S}} ||\mathbf{x}_i - \mathbf{x}_j||^2$$

4. *Repeat until convergence*
   Repeat Steps 2 and 3 until cluster assigns no longer change.

The final output of K-center selection is the subset of K centers $\mathbb{S} = \{\mathbf{x}_1, \cdots, \mathbf{x}_K\}$.

> ### Random Sampling Versus K-Center Selection
>
> Using instance selection methods like K-center methods can offer significant advantages over random sampling, even though they require additional computational resources. K-center methods strategically select a subset of instances that are well-distributed across the dataset, ensuring better representation of diverse data characteristics compared to random sampling. This improved representation can enhance model accuracy and generalization by covering a wider range of data variations, including rare or underrepresented classes.
>
> Although K-center methods involve more computation initially, they often lead to faster model convergence and reduced overall training time. By selecting a high-quality subset, these methods can make training more efficient, potentially offsetting the extra computational cost. Additionally, in large-scale applications where processing the entire labeled dataset is impractical and setting up active learning is not possible, K-center methods provide a scalable approach by reducing the dataset size while maintaining its effectiveness.

Tokenization and Data Efficiency in Modern AI Models

Tokenization is the process of representing data into smaller units (tokens), before obtaining either precomputed or learned vector representations (see "Tokenization makes transformers versatile" on page 39). This tokenized data is used specifically in transformer-based models that include LLMs and foundational models. In language tasks, tokenization involves breaking down text into tokens like characters, words, or subwords.

Tokenization is also useful in non-language datasets where the data is broken down into smaller tokens that can enhance processing and analysis. In image processing, tokenization involves dividing images into patches to facilitate feature extraction. For time-series data, tokens might correspond to segmenting data into time windows to analyze patterns over specific periods. Overall, tokenization is an essential process in how the data is represented and used by transformer-based models. The tokenization schemes can influence the efficiency and effectiveness of processing and analyzing various types of complex data.

Subword tokenization schemes are commonly used for language data. For a given text source, T is given as follows:

1. Initialize the vocabulary $V = \{c_1, c_2, \ldots, c_k\}$ where c_i are the unique characters in T.
2. While $|V|$ < desired vocabulary size:
   - Find the most frequent pair of tokens (a,b) in T.
   - Merge a and b into a new token ab.
   - Update the vocabulary V with the new token ab.
3. Encode T using the final vocabulary V to obtain tokens S.
4. Return S.

Example 4-2 shows the effect on the size of the dataset as a function of different tokenization schemes. The code is available in this chapter's Jupyter notebook (*https://github.com/raghavian/sustainable_ai*).

Example 4-2. Effect on the number of tokens generated from the FAIRYTALES dataset when using word-level, character-level, and subword tokenization schemes

```
Original text length: 381462 characters

Word Tokenization:
Number of tokens: 83132
Vocabulary size: 6420

Character Tokenization:
Number of tokens: 381462
Vocabulary size: 75

Simple Subword Tokenization:
Number of tokens: 291153
Vocabulary size: 87
```

Coreset Selection

Coreset selection is a more specific approach that focuses on creating a smaller set of instances (coreset) that approximates the behavior of the entire dataset *for a specific task*, such as training an ML model for a particular downstream task.

The goal of coreset selection is to retain a small set of instances that collectively capture the most important characteristics of the data and result in similar model performance compared to using the entire dataset. Coreset selection aims to minimize the loss in performance when using the coreset for training while significantly reducing the computational and memory requirements.

Herding

Herding refers to a technique used to iteratively select instances from a larger dataset in a way that progressively captures the essential characteristics of the data distribution with respect to a *specific task*. Herding is a greedy algorithm that adds one sample each time into the coreset that can minimize the distance between the centers of the coreset and the original dataset.

Given a dataset $\mathbb{X} = \{\mathbf{x}_1, \cdots, \mathbf{x}_N\}$ with N data points and a task-specific feature extractor such as a pretrained neural network $f(\cdot)$,[15] a smaller dataset $\mathbb{S} = \{\mathbf{x}_1, \cdots, \mathbf{x}_K\}$ of predetermined size K can be obtained using herding by the following steps:

1. *Initialize the coreset*
   Initialize the coreset $\mathbb{S} = \{\}$.
2. *Coreset selection*
   For k from 1 to K:
   a. Find the data point $\mathbf{x}_i$ that minimizes the squared Euclidean distance to the current coreset in the feature space induced by $f(\cdot)$:

$$\mathbf{x_k} = \operatorname{argmin}_{\mathbf{x}_i \in \mathbb{X}} \sum_{\mathbf{x}_j \in \mathbb{S}} || f(\mathbf{x}_i) - f(\mathbf{x}_j) ||^2$$

   b. Add the selected data point to the coreset: $\mathbb{S} = \mathbb{S} \cup \{\mathbf{x}_k\}$.
3. *Convergence*
   Repeat the selection iterations until the desired coreset size K is reached.

Importance-based coreset selection

The key insight used in importance-based coreset selection is that during training of an ML model, the importance of a data point is related to its contribution toward the error or loss. That is, data points with larger magnitude of errors are more important

15 Feature extractors can range from simple filters (Fourier, wavelet, etc.) to more complex ones such as pretrained neural networks.

and should be included in the coreset. So, samples with the largest importance during training are selected as the coreset.

Several classes of coreset selection methods are obtained based on how the importance of data points is determined. For instance, some methods count the number of times a sample is misclassified during training after having been correctly classified in the previous training epoch. These events are called *forgetting events*, and samples with larger forgetting are deemed to be more important.[16] Other classes of methods use the magnitude of the gradient induced by a training data point as an indication of its importance. Furthermore, for methods that provide uncertainty estimates, data points with higher uncertainty can be assumed to be more important to the training of the model and can be included in the coreset.

Given a dataset $\mathbb{D} = \{(\mathbf{x}_1, \mathbf{y}_1), \cdots, (\mathbf{x}_N, \mathbf{y}_N)\}$ with N labeled data points, a trainable neural network $f_\theta(\cdot)$ and a smaller dataset $\mathbb{S} = \{\mathbf{x}_1, \cdots, \mathbf{x}_K\}$ of predetermined size K can be obtained using importance-based coreset selection by the following steps:

1. *Initialization*

   Initialize the coreset $\mathbb{S} = \{\}$.

2. *Compute the training loss*

   Estimate the training loss between the true labels and the model's predicted output using the neural network's current parameters: $\mathscr{L}(\mathbf{y}, f_\theta(\mathbf{x}))$.

3. *Importance ranking*

   Identify the contribution of each data point to the overall loss, $\ell_i = \mathscr{L}(\mathbf{y}_i, f_\theta(\mathbf{x}_i))$. Rank the data points based on their loss values from highest to lowest $\mathbb{D}_{ranked}$.

4. *Coreset selection*

   The coreset $\mathbb{S}$ is constructed by selecting the first K data points from the importance ranked dataset: $\mathbb{S} = \mathbb{D}_{ranked}\{1 \cdots K\}$.

The selected coreset $\mathbb{S}$ contains data points that contribute significantly to the overall loss, making it possible to train the model effectively while using a smaller subset of the data. Note that the procedure mentioned earlier can be adapted to other importance-based coreset selection methods by changing the importance estimation in step 3. Instead of ranking based on loss contributions, ranking can also be made

16 Mariya Toneva et al., "An Empirical Study of Example Forgetting During Deep Neural Network Learning," *International Conference on Learning Representations*, November 15, 2019 (*https://arxiv.org/abs/1812.05159*).

based on gradient or uncertainty. Example 4-3 uses DeepCore (*https://oreil.ly/Zr91F*), an open source package with several coreset method implementations.[17]

> **Instance Selection Methods for Coreset Selection**
>
> The key difference between instance-selection and coreset-selection methods is that the former is agnostic to the downstream task, whereas the latter is tuned for a specific task of interest. Instance-selection methods attempt to capture the original dataset characteristics with a smaller subset of data points. Coreset-selection methods aim to maintain the same performance on some task (e.g., training performance of ML models) with the smaller subset as compared to the original dataset. Instance-selection methods such as K-center selection can also be used for coreset selection if the distance measure is made specific to the downstream task. Instead of computing distances in the data space, performing K-center selection in a feature space that is specific to the task can yield a coreset that is better suited for the task of interest.

Example 4-3. Herding on AerialNIST dataset for training an MLP for classification using DeepCore package

```
git clone https://github.com/PatrickZH/DeepCore.git # Clone into DeepCore repository
cd DeepCore # Enter DeepCore directory

# Run Herding on AerialNIST to obtain 0.1% of the original dataset for training
# an MLP model
python -u main.py --fraction 0.1 --dataset AerialNIST \
--data_path ./data --selection Herding --model MLP --workers 10
```

Additional Compute for Coreset Selection Versus Sustainable AI

The objective of using methods like random sampling or K-center selection is to reduce the amount of data used to develop AI models, which can reduce the overall computational costs and also the corresponding energy consumption and carbon emissions. That the methods like random sampling and K-center are inexpensive makes them attractive methods for reducing the dataset size.

Coreset methods like herding are more computationally intensive than random sampling. Then what is the argument for using these more sophisticated coreset methods?

17 Chengcheng Guo et al., "DeepCore: A Comprehensive Library for Coreset Selection in Deep Learning," in *Lecture Notes in Computer Science*, (Springer Nature, 2022): 181–95 (*https://doi.org/10.1007/978-3-031-12423-5_14*).

One argument in favor of using coreset methods is that choosing better coresets can improve the convergence properties of DL models. This can then reduce the overall model development costs, which can justify the initial cost of creating the coreset in the first place. This is all the more evident when a coreset is used to perform hyperparameter tuning or neural architecture search, which are discussed in Chapter 5.

Learning with Compressed Data

Instance- and coreset-selection methods yield a subset of the original dataset to improve the computational efficiency of training ML models. This can reduce the AI waste due to the redundancy between data points in a given dataset. Another class of method that focuses on reducing the redundancy within and between data points is data compression. We look at two broad classes of data compression strategies that are used when developing ML models:

Compression of data points
: In this approach the total number of data points in a dataset is not reduced, but the size of each data point is reduced while retaining as much information as possible. This class of dimensionality reduction methods is widely used.

Compression of datasets
: Dataset compression or dataset condensation is akin to coreset selection, in that a dataset smaller than the original dataset is obtained. However, the key difference is that the new data points are not data points from the original dataset but are synthetic data points attempting to distill the information of the original dataset into fewer samples.

Data Point Compression

Dimensionality reduction is the process of reducing the number of features or dimensions in a dataset while attempting to preserve as much relevant information as possible. In ML, high-dimensional data can present challenges. As the number of features (dimensions) increases, computational complexity often grows, and it becomes more difficult to visualize and analyze the data. Additionally, the curse of dimensionality can lead to overfitting, where models perform well on the training data but generalize poorly to new, unseen data. The class of data point compression methods presented next can also alleviate some of these effects manifested due to the curse of dimensionality.

Random projection

Random projection refers to the technique used for dimensionality reduction using a specific class of projection matrices known as random projection matrices. A random projection matrix, as the name suggests, is composed of random values. When applied to data points, this matrix transforms the data into a lower-dimensional space where the relative distances between data points are preserved to a certain extent.

Dimensionality reduction via random projection transforms the original dataset with N data points of F dimensional features $\mathbf{X} \in \mathbb{R}^{N \times F}$ to a compressed dataset with K features $\widetilde{\mathbf{X}} \in \mathbb{R}^{N \times K}$ by the following steps:

1. *Initialize random projection matrix*
   Generate a random projection matrix $\mathbf{R} \in \mathbb{R}^{F \times K}$, where K is the reduced dimensionality. The elements of $\mathbf{R}$ are drawn from as suitable distribution, such as the Gaussian distribution or the Rademacher distribution.[18]

2. *Perform random projection*
   Project the original data points into the lower dimensional space using the random projection matrix: $\widetilde{\mathbf{X}} = \mathbf{XR}$.

The extent of dimensionality reduction is controlled by K. Aggressive dimensionality reduction using random projection can lead to information loss, while milder reductions may better preserve the relations between the data points.

Principal component analysis

Principal component analysis (PCA) is a widely used dimensionality reduction method. PCA aims to find a new set of orthogonal axes (principal components) in the original feature space that captures the most variance in the data. It achieves this by finding the directions along which the data vary the most. While it captures the variance well and provides guarantees in terms of variance explained, it might not always preserve distances optimally. PCA involves the computation of eigenvectors and eigenvalues of the covariance matrix, which can be computationally intensive, especially for large datasets.

PCA-based dimensionality reduction transforms the original dataset with N data points of F dimensional features $\mathbf{X} \in \mathbb{R}^{N \times F}$ to a compressed dataset with K features $\widetilde{\mathbf{X}} \in \mathbb{R}^{N \times K}$ by the following steps:

1. *Center the data*
   Compute the mean vector $\overline{\mathbf{x}}$ by averaging the rows of $\mathbf{X}$; i.e., $\mathbf{X}_{\text{centered}} = \mathbf{X} - \overline{\mathbf{x}}$.

2. *Compute the covariance matrix*
   Compute the covariance matrix $\mathbf{C} \in \mathbb{R}^{F \times F} = \frac{1}{(N-1)}\mathbf{X}_{\text{centered}}\mathbf{X}_{\text{centered}}^T$.

18 Rademacher distribution is a discrete probability distribution that takes on the values +1 and -1 with equal probability, i.e., for a binary discrete random variable $X \in \{+1, -1\}, P(X = +1) = P(X = -1) = 0.5$.

3. *Eigenvalue decomposition*

   Perform the eigenvalue decomposition of $\mathbf{C}$ to find its eigenvectors $\mathbf{v}_i$ and corresponding eigenvalues λ_i. Sort the eigenvectors in decreasing order of their eigenvalues.

4. *Select principal components*

   Choose the top K eigenvectors corresponding to the largest K eigenvalues.

5. *Projection matrix*

   Form a projection matrix, $\mathbf{P} \in \mathbb{R}^{F \times K}$ by concatenating the selected eigenvectors as columns. To project the data into the new low-dimensional space:

$$\widetilde{\mathbf{X}} = \mathbf{X}_{\text{centered}}\mathbf{P}$$

The matrix $\widetilde{\mathbf{X}}$ represents the data in the lower-dimensional space, where each row corresponds to the reduced representation of a data point.

Figure 4-9 illustrates the projection of data from 3D to 2D using random projection and PCA. For this simple dataset, both methods are able to capture the key properties of the original 3D data in the 2D space.

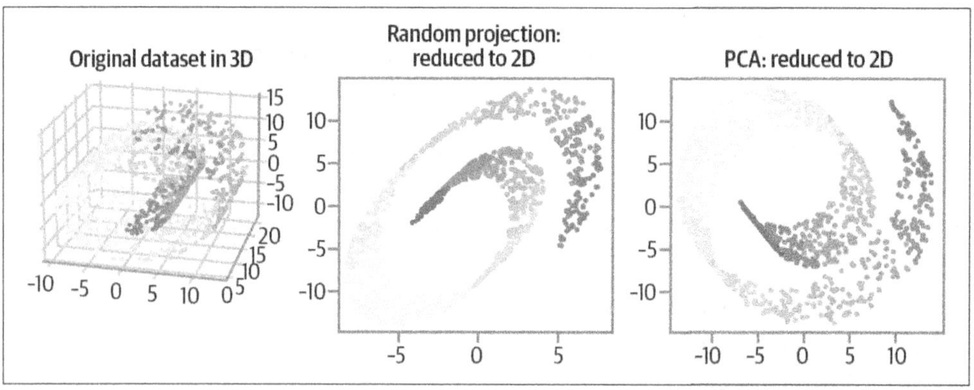

Figure 4-9. Visualizing the dimensionality reduction for a toy dataset in 3D to 2D using random projection and PCA.

Autoencoders

Dimensionality-reduction methods such as PCA scale poorly as the number of data points increases.[19] In this section, we look at a class of dimensionality-reducing DL models—autoencoders—that scales better for large-scale data compared to

19 Eigen decomposition of the covariance matrix is expensive and scales poorly with number of data points.

methods like PCA. Specifically, we look at the undercomplete autoencoders already discussed in "Learning Representation Spaces" on page 24 for obtaining compact data representations.

Undercomplete autoencoders are a class of unsupervised ML models that use an encoder-decoder architecture. The encoder takes the original, large data and compresses it into a much smaller, condensed representation. It learns to pick out only the most important features. The decoder takes the compressed representation and tries to reconstruct the original data from it.

The goal is to train both parts together until the decoder can create a near-perfect reconstruction. (See discussions related to representation learning in Chapter 2.) For the decoder to succeed, the encoder must have learned to create a meaningful summary in the first place. The connection between them is called a *bottleneck* because it forces the model to focus on the most essential features of the data.

Once the model is trained, you can discard the decoder and use the encoder by itself as a powerful tool for dimensionality reduction. Unlike older methods such as PCA, which can capture only simple, linear relationships, autoencoders can learn complex, nonlinear patterns (like curves and other intricate shapes) in the data.

In short, an autoencoder transforms a large dataset into a much smaller one by learning to represent it in a more efficient way, as shown in Figure 4-10. This is achieved by the following steps:

1. *Autoencoder architecture*
   a. The encoder neural network f_θ projects the input data $\mathbf{X}$ to a low-dimensional space $\widetilde{\mathbf{X}}$, i.e., $\widetilde{\mathbf{X}} = f_\theta(\mathbf{X}) \in \mathbb{R}^{N \times K}$.
   b. The decoder neural network g_φ projects the low-dimensional data back into the data space $\widehat{\mathbf{X}}$, i.e., $\widehat{\mathbf{X}} = f_\varphi\left(\widetilde{\mathbf{X}}\right) \in \mathbb{R}^{N \times F}$.
   c. Weights of the neural networks are randomly initialized.
2. *Training the autoencoder*
   The autoencoder is trained to minimize the reconstruction error using an appropriate loss function, such as mean squared error: $\mathscr{L} = ||\mathbf{X} - \widehat{\mathbf{X}}||^2$. During training, the parameters of the neural network are updated to minimize the loss.
3. *Dimensionality reduction*
   As the encoder creates a form of information bottleneck ($K<F$), the encoder learns to capture the most essential features. Once the autoencoder is trained, dimensionality reduction on new data can be performed using the encoder:

$$\widetilde{\mathbf{X}} = f_\theta(\mathbf{X})$$

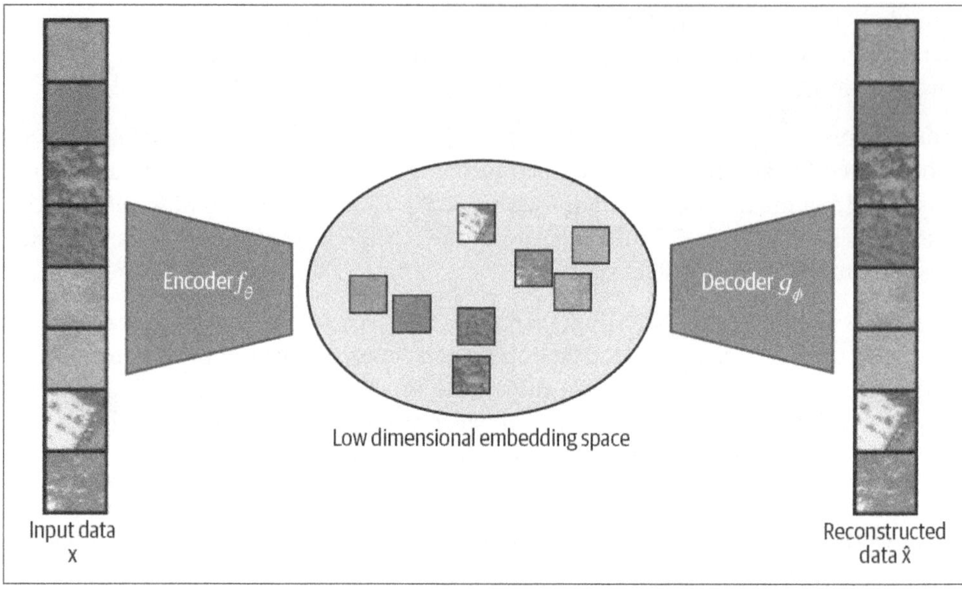

Figure 4-10. A high-level overview of the undercomplete autoencoder. After training the encoder-decoder pair jointly, only the encoder is used to obtain the low-dimensional representation.

Global Tree Identification in a Low-Dimensional Space

Building on top of the active learning and instance selection methods discussed so far, we might have a well-curated, labeled dataset based on the satellite images. Instead of working with 5 million images of 1,000 × 1,000 resolution, we might now be using a fraction, say about 100,000 images.

If we consider a CNN or a vision transformer (see Chapter 2 for details), processing 100,000 images that are of 1,000 × 1,000 resolution can also be computationally expensive. The dimensionality reduction methods presented in the previous section can reduce the feature dimension from 1,000 × 1,000 to something much smaller, without losing important information.

Processing in these reduced feature spaces can be efficient making the global tree identification task less resource-intensive.

Dataset Condensation

In the previous section, we looked at methods that reduce the dimensionality of individual data points by projecting them into linear (random projection, PCA) and nonlinear (autoencoders) spaces. These methods do not reduce the number of data points in a given dataset but only compress the individual data points. This reduces the training computational costs but has the disadvantage that information lost per sample cannot be compensated (if possible at all) by other data points in the dataset.

We now look at the class of methods focused on distilling the information in large datasets into few, synthetic samples using techniques known as *dataset condensation*. Dataset condensation methods are similar to the coreset selection methods in that they attempt to distill information contained in a dataset into fewer samples *for a specific task*. The key difference compared to coreset selection methods, however, is in the fact that the samples obtained using dataset condensation are not necessarily instances in the dataset. Dataset condensation methods are allowed to synthesize new data points that are derived from the training set. This offers additional flexibility as more information could be crammed into fewer samples.

More formally, given a dataset $\mathbb{X} = \{\mathbf{x}_1,\cdots,\mathbf{x}_N\}$ with N data points, the task of obtaining a smaller dataset $\mathbb{S} = \{\mathbf{s}_1,\cdots,\mathbf{s}_K\}$ of predetermined size K can be formulated as:

$$\mathbb{S} = \text{argmin}_{\mathbb{T}} \mathscr{L}(\mathbb{T},\mathbb{X}),$$

where $\mathscr{L}$ is some objective measure of performance that captures the quality of dataset condensation and $\mathbb{T}$ is any instance of a synthetic dataset with K samples. Depending on the choice of $\mathscr{L}$, different dataset condensation methods can be obtained. Figure 4-11 shows a high-level overview of the process of dataset condensation methods.

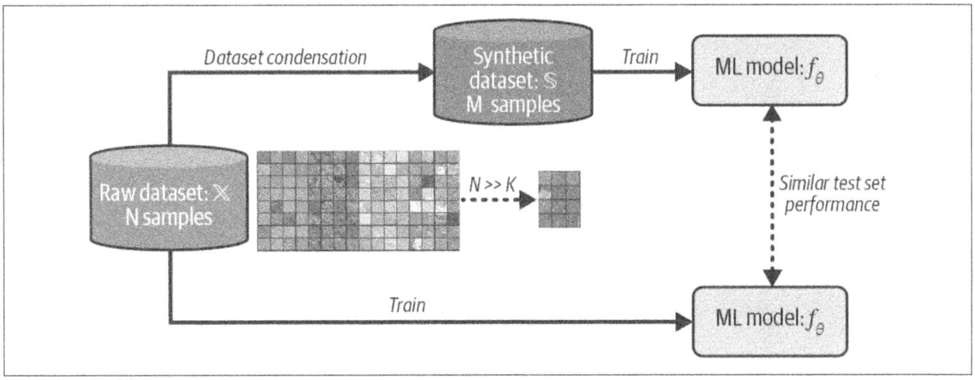

Figure 4-11. Dataset condensation methods distill a smaller dataset from a larger, raw dataset with the goals of achieving similar test performance on the downstream task. (Source: based on Yu et al., "Dataset Distillation: A Comprehensive Review" [2023] (https://arxiv.org/abs/2301.07014).)

A general framework for dataset condensation is prescribed by the following steps:

1. *Initialize synthetic data*
   Initialize the synthetic dataset $\mathbb{S}$ with K random, real, or coreset data points.
2. *Get a network*
   Choose a neural network of task-specific interest f_θ with random or pretrained or intermediate checkpoint weights θ.
3. *Update network parameters*
   Update θ via $\mathbb{X}$or $\mathbb{S}$ for some steps.
4. *Update synthetic dataset*
   Update synthetic data, $\mathbb{S}$, to minimize the chosen objective measure: $\mathscr{L}(\mathbb{S},\mathbb{X})$.
5. *Iterate until convergence*
   Repeat steps 2–4 until some convergence criterion.

The resulting dataset consists of synthetic data that captures representative features in the original dataset. Figure 4-12 illustrates the synthetic data obtained using one of the dataset condensation methods for the CIFAR10 dataset.

Dataset condensation methods can be categorized into three main types based on the type of objective measure, $\mathscr{L}$, used for matching the synthetic dataset with the raw dataset, which are presented next.

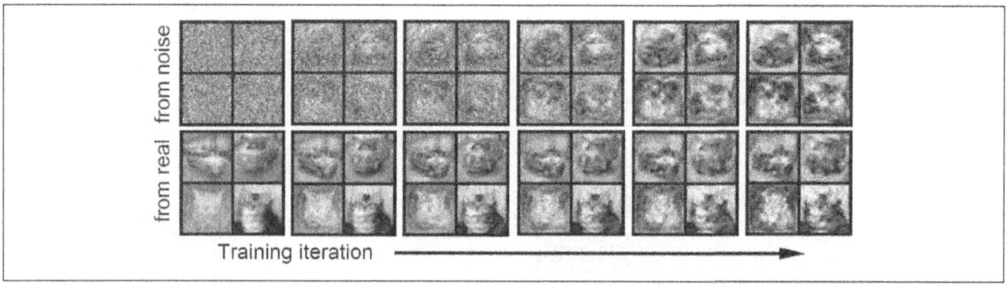

Figure 4-12. Evolution of the synthetic data generated using one of the dataset condensation methods. (Source: adapted from the DatasetCondensation GitHub (https://oreil.ly/JT90U).)

Dataset condensation with performance matching

Performance matching aims to obtain a new, synthetic dataset that is of reduced size but that performs almost as well as the original dataset.[20]

20 Performance matching was introduced in the seminal work of Wang et al., "Dataset Distillation" (2020) (*https://arxiv.org/abs/1811.10959*).

Consider a dataset $\mathbb{D} = \{(\mathbf{x}_1,\mathbf{y}_1),\cdots,(\mathbf{x}_N,\mathbf{y}_N)\}$ with N labeled data points. Denote a family of trainable neural networks $f_{\theta_0}(\cdot)$ where $\theta_0 \sim \Theta$ is the distribution for initialization of network parameters. The downstream supervised loss function to train the neural networks is given as $\mathscr{L}_s$ with T optimization steps. A smaller dataset $\mathbb{S} = \{\mathbf{s}_1,\cdots,\mathbf{s}_K\}$ of predetermined size K can be obtained using performance-matching-based dataset condensation by the following steps:

1. *Initialize synthetic data*
   Initialize the synthetic dataset $\mathbb{S}$ with K random data points.
2. *Outer optimization*
   Perform the outer optimization for T steps:
   a. Retrieve batch of random neural networks: sample a batch of P neural networks with random weights $\theta_p \sim \Theta$.
   b. Sample batch of original data: randomly sample K original data points, $\mathbb{X}_t$.
   c. Inner optimization: perform the inner optimization P times for each of the sampled neural networks:
      - Update network parameters: using loss computed based on synthetic data, $\mathscr{L}_s^{\mathbb{S}}\left(f_{\theta_p}(\mathbf{S}),Y\right)$ update neural network parameters to θ'_p.
      - Evaluate on real data: obtain loss on the real data, $\mathscr{L}_s^{\mathbb{X}}\left(f_{\theta'_p}(\mathbf{X}_t),\mathbf{Y}\right)$.
      - Update synthetic data: update synthetic data $\mathbb{S}$ to match the performance on real data $\mathscr{L}_s^{\mathbb{X}}$.

The inner- and outer-optimizations in step 2 of the procedure form the bi-level optimization, which is at the core of several dataset condensation methods. In performance-matching-based dataset condensation, few synthetic data samples are optimized to match the performance of several neural networks on the original data. Also note that the dataset condensation budget K is usually shared equally between all the classes; that is, if the original dataset has C classes, then performance matching yields K/C synthetic images per class.

> **Performance Matching to Parameter Matching**
>
> In performance matching, the synthetic dataset is optimized to match the downstream task performance of a neural network that is trained on the original dataset. In parameter-matching-based dataset condensation methods, by contrast, the matching objective is modified to focus on parameter updates. The updates to parameters, in turn, are captured by matching the gradients computed with respect to the neural network parameters. The original gradient matching work uses an explicit distance between the gradients estimated at each layer when trained using the synthetic data and the original dataset.[21] That is, for an L-layered neural network, the gradient matching objective is given as:
>
> $$\mathscr{L}(\mathbb{S},\mathbb{X}) = D\left(\Delta_\theta \mathscr{L}_s^{\mathbb{S}}, \Delta_\theta \mathscr{L}_s^{\mathbb{X}}\right)$$
>
> where Δ_θ is the gradient with respect to the network parameters.

Dataset condensation with distribution matching

Performance-matching- and parameter-matching-based dataset condensation methods match some form of training effects (performance, gradients, parameter updates) for synthetic datasets to those of the real datasets. The distribution-matching-based dataset condensation methods directly aim to approximate the distribution of the real data using fewer synthetic samples in the synthetic dataset, via metrics such as maximum mean discrepancy (MMD).[22] For efficient and expressive distribution matching, most existing methods perform the distribution matching not in the image space but using some form of an embedding space, such as the intermediate feature maps obtained from neural networks.

Given a dataset $\mathbb{D} = \{(\mathbf{x}_1,\mathbf{y}_1),\cdots,(\mathbf{x}_N,\mathbf{y}_N)\}$ with N labeled data points, a family of embedding functions $f_\theta(\cdot)$ where $\theta \sim \Theta$ is the distribution of embedding functions, a smaller dataset $\mathbb{S} = \{\mathbf{s}_1,\cdots,\mathbf{s}_K\}$ of predetermined size K can be obtained using distribution-matching-based dataset condensation by the following steps:

21 Zhao et al., "Dataset Condensation with Gradient Matching," *arxiv.org*, March 8, 2021 (*https://arxiv.org/abs/2006.05929*).

22 Tong Chen and Raghavendra Selvan, "A Discrepancy-Based Perspective on Dataset Condensation," *arxiv.org*, September 12, 2025 (*https://arxiv.org/abs/2509.10367*).

1. *Initialize synthetic data*
   Initialize the synthetic dataset $\mathbb{S}$ with K random data points.

2. *Sample embedding functions*
   Obtain embedding functions, $f_{\theta_i}: \theta_i \sim \Theta$.

3. *Embed real and synthetic data*
   Obtain embeddings for the real and synthetic data using the family of embedding functions: $f_{\theta_i}(\mathbf{X}), f_{\theta_i}(\mathbf{S})$.

4. *Compute distance between distributions*
   Compute distance between embeddings of real and synthetic data:

$$\mathscr{L}(\mathbb{S},\mathbb{X}) = ||\frac{1}{N}\sum f_{\theta_i}(\mathbf{X}) - \frac{1}{K}\sum f_{\theta_i}(\mathbf{S})||^2$$

5. *Update synthetic data*
   Update synthetic data $\mathbb{S}$ to minimize the distribution distance measure $\mathscr{L}$.

Random Neural Networks as Feature Extractors

Randomly initialized neural networks turn out to be useful feature extractors. They already consist of certain structures at initialization that are also manifested in the trained models. This is most evident in models that have strong inductive biases. For instance, CNNs operating on images assume local correlations between pixels, which are encoded as shareable kernels across the images. Using such randomly initialized CNNs can extract useful image features.[23] This can be seen as a generalization of random projections that are highly nonlinear.

23 Ehsan Amid et al., "Learning From Randomly Initialized Neural Network Features," *arXiv.org*, February 13, 2022 (*https://arxiv.org/abs/2202.06438*).

Data and Dataset Compressed: What Comes Next?

We have explored several classes of methods to reduce the size of the training datasets in this chapter. While some methods focused on selecting informative samples (instance/coreset selection), others focused on compressing individual data points (PCA/autoencoders) or even compressing entire datasets (dataset condensation). We next summarize some of the caveats and considerations of using these methods:

Why can we not always use compressed data?

Compression loses information, and some tasks are not tolerant to this loss.

Data compression, as described in this chapter, is lossy. Any gain in efficiency achieved using the compression of data points and datasets comes with some loss of information. While some methods can asymptotically capture all of the information in the original data, there is no guarantee that with a reduced budget any of the methods are able to capture *all* of the information in the dataset. As a consequence, using compressed data in all scenarios is not recommended, as the information lost due to compression could be informative for the downstream tasks. Compressed data can be used to accelerate learning, and in applications that are not critical, one might be able to get away without any serious performance issues. In all other cases, models should be validated on at least a subset of the original data, and users should be made aware of the performance trade-offs.

Can the loss in information be quantified?

Not always. Only some methods have this feature.

Methods like PCA inherently have ways to quantify the loss in information measured as the ratio of explained variance. Other classes of methods might not have these features. As a general rule, the performance gap on some chosen downstream task should be compared with and without compression using a smaller subset of real data to provide meaningful insight into the trade-off between efficiency and performance.

Does compression come at no cost?

There is always a trade-off. There will never be free lunch.[24]

Other than the performance trade-off, most of the data compression methods also incur additional computational costs. Sometimes these costs can be small, as in instance selection methods. Sometimes they can be massive, such as in dataset condensation with performance matching that uses a bi-level optimization. These

24 In the same spirit as D.H. Wolpert and W.G. Macready's "No Free Lunch Theorems for Optimization" (1997) (*https://doi.org/10.1109/4235.585893*).

computational costs should be taken into account before advocating for data compression.

Is dataset condensation only for image data?

Mostly yes. But there are ongoing attempts for other modalities.

Current dataset condensation methods are primarily focused on image datasets, but this is poised to change. Efforts toward condensing other types of data are ongoing. For instance, graph data condensation might actually be better suited than condensing image datasets due to the inherent sparsity of graph data.[25] Condensing large-scale (tokenized) language datasets within the paradigm of dataset condensation is not yet common.

Compressing data points versus datasets: is one preferable over the other?

No. These choices should be made after carefully considering the downstream tasks.

The goal of data compression is to reduce redundancy. Redundancy at the data point level due to dependent features or irrelevant features warrants compression of data points. On the other hand, prevalence of similar data points within a dataset lends itself well to compressing datasets. However, this should be known *a priori* to the users; without this prior knowledge, there is no clear way of choosing one class of methods over the other.

How is data compression related to sustainable AI?

Data/dataset compression alone can't lead us to sustainable AI. It is only one part of the solution.

Using compressed data can reduce the training computational costs, as using compressed data can lead to faster convergence in some instances. In addition, training large-scale AI models on smaller, compressed datasets can substantially reduce the computational costs. This reduction of computations can result in reduction in the carbon footprint of developing AI models.

Is compression the only way to improve sustainability of AI from a data point of view?

No. It's just one important way.

Data compression provides a set of technical tools to make informed trade-off decisions between performance and efficiency. Another highly important data-related action that can improve the sustainability of AI methods is to endorse *open data* as outlined within the FAIR principles (*https://oreil.ly/CJuaq*) (see

25 For some extreme dataset compression on graph datasets, see works such as Jin et al.'s "Graph Condensation for Graph Neural Networks" (2022) (*https://arxiv.org/abs/2110.07580*).

Figure 4-4). In Chapter 9, we will elaborate more on these behavioral changes that can also be helpful.

Data Parsimony for Global Tree Identification

We have looked at the pros and cons of performing data and dataset compression in this chapter. Returning to the question of global tree identification from satellite images ("Curating Datasets Frugally for Global Tree Identification" on page 84), how can one achieve reasonable results while minimizing AI waste from the data point of view?

- Active learning for dataset curation can minimize the labeling effort and also be used to choose the most informative data points.
- Coreset selection methods can be used on top of the labeled coreset to subsample datasets. This coreset can be used to perform hyperparameter tuning of the neural networks, which can be computationally intensive.
- In choosing the network architectures, one could resort to using models that operate on low-dimensional representation of the data. Dimensionality reduction methods like autoencoders have shown to capture useful features in fewer dimensions compared to the original input dimensions.

Using these methods together can drastically reduce the compute needed to solve an inherently large-scale problem such as the global tree identification.

CHAPTER 5
Automating Model Selection

The adage "pull out all the stops," meaning you exhaust all resources to achieve a goal, might apply to how models are currently designed in DL. This work involves adjusting multiple configurations of a DL model, somewhat like an organist using a variety of stops to produce different sounds. Obtaining the appropriate class, configuration, and parameters for a particular downstream task from the massive space of possibilities is known as *model selection*. This step of model selection is tedious, and requires several orders of magnitude more compute resources than training the final model, as illustrated in Figure 5-1. Further, the process of model selection in DL is known to be as much art as it is science, requiring significant human effort.[1]

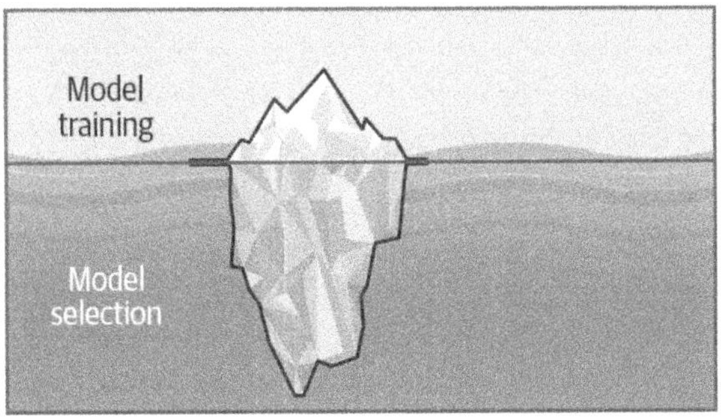

Figure 5-1. The proverbial "tip of the iceberg" captures the seldom-addressed costs of performing model selection in DL. The vast hypothesis space increases the model selection costs many folds over compared to the training cost of a single model.

1 Barret Zoph and Quoc V. Le, "Neural Architecture Search With Reinforcement Learning," *arXiv.org*, February 15, 2017 (*https://arxiv.org/abs/1611.01578*).

In this chapter, we will understand why model selection is a computationally expensive process, look at some fundamental concepts of model selection, identify the AI waste involved in this step, and try out various tools for model selection. We will look at methods for automated model selection, with the objective of improving the overall efficiency of AI methods while offering tips on how to achieve a reasonable tradeoff between performance and efficiency.

Motivation

DL model selection is a difficult task due to the plethora of choices to be made related to the class of models, architectures of the chosen model class, activation functions, connectivity patterns, regularization techniques, and so on. This range of choice results in a vast, if not infinite, set of possible models known as the *hypothesis space*. The task of model selection is then to choose the appropriate model for the downstream task from this hypothesis space. The scale and complexity of this space make even exhaustive exploration tedious, cumbersome, and resource-intensive.

Consider the space of feed-forward CNNs for image classification, which consists of models like ResNet.[2] Training a single model like ResNet on a benchmark dataset like CIFAR-10 on a standard GPU can take about five minutes. However, a comprehensive exploration of the hypothesis space where models like ResNet reside can be prohibitively expensive from a compute point of view. As a simplified example, the space of CNNs could consist of 423,000 unique architectures according to the NAS-Bench-101 dataset.[3] The authors of NAS-Bench-101 report that the compute required to train all the models in this space amounted to a staggering 100TPU years! Standard model selection using exhaustive exploration even only of the hyperparameters for a specific model can incur several orders of magnitude more compute than training one model. Training resource costs are only the tip of the iceberg, as the bulk of the compute could be used up in model selection (Figure 5-1).

Obtaining appropriate DL models from the vast hypothesis spaces is an important step to achieve satisfactory performance on downstream tasks. However, performing model selection conventionally using exhaustive exploration can be infeasible in most cases and is rife with AI waste (see Chapter 3). We can reduce the disproportionate resource consumption between model selection and training by restricting the hypothesis spaces, using smarter exploration of the hypothesis space, and avoiding redundant computations.

2 Kaiming He et al., "Deep Residual Learning for Image Recognition," *arXiv.org*, December 10, 2015 (*https://arxiv.org/abs/1512.03385*).

3 Chris Ying et al., "NAS-Bench-101: Towards Reproducible Neural Architecture Search," *arXiv.org*, May 14, 2019 (*https://arxiv.org/abs/1902.09635*).

Exhaustive exploration of a hypothesis space is seldom performed in practice, due to the exorbitant computational resources needed. Most AI practitioners use some domain knowledge or inherit model choices from existing literature. This reduces the AI waste to some degree, however, at the expense of knowing if the chosen model is the best possible one. Many of the methods presented here offer a more informed trade-off between reducing AI waste for model selection and obtaining performant models.

Novel Materials Discovery Task

Automating the discovery of novel molecules with certain properties can be extremely useful. For instance, novel nanomaterials for batteries that don't require rare earth minerals or to discover drugs that are effective and fast to develop can all benefit from the use of ML/AI models. However, unlike GenAI for text and images, modeling the chemical space where molecules live is highly complex. Figure 5-2 depicts a set of base structures when modeling a specific class of nanomaterials.

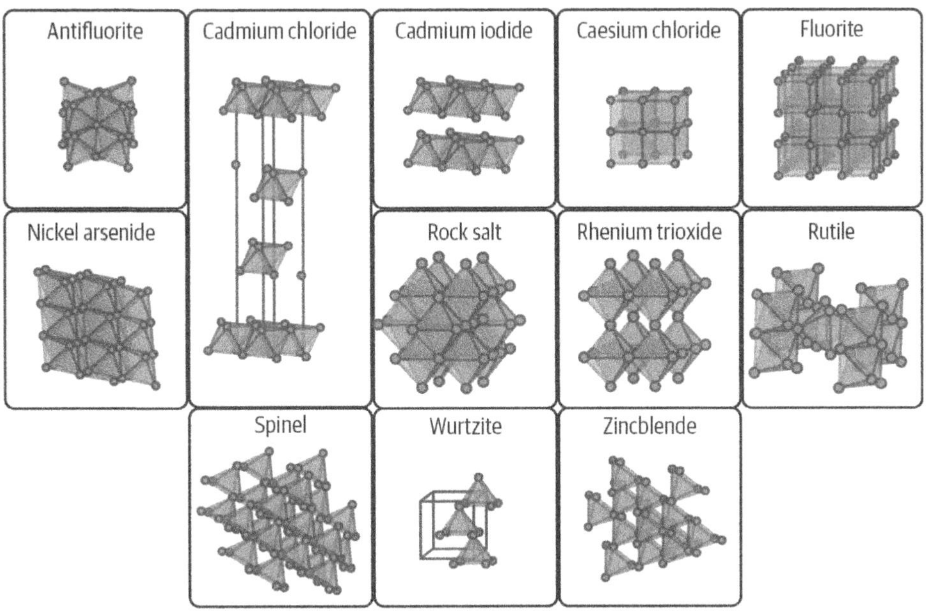

Figure 5-2. Different nanomaterial structures. (Source: adapted from Friis-Jensen et al. [2024] (https://arxiv.org/abs/2402.13221).)

GenAI for molecules poses interesting challenges in terms of the types of models to develop and the amount of data to use. How does one go about choosing a model appropriate for dealing with molecular data? We will use this task as the running example in this chapter.

The Model Selection Hierarchy: MC³-Space

Decomposing the hypothesis space into hierarchical levels with the MC³-space concept—model class, configuration, and complements—can make DL model selection more systematic. This approach provides a structured framework for neural network design. I introduce the MC³-space in this book to provide a structured framework for neural network design:

1. *Model class*

   At the highest level, DL practitioners should choose the model class, taking into account the type of task at hand. Depending on the type of input data and the desired output, it's usually straightforward to select the model class. Common DL model classes include MLP, RNN, CNN, and Transformers. (See "Neural Network Zoo" on page 32 for an introduction to these models.)

2. *Model configuration*

   After determining the model class, the next step is to decide on the model configuration. A general rule based on the principle of *Occam's razor* is to begin by designing simpler models. Practitioners can then gradually increase complexity by adjusting design parameters as needed. Common model configuration parameters include depth, width, activations, feature channels, and number of attention heads.

3. *Model complements*

   After obtaining a basic model, practitioners can introduce additional elements to enhance performance. These primarily improve model convergence and/or generalization. Expected or observed overfitting influences the decision to include these components. Among a broad array of potential model complements, we focus on those influencing the optimization or the generalization of the chosen models. Commonly used model complements include dropout, batch norm, layer norm, and weight initializations.

Figure 5-3 illustrates a high-level overview of the MC³-space concept for model selection. We can view the DL hypothesis space using hierarchical concepts of model class, model configuration, and model complements. According to the MC³-space concept, each point within the hypothesis space belongs to a particular model class, has a specific model configuration, and has model complements. The task of model selection then is to explore this space to obtain the model that is best in some measure of performance.

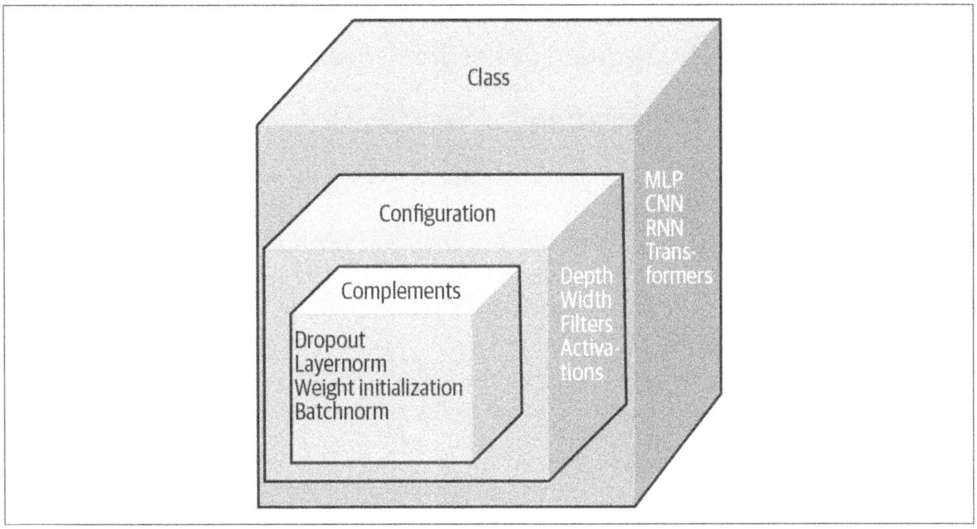

Figure 5-3. Overview of the MC³-space concept for model selection showing a nonexhaustive set of options at each level.

Model Selection Parameters, Hyperparameters, and Model Parameters

The distinction between model selection parameters, training hyperparameters, and model parameters can sometimes be unclear. We'll assume all parameters that do not influence the structure of a chosen neural network are the hyperparameters. Once a specific instance of an untrained model is chosen and the hyperparameters for the training procedure are fixed, the model parameters then correspond to the tunable weights of this model.

For example, we could choose a two-layered MLP with 32 hidden units, a dropout layer with dropout rate 0.65, and a total of 400 trainable weights. We could use a stochastic gradient descent algorithm with a batch size of 4 using a learning rate of 0.1. In this instance, MLP, 2-layers, and 32 hidden units are the model selection parameters defined by the MC³-space. The other parameters that don't alter the network structure, such as SGD, batch size, learning rate, and dropout rate, are the hyperparameters. The four hundred trainable weights are the model parameters.

Beyond the elements in the MC³-space that define the hypothesis space, we can optimize additional parameters related to the model training. Commonly called *hyperparameters* in the model of DL model selection, these may include the learning rate of the optimizer, batch size of training data, and the optimizer itself. Some of the model complements can take up different values, which can also be optimized as part of the hyperparameter tuning. For instance, the specific value of the dropout rate can be tuned, as the specific value does not change the structure of any given neural network.

Model Selection as Optimization

The vastness of the hypothesis space in DL makes exhaustive exploration infeasible. Expressive encoding of the hypothesis space, appropriate goodness-of-fit measures, and efficient algorithms to explore the hypothesis space can be used to automate model selection to a large extent. Automated model selection requires formalizing notions of search space, optimization criteria, and discrete optimization methods, as illustrated in Figure 5-4. Choosing the right search space, optimization strategy, and optimization criteria are crucial to automating model selection. Once model selection is automated, strategies to improve them further to reduce AI waste can also be incorporated.

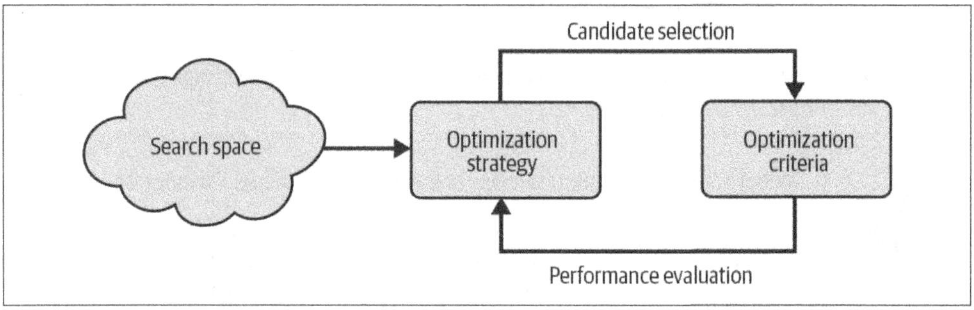

Figure 5-4. Overview of the three model selection steps posed as discrete optimization.

Search space

Because hyperparameters and neural network architectures consist of values that are represented by nonnumerical values such as activation functions, normalization operations, and regularization techniques, direct optimization using existing numerical methods is not feasible. These variables should be mapped to real numbers. Consider model selection parameters such as activation functions consisting of several candidates: `sigmod`, `relu`, `leaky-relu`, and `elu`. We can map these discrete numbers to optimize neural network configurations with these activation functions. One possible mapping could be `sigmoid:0`, `relu:1`, `leaky-relu:2`, and `elu:3`.

Encoding neural networks architectures into meaningful and compact spaces is an open area of research. Currently, the most popular strategy is to use directed acyclic graphs (DAGs) to encode neural network architectures. In these DAGs the nodes can correspond to the individual operators that are part of the neural network architecture, and the edges capture the connectivity, as detailed in "Neural Architecture Search" on page 129.[4]

Optimization criteria

The objective of model selection is to obtain neural network architectures or training settings that perform well according to a specific performance measure. The most common optimization criteria for model selection are training the model using a chosen set of parameters and then validating on a validation set. The performance on the validation set is used to alter or retain a subset of parameters until a network of desirable performance is obtained.

> **Multiobjective Optimization for Model Selection**
>
> In addition to validation performance, other objectives that can steer toward reducing AI waste can also be included. Compute requirements or energy consumption can be directly included as criteria when performing multiobjective optimization.[5]

Optimization strategy

The optimization strategy defines the approach to exploring the designed search space. When search spaces are small enough, we can evaluate all possible models and select the best candidate according to the optimization criteria. The search space is typically too large, however, for this approach to be feasible. Most optimization strategies used for model selection attempt to trade off between exploring new regions in the search space and exploiting existing structures to obtain the best candidate model. The most common optimization strategies are random search, Bayesian optimization, evolutionary methods, reinforcement learning, and gradient-based methods. We will cover some of these methods later in this chapter.

Based on the scope of the search space, we can perform systematic and automated model selection at two levels:

Hyperparameter optimization
: This step optimizes parameters that do not directly affect the architecture or design of the neural network. *Hyperparameter optimization* (HPO) is used for tuning the parameters that control the training setup of a chosen architecture or some specific values of a *model complement*. For instance, a network could be

---

4 Thomas Elsken et al., "Neural Architecture Search: A Survey," *arXiv.org*, April 26, 2019 (*https://arxiv.org/abs/1808.05377*).

5 Pedram Bakhtiarifard et al., "EC-NAS: Energy Consumption Aware Tabular Benchmarks for Neural Architecture Search," *ICASSP 2022 - 2022 IEEE International Conference on Acoustics, Speech and Signal Processing (ICASSP)*, March 18, 2024, 5660–64 (*https://doi.org/10.1109/icassp48485.2024.10448303*).

designed to comprise a dropout layer, but the specific dropout rate in the range [0,1] can be optimized using HPO. Additional model training parameters such as the learning rate, batch size, and even optimizers can be treated as hyperparameters and optimized.

Neural architecture search
: This step involves designing and configuring neural network architectures composed of various elements. The automated design of neural networks from a search space is known as *neural architecture search* (NAS). While exploring all possible neural network architectures is impractical (due to scaling issues), current NAS methods focus on a specific model class. For example, the NASBench-101 dataset explores the space of feedforward CNNs, and the resulting architecture will be a candidate from this search space.

Next we'll look closely into HPO and NAS, two essential model selection steps. Some of the concepts related to the search space, optimization criteria, and optimization strategies for performing HPO and NAS are interchangeable, and in some scenarios can be performed jointly.[6]

Model Class for the Novel Materials Discovery Task

Molecules present an interesting challenge in how they are represented. While images can be represented in multidimensional arrays and text as a set of tokens, these are not immediately useful to represent molecules. Representing molecules as graphs—where each atom is a node and pairwise relations are edges—has been the most common representation.[7]

If we use graph-based representations for molecules, the choice of model class (the outer most layer of the MC^3-space in Figure 5-3) can be narrowed to the use of GNNs. As discussed in "Graph neural networks ("Relationships, not grids")" on page 37, GNNs are well suited for dealing with graph structured data. Choosing the model class as GNNs immediately reduces the complexity of the MC^3-space. The inductive bias here about how molecules are better represented as graphs can reduce the complexity of model selection.

6 Xiaoliang Dai et al., "FBNetV3: Joint Architecture-Recipe Search Using Predictor Pretraining," *arXiv.org*, March 30, 2021 (*https://arxiv.org/abs/2006.02049*).

7 Yuyang Wang et al., "Graph Neural Networks for Molecules," in *Machine Learning in Molecular Sciences*, ed. Chen Qu and Hanchao Liu (Springer Cham, 2023), 21–66 (*https://doi.org/10.1007/978-3-031-37196-7_2*).

Hyperparameter Optimization

For a given DL model in the MC³-space, performing HPO allows us to optimize the specific values of some of these parameters and the training settings. More formally, if we aim to find the optimal values for a set of hyperparameters φ that optimize a specific objective function $\mathscr{L}(\varphi)$, the goal of HPO is to find $\varphi^{*} = \arg\min_{\varphi} \mathscr{L}(\varphi)$.

Let's examine some of the common model selection techniques used for obtaining the best hyperparameter configurations.

Grid Search

Grid search is the simplest model selection method that relies on exhaustive evaluations of all possible parameter configurations provided as a finite grid of points. While grid search is exhaustive within this grid, it is feasible for optimizing only a small number of parameters, as it scales poorly in the number of parameters. Further, the resolution of the grid also influences the computational costs of performing grid search. The number of combinations to be evaluated in grid search grows exponentially with the number of hyperparameters. For a search space with M hyperparameters where each parameter can take k unique values, the total number of parameter configurations to be evaluated in grid search is k^{M}.

Figure 5-5 shows an increasing number of hyperparameters, where each parameter can take $k = 2$ values; even for reasonable number of hyperparameters (< 20), the search space explodes (10^{6}). Grid search scales exponentially with the number of hyperparameters.

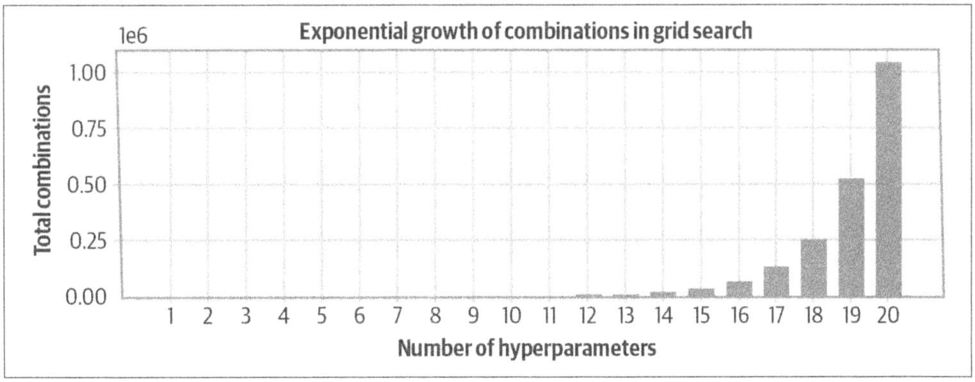

Figure 5-5. The total number of hyperparameter combinations in the vertical axis plotted against increasing number of hyperparameters. Each hyperparameter in this illustration can take two unique values.

Consider a set of M hyperparameters $\varphi = [\varphi_1, \varphi_2, ..., \varphi_M]$, where each hyperparameter φ_i can take on a set of values $V_i = \{v_{i1}, v_{i2}, ..., v_{ik_i}\}$. If the objective function to be optimized is $\mathscr{L}(\varphi)$, then the optimal hyperparameter configuration φ^* can be obtained using grid search by the following steps:

1. *Create a parameter grid*

   Generate all possible combinations of parameters:

$$\varphi = \{(\varphi_1, \varphi_2, ..., \varphi_M) \in V_1 \times V_2 \times ... V_M\}$$

2. *Iterate over hyperparameter combinations*
   - For each hyperparameter value combination in φ, train a model on training data.
   - Evaluate the model on the validation set using the objective function $\mathscr{L}(\varphi)$.

3. *Select best hyperparameters*

   Choose the set of hyperparameters that yield the best performance. For a minimization objective, the best configuration is obtained as $\varphi^* = \arg\ \min_\varphi \mathscr{L}(\varphi)$.

4. *Final model*

   The optimal set of hyperparameters is given by φ^*, and the corresponding performance score is $\mathscr{L}(\varphi^*)$.

Although grid search is inefficient, it can be used in small search spaces if obtaining *the* optimum is important, as illustrated in Figure 5-6. In this toy example of the scaling of grid search, the parameters of a linear regression model are sampled on a finite grid of slope-intercept values, each point is evaluated, and the validation loss is reported. After all points on the grid are evaluated, the parameter combination with the lowest error is used to train the final model. Once the evaluation on the grid is completed, the parameters that yield minimum loss are reported as the optimal parameters. Note that the resolution of the grid can have an impact on the quality of the solutions obtained.

On the scale of trade-off between exploration and exploitation, grid search skews heavily toward exploitation. It relies mainly on evaluating hyperparameter configurations predefined by users and does not explore any other parameter regimes. If the chosen grid is coarse, then the optimal parameter configuration may not be reached, yet finer grids (large k) cost more evaluations.

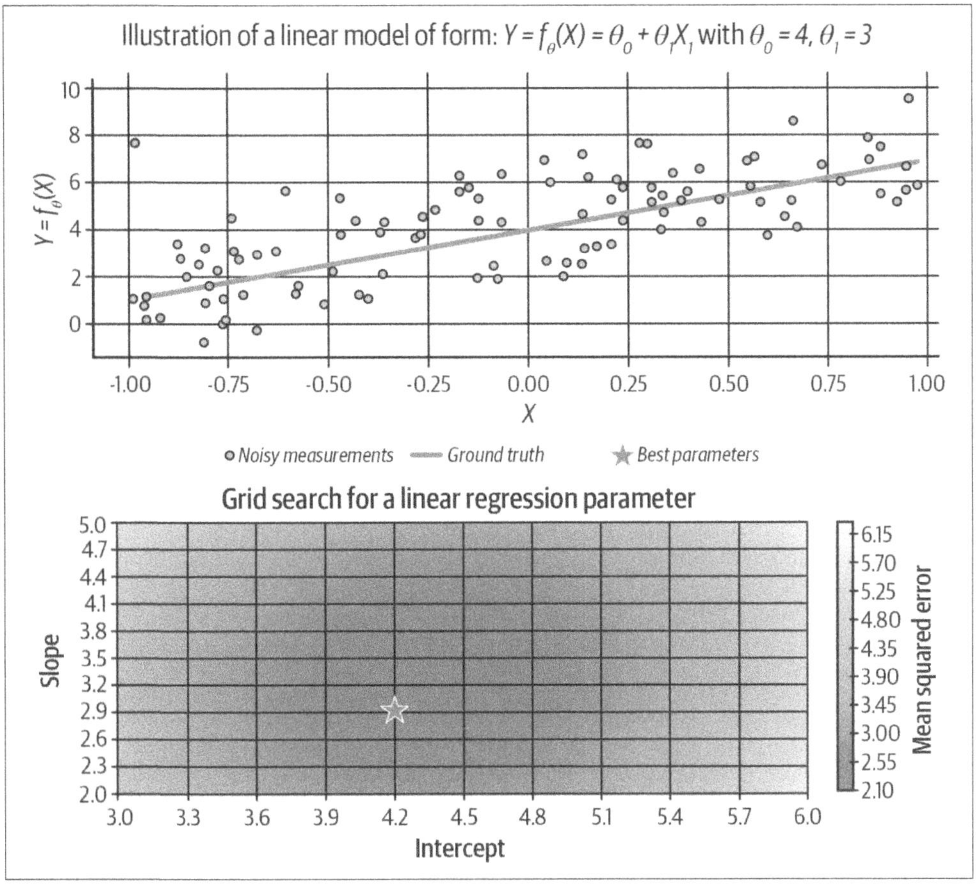

Figure 5-6. Exploring all possible intercept-slope combinations to solve linear regression using grid search. Each intersection in the 2D grid evaluates a parameter combination and estimates the mean squared error.

Random Search

When the search space for hyperparameters is massive, grid search is untenable. In such situations, *random search* can be an effective strategy. Random search explores random combinations of hyperparameters. For a given compute budget (hyperparameter combination evaluations), random search is better than grid search at exploring the search space. On the exploration-exploitation scale, random search skews toward the exploration end, as it cannot exploit any prior information.

Consider a set of M hyperparameters $\varphi = [\varphi_1, \varphi_2, ..., \varphi_M]$, where each hyperparameter φ_i, can take on a set of values $V_i = \{v_{i1}, v_{i2}, ..., v_{ik_i}\}$. If the objective function to be optimized is $\mathscr{L}(\varphi)$, then the optimal hyperparameter configuration φ^* can be obtained using random search with a budget of N evaluations by the following steps:

1. *Set the number of random samples*
   Define the number of random combinations or iterations N.

2. *Generate random hyperparameter combinations*
   For $n = 1...N$, randomly select values for each hyperparameter: $\varphi^{(n)} = \left(\varphi_1^{(n)}, \varphi_2^{(n)}, ..., \varphi_M^{(n)}\right)$, where $\varphi_i^{(n)}$ is randomly chosen from V_i.

3. *Iterate over random hyperparameter combinations*
   For each randomly generated combination $\varphi^{(n)}$:

   - Train a model with hyperparameters $\varphi^{(n)}$ on the training data.
   - Evaluate the model on the validation set using the objective function $\mathscr{L}\left(\varphi^{(n)}\right)$.

4. *Select best hyperparameters*
   Choose the set of hyperparameters that yield the best performance as follows:

$$\varphi^* = \arg\min_{\varphi^{(n)}} \mathscr{L}\left(\varphi^{(n)}\right)$$

5. *Final model*
   The optimal set of hyperparameters is given by φ^*, and the corresponding performance score is $\mathscr{L}(\varphi^*)$.

Random search can be optimal only when the number of iterations are equal to the number of hyperparameter configurations, i.e., $N = k^M$. While random search can stumble upon good hyperparameter configurations, it is not guaranteed to find the optimal set of hyperparameters when $N < k^M$. The key advantage of random search over grid search is in the regime of limited computed budget. Random search can explore the space more effectively, as shown in Figure 5-7. This strategy can be particularly useful when a subset of the hyperparameters have smaller influence on the overall performance.

Example 5-1 shows the difference between grid search and random search for optimizing the hyperparameters of an MLP, using standard libraries in scikit-learn. Grid search should take an order of magnitude longer than random search for this simple example.

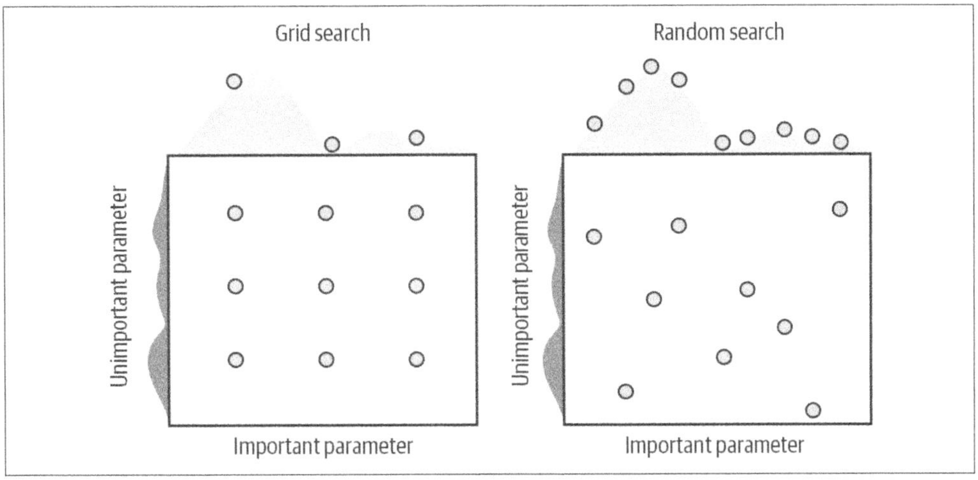

Figure 5-7. Effective exploration capacity when using grid search compared to random search. (Source: adapted from Bergstra and Bengio, "Random Search for Hyper-Parameter Optimization," 2012 (https://dl.acm.org/doi/10.5555/2188385.2188395).)

Example 5-1. The difference between grid search and random search

```
from sklearn.neural_network import MLPClassifier
from sklearn.model_selection import GridSearchCV, RandomizedSearchCV
from sklearn.datasets import load_iris
from sklearn.model_selection import train_test_split
import time

# Load the Iris dataset
iris = load_iris()
X = iris.data
y = iris.target

# Split the data into training and testing sets
X_train, X_test, y_train, y_test = \
train_test_split(X, y, test_size=0.2, random_state=42)

# Define the parameter grid for grid search
param_grid = {
    'hidden_layer_sizes': [(50,), (100,), (50, 50), (100, 50, 100)],
    'activation': ['relu', 'tanh'],
    'alpha': [0.0001, 0.001, 0.01],
    'learning_rate': ['constant', 'invscaling', 'adaptive']
}
print("Exploring the following parameter grid:")
print(param_grid)

max_iter = 1000
cv = 5
```

```
# Create grid/random search objects for MLPClassifier and fit it to the data
grid_search = GridSearchCV(MLPClassifier(max_iter=max_iter),
                           param_grid=param_grid, cv=cv)
random_search = RandomizedSearchCV(MLPClassifier(max_iter=max_iter),
                           param_distributions=param_grid, n_iter=10, cv=cv)

for search_name, search in zip(['Grid','Random'],[grid_search, random_search]):
    tic = time.time()
    search.fit(X_train,y_train)
    toc = time.time()
    # Print the best hyperparameters found
    print("Best hyperparameters found via "+search_name+" search:")
    print(search.best_params_)
    print("Time to perform search: %.2f s"%(toc-tic))
```

This should output the following:

```
Exploring the following parameter grid:
{'hidden_layer_sizes': [(50,), (100,), (50, 50), (100, 50, 100)],
'activation': ['relu', 'tanh'], 'alpha': [0.0001, 0.001, 0.01],
'learning_rate': ['constant', 'invscaling', 'adaptive']}
Best hyperparameters found via Grid search:
{'activation': 'relu', 'alpha': 0.0001,
'hidden_layer_sizes': (50,), 'learning_rate': 'constant'}
Time to perform search: 107.49 s
Best hyperparameters found via Random search:
{'learning_rate': 'invscaling', 'hidden_layer_sizes': (100,),
'alpha': 0.0001, 'activation': 'relu'}
Time to perform search: 13.68 s
```

Bayesian Optimization

Grid search exploits a predefined grid of hyperparameters, whereas random search explores the search space. Neither method attempts to balance the strengths of exploitation and exploration strategies to limit the search space.

Bayesian optimization navigates complex search spaces to find the best set of parameters by building a model of the space of hyperparameters to efficiently sample configurations that can yield better candidates for evaluations.[8] Bayesian optimization uses a combination of exploration and exploitation strategies iteratively to suggest new parameter configurations based on past evaluations that converge toward the optimal solution with fewer function evaluations.[9]

8 J. B. Mockus and L. J. Mockus, "Bayesian Approach to Global Optimization and Application to Multiobjective and Constrained Problems," *Journal of Optimization Theory and Applications* 70, no. 1 (1991): 157–72 (*https://doi.org/10.1007/bf00940509*).

9 Ruben Martinez-Cantin, "BayesOpt: A Bayesian Optimization Library for Nonlinear Optimization, Experimental Design and Bandits," *Journal of Machine Learning Research* 15 (November 2014): 3915–19 (*https://oreil.ly/zb5qk*).

Bayesian optimization explores the hyperparameter space without evaluating all configurations, as grid search does, by approximating the true objective function with a surrogate model. Probabilistic methods like Gaussian processes are typically used to implement these surrogate models, which help identify promising regions in the hyperparameter space. Another key component in Bayesian optimization is the *acquisition function*; it plays a key role in Bayesian optimization by using information from the surrogate model to select the next candidate for evaluation. Acquisition function often uses expected improvement or upper confidence bounds to transform the probabilistic information from the surrogate model into choices for acquiring the next candidates for evaluation.

> **Surrogate Models and Acquisition Functions in Bayesian Optimization**
>
> Surrogate models and acquisition functions are two crucial elements in Bayesian optimization. Surrogate models approximate the objective function based on observed data to guide the selection of next hyperparameters to be evaluated. Acquisition functions are used in Bayesian optimization to help decide which hyperparameter configurations to evaluate next based on the surrogate model's predictions and uncertainty.
>
> The specific choice of surrogate models and acquisition functions can be important when performing Bayesian optimization. Relying on surrogate models can be restrictive and computationally expensive and has given rise to a new class of *model-free* optimization methods.[10]

Consider a set of M hyperparameters $\varphi = [\varphi_1, \varphi_2, \ldots, \varphi_M]$, where each hyperparameter φ_i, can take on a set of values $V_i = \{v_{i1}, v_{i2}, \ldots, v_{ik_i}\}$. If the objective function to be optimized is $\mathscr{L}(\varphi)$, then the optimal hyperparameter configuration φ^* can be obtained using Bayesian optimization by the following steps:

1. *Initialization*

   Define the objective function $\mathscr{L}(\varphi)$ and choose the initial set of hyperparameters $\varphi_{i=1}^{N}$.

2. *Create initial data for surrogate model*

   Evaluate the initial configurations to obtain the dataset $D = \{(\varphi_i, \mathscr{L}(\varphi_i))\}_{i=1}^{N}$.

10 Jiaming Song et al., "A General Recipe for Likelihood-Free Bayesian Optimization," *Proceedings of the 39th International Conference on Machine Learning: PMLR*, 162 (June 28, 2022): 20384–404 (*https://oreil.ly/uEOGn*).

3. *Initialize surrogate model*
   Initialize a surrogate probabilistic model $s_\psi(\cdot)$ to approximate the objective function with parameters ψ.

4. *Update surrogate model*
   Update the surrogate model parameters ψ on D.

5. *Select next hyperparameters to evaluate*
   Use an acquisition function (e.g., expected improvement, upper confidence bound) $\alpha(\cdot)$ to suggest the next set of hyperparameters to evaluate:

$$\varphi_{\text{next}} = \arg \max_{\varphi} \alpha\left(\varphi ; s_\psi , D\right)$$

6. *Evaluate objective function*
   Evaluate the objective function for the selected hyperparameters: $\mathcal{L}(\varphi_{\text{next}})$.

7. *Update surrogate model with new observations*
   Update the surrogate model $s_\psi(\cdot)$ with the new observed hyperparameter-performance pair $(\varphi_{\text{next}}, \mathcal{L}(\varphi_{\text{next}}))$.

8. *Repeat steps 4–6*
   Iterate by selecting new hyperparameters based on the updated surrogate model until a stopping criterion is met (e.g., maximum number of iterations).

9. *Select best hyperparameters*
   Choose the set of hyperparameters that yield the best performance as $\varphi^* = \arg \min_\varphi \mathcal{L}(\varphi)$.

10. *Final model*
    The optimal set of hyperparameters is given by φ^*, and the corresponding performance score is $\mathcal{L}(\varphi^*)$.

Designing the surrogate models and acquisition functions for Bayesian optimization might not be straightforward. Furthermore, maintaining the surrogate models to approximate the objective function and performing the acquisition function evaluations can incur additional computational overhead when dealing with large datasets.

Example 5-2 shows the procedure for using packages like Bayes-Opt to perform Bayesian optimization, and the results are visualized in Figure 5-8. A dense space of parameters can be effectively explored using Bayesian optimization.

Example 5-2. Bayesian optimization for optimizing a set of hyperparameters can be performed using packages such as Bayes-Opt (https://oreil.ly/nz56x).

```
from bayes_opt import BayesianOptimization
from sklearn.neural_network import MLPClassifier
from sklearn.datasets import load_iris
from sklearn.model_selection import train_test_split, cross_val_score
from sklearn.metrics import accuracy_score
import numpy as np

# Data
X, y = load_iris(return_X_y=True)
X_train, X_test, y_train, y_test = \
train_test_split(X, y, test_size=0.2, stratify=y, random_state=42)

# Helpers to map continuous search space to valid hyperparams
decode_hls   = lambda x: (int(round(x)),)
decode_alpha = lambda x: 10**x
def decode_lr(x): return ["constant","invscaling","adaptive"][int(x)]

# Objective: mean CV accuracy
def objective(hidden_layer_sizes, alpha, learning_rate):
    clf = MLPClassifier(
        hidden_layer_sizes=decode_hls(hidden_layer_sizes),
        alpha=decode_alpha(alpha),
        learning_rate=decode_lr(learning_rate),
        max_iter=300, random_state=42
    )
    return cross_val_score(clf, X_train, y_train, cv=5).mean()

# Search space: note log10(alpha) and categorical lr encoded as [0,1,2]
pbounds = {"hidden_layer_sizes": (1,100), "alpha": (-4,0), "learning_rate": (0,2.99)}

opt = BayesianOptimization(f=objective, pbounds=pbounds, random_state=42, verbose=0)
opt.maximize(init_points=5, n_iter=25)

# Decode best params and test
p = opt.max["params"]
best = MLPClassifier(
    hidden_layer_sizes=decode_hls(p["hidden_layer_sizes"]),
    alpha=decode_alpha(p["alpha"]),
    learning_rate=decode_lr(p["learning_rate"]),
    max_iter=500, random_state=42
).fit(X_train, y_train)

print("Best CV score:", round(opt.max["target"],4))
print("Test accuracy:", round(accuracy_score(y_test, best.predict(X_test)),4))
print("Best params:", {
    "hidden_layer_sizes": decode_hls(p["hidden_layer_sizes"]),
    "alpha": decode_alpha(p["alpha"]),
    "learning_rate": decode_lr(p["learning_rate"])
})
```

This should result in output similar to the following:

```
Best CV score: 0.975
Test accuracy: 1.0
Best params: {'hidden_layer_sizes': (95,), 'alpha': 0.00314891164795686,
'learning_rate': 'adaptive'}
```

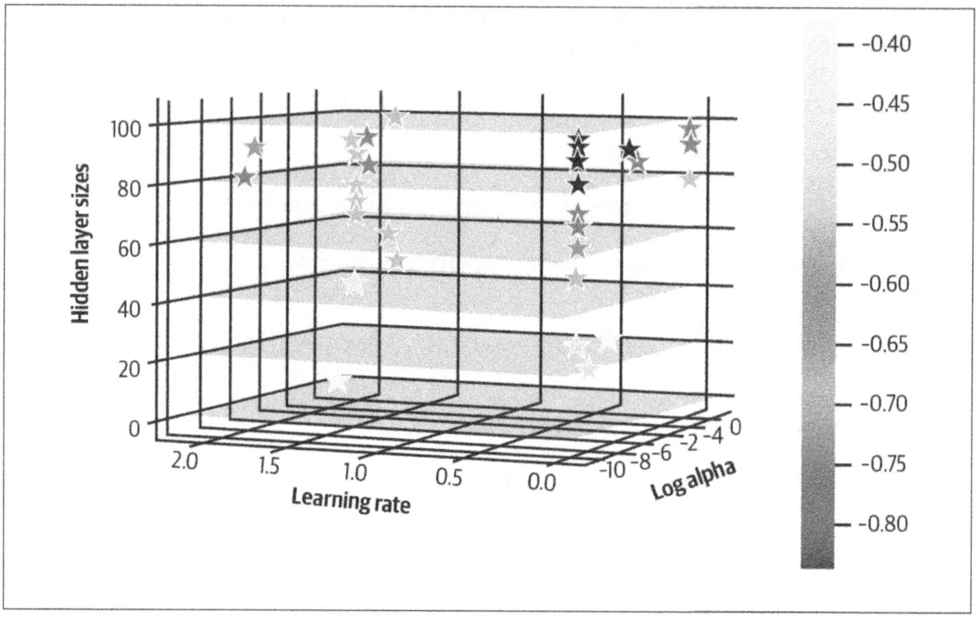

Figure 5-8. Three parameters used to design an MLP are optimized using Bayesian optimization: hidden layer sizes, learning rate, and log alpha. Within a few evaluations, the optimal model configuration that clusters around more complex models (with larger number of hidden layers) is achieved.

HPO and More for the Novel Materials Discovery Task

The specific instantiation of the GNNs to be used for the Novel Materials Discovery task can have a huge impact on its performance. GNNs are more complex than MLPs but less complex than transformers (with respect to the different model configurations).

We could parameterize GNN layer, depth, width, and non-linearity as the main model configuration parameters and deploy HPO methods like random search to discover the most useful GNN *model configuration*. In addition, the *hyperparameters* such as optimizer, batch size, and learning rate can be tuned using the same HPO.

Searching model configuration and hyperparameters jointly can reduce the complexity of model selection because we can resort to using the same HPO methods effectively.

Neural Architecture Search

Optimizing the hyperparameters of ML models, in particular those of DL models, can be tedious and computationally expensive. Fortunately, multiple methods offer a trade-off between exploration and exploitation. The second step used along with HPO in automating model selection is NAS.[11] Based on the MC^3-space visualized in Figure 5-3, regions of the hypothesis space controlling neural network architectures are spanned primarily by the model class and model configurations, whereas HPO was concerned with model complements.

Consider the model class of MLPs; the main parameters controlling the architectures of these classes of fully connected neural networks are the `depth` (D) and `width` (W) parameters. This simple hypothesis space then consists of $D \cdot W$ possible architectures to choose from. Inclusion of other model configuration elements like the choice of activation functions, skip connections, and so on, can expand this hypothesis space further. Moving to other model classes like CNNs can make the space more complex. For example, the NAS-Bench-101 dataset comprises a hypothesis space with 423,000 unique CNN architectures. More recent methods are operating on more complex hypothesis spaces with about 2×10^{19} different neural network architectures![12]

Given such large search spaces, obtaining optimal architectures is a challenging task. NAS methods can be used to automatically design neural networks from a space of architectures using discrete optimization where the optimization can be performed over the MC^3-space. NAS requires encoding of MC^3-space of model selection into a discrete space suitable for exploration. For a given search space, NAS uses various classes of discrete algorithms to explore and obtain the neural network candidates.

As with HPO, formulating notions of search space, optimization strategy, and optimization criteria (depicted in Figure 5-4) is also important for NAS. The key differences are in how the search space for NAS is prescribed, as the HPO space is of *relatively* lower complexity than that of NAS due to the diversity in model classes and model configurations.

11 Zoph and Le, "Neural Architecture Search With Reinforcement Learning" (*https://arxiv.org/abs/1611.01578*).

12 Han Cai et al., "Once-for-All: Train One Network and Specialize It for Efficient Deployment," *arXiv.org*, April 29, 2020 (*https://arxiv.org/abs/1908.09791*).

> ### Carbon Cost of NAS
>
> By definition, NAS requires several orders of more compute than training a model once until convergence. While there are no clear estimations of the carbon footprint of NAS, some attempts have been made to obtain some estimations for specific choices of NAS space, tasks, and datasets.
>
> For example, the authors in the CE-NAS paper estimate the total compute cost of six popular NAS methods to be about 440GPU years![13] The corresponding carbon footprint can be about 45,100kgCO_2e.

NAS Search Space

Encoding neural network architectures into a search space that is easy to optimize is not straightforward. This is primarily due to the diversity in the MC^3-space pertaining to designing a neural network. Currently, the most widely used search spaces use DAG-based representations, as shown in Figure 5-9, to encode neural networks.[14] In these DAGs, nodes represent low-level operators, and the directed edges capture the connectivity. The nodes can also be comprised of more complex blocks of neural network operations, or sometimes even small neural networks. Figure 5-9 visualizes these hierarchical representations of neural networks in a search space consisting of hierarchies of DAGs. At the lowest level, individual operators such as fully connected layers, convolution layers, activation functions, dropout layers, and so on, can be encoded. These elements can then be put together into diverse configurations to form cells, which could be MLPs, CNN blocks, or multihead attention layers. These cells can be further stacked into complex neural network architectures at the final level.

Neural network architectures are designed by combining individual operations, blocks of operations, or cells, in many configurations resulting in massive search spaces. The leftmost dashed box in Figure 5-9 consists of individual operations that can then be used to compose smaller units of a neural network (second dashed box). Individual elements and smaller blocks of operations can be combined to obtain complete architectures (rightmost dashed box). You can think of the lowest operations as letters in an alphabet that can be combined into words or sentences, resulting in expressive prose or, in this case, expressive neural network architectures.

---

13 Yiyang Zhao et al., "CE-NAS: An End-to-End Carbon-Efficient Neural Architecture Search Framework," *arXiv.org*, July 18, 2024 (*https://arxiv.org/abs/2406.01414*).

14 Elsken et al., "Neural Architecture Search: A Survey" (*https://arxiv.org/abs/1808.05377*).

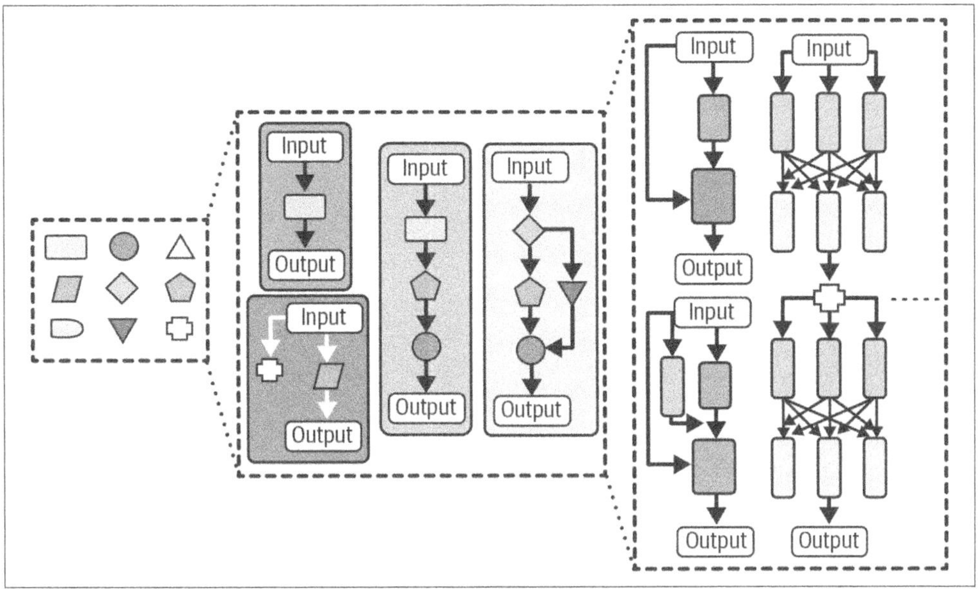

Figure 5-9. A hierarchically encoded NAS search space.

In recent literature, newer representations of NAS search spaces are being formulated based on a single large neural network. This *supernetwork* then consists of smaller subnetworks that can be accessed as different pathways within the supernetwork.[15]

NAS As Optimization

Obtaining optimal neural network architectures from the NAS search space can be formulated as a multivariable optimization based on the following elements:

Discrete variables (architectural choices)
: Representing architectural decisions like layer types, connectivity patterns, and number of layers.

Categorical variables (specific settings)
: Encompassing choices like activation functions (e.g., `ReLU`, `sigmoid`).

Continuous variables (hyperparameters)
: Containing hyperparameters such as learning rates, dropout rates, and so on, which can be optimized using HPO.

15 Cai et al., "Once-for-All: Train One Network and Specialize it for Efficient Deployment," (*https://arxiv.org/abs/1908.09791*).

Many of the techniques used for HPO such as random search and reinforcement learning are also applicable to NAS.

Formally, the goal of NAS is to find the optimal neural network architecture A that optimizes certain performance metric $P(A)$.[16] If the space of architectures $\mathcal{A}$ consists of M possible architectures, i.e., $\mathcal{A} = \{A_1, A_2, \cdots, A_M\}$, then the goal of NAS is to find $A^* = \arg\max_{A \in \mathcal{A}} P(A)$.

NAS Using Random Search

Random search–like methods used for HPO can also be used for NAS with a few modifications. NAS using random search can be computationally intensive as the search spaces can be massive, and obtaining optimal networks in these spaces only by exploration can be inefficient. For small enough search spaces or with a large number of iterations, random search can still be quite useful for NAS.

Consider a space of neural network architectures, $\mathcal{A} = \{A_1, A_2, \ldots, A_M\}$, consisting of M unique architectures. If the objective function to be optimized is $P(A)$, then the optimal architecture, A^*, can be obtained using N iterations of random search by the following steps:

1. *Initialization of best architecture and performance*
   Set $A^* = \{\ \}, P(A^*) = -\infty$.

2. *Perform random search*
   For $i = 1, \ldots, N$:
   - Generate a random architecture: $A_i \in \mathcal{A}$.
   - Evaluate the performance metric: $P(A_i)$.
   - If $P(A_i) > P(A^*)$:
     — Update best performance: $P(A^*) \leftarrow P(A_i)$.
     — Update best architecture: $A^* \leftarrow A_i$.

3. *Output*
   Output the best-performing architecture found after N evaluations, A^* with performance $P(A^*)$.

16 Here the architecture A corresponds to the parameterized model f_θ. The model parameters θ are optimized during model training.

NAS Using Evolutionary Algorithms

The design of neural networks requires careful combinations of a multitude of operators. Instead of exploring entire NAS spaces, starting from a subset of architectures, optimizing some parts of these networks until the desired performance is achieved can be a better approach. This is the core idea in using *evolutionary algorithms*, which attempt to mimic genetic evolution.

In NAS, evolutionary algorithms optimize the design of neural network architectures by mimicking the process of natural selection. Each potential architecture is represented as a "chromosome," a structure that encodes key properties like the number of layers, layer types, number of units in each layer, activation functions, and other architectural decisions. The algorithm begins with a randomly generated population of architectures, each evaluated based on its performance on a specific task (e.g., accuracy, loss, or other relevant metrics).

The evolutionary algorithm then selects the best-performing architectures as "parents." These parents undergo crossover, where portions of their "chromosomes" are exchanged to create new offspring architectures that combine characteristics from both parent networks. This process encourages the exploration of different architectural configurations. Additionally, mutation introduces small, random changes in the offspring's architecture, such as altering the number of layers or switching activation functions, to promote diversity and avoid premature convergence to suboptimal solutions.

After generating the offspring, the algorithm evaluates their performance and replaces the less fit individuals in the population with the new, potentially better-performing architectures. This process repeats over multiple generations, with the population evolving as architectures with higher performance are consistently selected, recombined, and mutated. Through this iterative process, genetic algorithms gradually discover neural network architectures that perform well on the given task, optimizing the search for high-performing models in a complex and vast search space.

Evolutionary algorithms are some of the widely used NAS methods as they rely on a more systematic exploration of the NAS spaces. Several variations of the basic evolutionary method described previously are widely used for NAS, as these methods can explore a wide selection of architectures depending on the choice of the genetic operations.

Efficiency and NAS

NAS is computationally expensive with a large resource footprint, stemming primarily from the massive NAS spaces comprising millions of neural network architectures. Furthermore, evaluating the performance of individual neural network architectures entails full training and validation on a given dataset. Performing these expensive training runs for each candidate architecture to assess their goodness-of-fit adds to the AI waste (see Chapter 6 for more on training costs).

While automating model selection with NAS is desirable, large resource costs can be deterrents. In an effort to improve the efficiency of NAS and to advance development of novel NAS algorithms, without retraining entire search spaces, *NAS benchmarks* are gaining popularity within the NAS community. The main goal of NAS benchmarks is to provide datasets with performance metrics for each architecture in a NAS search space. These NAS benchmarks usually consist of architecture specification, training accuracy, validation accuracy, and other metrics. The promise of NAS benchmarks is that the learnings from these fixed architecture and dataset combinations can also generalize to newer NAS search spaces or tasks.

NAS tabular benchmarks

One of the first tabular benchmark datasets for NAS was the NAS-Bench-101.[17] The authors of NAS-Bench-101 performed a one-time expensive exploration of a predefined NAS space, collected relevant performance metrics, and published this as a tabular dataset. The hope was that other researchers could use this dataset to develop novel NAS algorithms without having to recompute the entire search space.

The NAS-Bench-101 search space consisted of 423,000 unique CNN architectures. The one-time cost of making this dataset, however, required more than 100TPU years of compute, which implies proportional energy and carbon costs. The model classes explored in such tabular benchmarks are limited to a small subset (MLPs/CNNs/transformers) and can become outdated.

Table 5-1 provides an overview of different NAS benchmarks, their sizes, and the reported metrics. These are only a subset of recent benchmarks, and each benchmark dataset has unique features that can be useful in specific settings.

Table 5-1. Overview of popular NAS benchmarks

Benchmark	Size	Type	Metrics
`NAS-Bench-101`	423,000	Tabular	Accuracy
`NAS-Bench-201`	6,000	Tabular	Accuracy and loss
`NAS-Bench-301`	10^{18}	Surrogate	Accuracy
`NATS-Bench`	32,000	Tabular	Accuracy and loss
`HW-NAS-Bench`	10^{21}	Tabular	Latency and inference energy

17 Chris Ying et al., "NAS-Bench-101: Towards Reproducible Neural Architecture Search" (*https://arxiv.org/abs/1902.09635*).

Benchmark	Size	Type	Metrics
`NAS-Bench-x11`	10^{18}	Surrogate	Accuracy and loss
`EC-NAS`	423,000	Tabular	Accuracy, latency, and training/inference energy
`EA-HAS-Bench`	6×10^7	Surrogate	Accuracy and training energy

NAS benchmarks for surrogate models

Evaluating a NAS search space—even once—can be prohibitively expensive. Newer NAS benchmark datasets are increasingly relying on approximating the goodness-of-fit of architectures using surrogate models. These surrogate model-based NAS benchmarks use architectural specifications, learning curves, or a smaller NAS space, to approximate the performance of the larger NAS search spaces. Surrogate models also allow easy inclusion of newer model classes, as they require only redefining the surrogate models.

NAS is computationally expensive, requiring thousands of hours of compute time. Using precomputed statistics for a large NAS search space and exploring several NAS algorithms implemented in Bag of Baselines (*https://oreil.ly/3gfKd*) using the EC-NAS Benchmark dataset (*https://oreil.ly/IYRzI*) can be tried in this chapter's Jupyter notebooks (*https://github.com/raghavian/sustainable_ai*).

NAS for the Novel Materials Discovery Task

Most existing NAS literature formulates the search space and explores them for a specific downstream task (in most cases, it is classification). In our task of discovering novel materials, we are looking for a generative model.

There are no widely used NAS methods for discovering generative models when using GNNs. NAS for GNNs has also focused primarily on classification.[18]

So, for this generative task at hand, NAS might not be useful. We should focus on a combination of strong HPO and model configuration optimization to get to the most useful generative model.

18 Kaixiong Zhou et al., "Auto-GNN: Neural Architecture Search of Graph Neural Networks," *arXiv.org*, September 10, 2019 (*https://arxiv.org/abs/1909.03184*).

Model Selection in the Era of Foundational Models

The recent class of foundational models that include LLMs expand the MC^3 space to an even larger scale. This is because the most useful models can end up having billions of model parameters. Arriving at the final configuration for a model at this scale can pose pose additional challenges simply due to their scale.

As we've seen, model selection consisting of HPO and NAS is computationally intensive by design. The methods discussed this far present mitigation strategies that can allow DL practitioners to reduce the AI waste when selecting models for their downstream tasks. However, for LLMs even these strategies might not be optimal simply due to their scale. Furthermore, many foundational models consist of transformers, a key component that has two unique properties:

Resilient architecture
: The original transformer architecture, which is a key component in several LLMs, has not undergone drastic improvements since its original release in 2017.[19] This appears to be the case with extremely over-parameterized models as they seem to also adapt the implicit architecture during training. This has been speculatively described as the *Lottery Ticket Hypothesis* (LTH), which posits that within large, randomly initialized networks, there exist smaller, trainable subnetworks (winning tickets).[20] The larger the network, the higher the likelihood of containing such winning tickets, simply due to the increased number of possible subnetworks. Thus, as models scale up (which can be easily achieved for transformers), the probability of finding effective sparse subnetworks increases.

Parameter redundancy
: Large-scale models often have significant parameter redundancy. The LTH leverages this redundancy by pruning less important weights and identifying a smaller subnetwork that can be trained to achieve comparable performance. In massive models, this redundancy means there are more opportunities to find these smaller subnetworks.

Given this, most emphasis has been placed on HPO (and not NAS) for foundational models. Performing HPO for foundational models is also expensive. Techniques inspired from *transfer learning* (see Chapter 6 for details) have been used to reduce the computational overhead of HPO of large models. For instance, the *Maximal*

19 Ashish Vaswani et al., "Attention Is All You Need," *arXiv.org*, (June 12, 2017): 5998–6008 (*https://arxiv.org/pdf/1706.03762v5*).

20 Jonathan Frankle and Michael Carbin, "The Lottery Ticket Hypothesis: Finding Sparse, Trainable Neural Networks," *arXiv.org*, March 9, 2018 (*https://arxiv.org/abs/1803.03635*).

Update Parameter (muP) technique performs HPO for a smaller model and transfers these hyperparameters to the larger models, showing robust performance.[21]

> **Is HPO > NAS for LLMs?**
>
> The question of whether LLMs benefit from NAS and only HPO is debatable. This could simply be an artifact of how the DL community has seen more benefits by primarily scaling up the model size and datasets. Performing HPO is relatively cheaper and has garnered more attention than NAS. We can't definitively say that there are no other better architectures for LLMs or other foundational models.

Mixture of Experts

A *mixture-of-experts* (MoE) model is a neural architecture designed to increase model capacity without a proportional increase in computation. Instead of processing every input through the entire network (as dense models do), an MoE splits part of the network into multiple independent subnetworks called *experts*. These experts are typically smaller networks with separate parameters. Instead of processing every token through the same dense layers, the model uses a learned router (another neural network) to decide which experts should handle each token.[22] This router examines the token's hidden state and assigns it to the top K experts, often just one or two based on a scoring function. Figure 5-10 depicts how sparsely activated MoE handles different tokens. Even when there are K expert networks, only one is activated based on the scoring of the routing network.

The model routes the token only through the selected experts, keeping the computation budget roughly constant while dramatically increasing parameter count. During training, the model learns both the router and the experts jointly, allowing each expert to specialize. With this setup, MoEs unlock more capacity per token without paying the full computational cost, making them highly attractive for scaling large transformer models.

The model comprises several smaller expert networks and, depending on the token, only a subset of these experts are activated in each computation. In Figure 5-10, K expert networks is available but the router network activates only one (top-1) expert. For token-1, this is the first expert; for token-2, this is the expert-K.

21 Greg Yang et al., "Tensor Programs V: Tuning Large Neural Networks via Zero-Shot Hyperparameter Transfer," *arXiv.org*, March 7, 2022 (*https://arxiv.org/abs/2203.03466*).

22 Noam Shazeer et al., "Outrageously Large Neural Networks: The Sparsely-Gated Mixture-of-Experts Layer," *arXiv.org*, January 23, 2017 (*https://arxiv.org/abs/1701.06538*).

Figure 5-10. Sparse routing in MoE configuration.

Technically, sparsely activated MoEs do not belong to the classical model selection discussions. However, at some abstraction, it is similar to model selection. The router evaluates each token's representation and decides which subset of experts to activate. This sounds similar to the classic task in model selection: choosing the best model (or set of models) given some data. However, it is more accurate to view it as learned conditional computation.[23]

Model Selection Automated: What Comes Next?

In this chapter, we have seen that model selection has to be automated simply due to the scale of the hypothesis space. Automatic model selection can be performed in two steps: HPO and NAS. Each of these steps is resource-intensive and involves AI waste at different stages. The various classes of methods presented can be used to automatically select models that can achieve certain objectives while being cognizant of the resource footprint of ML/AI model selection. Certain factors should be taken into account when automatically choosing models:

If automatic model selection is computationally expensive, why do it in the first place?

Automatic model selection can reduce individual user biases when designing models.

The massive hypothesis space of ML/AI methods offer diverse models to choose from. Exploring these hypothesis spaces manually can be tedious and in many instances infeasible. When ML practitioners are constrained to perform model selection manually, they can introduce biases into the model selection process. When these biases are easy to quantify—such as when choosing hyperparameters

23 Andrew Davis and Itamar Arel, "Low-Rank Approximations for Conditional Feedforward Computation in Deep Neural Networks," *arxiv.org*, January 28, 2014 (*https://arxiv.org/abs/1312.4461*).

for simpler models—it might not be a problem. However, when faced with designing neural network architectures that have a plethora of model classes, configurations, and complements to choose from, subjective choices can take over. Automatic model selection offers systematic procedures to design these complex models that can be reproduced by others. Scale of the hypothesis space and systematizing model selection are the key benefits of performing expensive automatic model selection.

Isn't exploitation better than crude exploration during model selection?
It depends on the knowledge that is present to be exploited.

Based on the HPO and NAS methods described in this chapter, one could argue that brute-force exploration methods are always inferior to methods that rely on knowledge exploitation. This can be true in a majority of the cases; however, in other instances, exploitation can be problematic, as the knowledge or the user bias need not always be informative. If there is a substantial amount of high-quality, relevant information available, exploiting that knowledge might lead to better results without the need for extensive exploration.[24] However, if the available knowledge is limited, outdated, or insufficient, then exploration might be necessary to uncover new insights, data patterns, or model improvements that could potentially lead to better performance.

Which is the best HPO method for AI methods?
No one method can be cited as being the best. Any method that reasonably trades off exploration-exploitation can be useful.

There is no one-size-fits-all approach to HPO, or even model selection broadly, because different methods prioritize exploration-exploitation trade-off differently. The *best* method depends on various factors such as resource constraints, nature of the hypothesis space, type of data, and the performance objective. Achieving a balance across these factors will require careful considerations of the pros and cons of different HPO+NAS methods.

Methods for HPO and NAS are similar. Can these procedures be combined?
Yes. There are several methods trying to jointly perform HPO+NAS optimization.

The ML/AI hypothesis space can be decomposed using the MC^3-space comprising model classes, configurations, and complements. The distinction of performing HPO for choosing model complements, and NAS when choosing model class or configuration, can be overcome in joint HPO+NAS optimization. There are

24 Sophia N. Wilson et al., "Trading Carbon for Physics: On the Resource Efficiency of Machine Learning for Spatio-Temporal Forecasting," *arXiv.org*, September 29, 2025 (*https://arxiv.org/abs/2509.24517*).

several existing works that have investigated this idea.[25] Most recent NAS benchmark datasets assume the NAS and HPO spaces to be joint product space and employ the same optimization methods.

Have novel and useful architectures been discovered using NAS?

Rare instances do exist, but this has not been the norm.

Performing NAS in the space of all feasible neural network architectures is impossible. Current NAS methods constrain the search by carefully designing expressive NAS search spaces. The fact that these NAS search spaces are predefined can limit the discovery of novel architectures. For instance, a space conducive for feedforward CNNs could never have discovered the transformer architecture. And combining search spaces across model classes will further explode the hypothesis space. Most existing NAS methods aim to discover novel architectures within a known space with specified attributes. For instance, by posing efficiency as an additional constraint, the now popular EfficientNet architecture was discovered.[26]

Are models selected automatically versatile?

Not always. They are usually selected on single datasets and might not generalize to other datasets.

The objective optimized when performing NAS or HPO is related to the estimated performance on a single dataset in most cases. The neural network architectures or hyperparameter settings obtained can yield good performance mainly on datasets *similar* to the ones used during HPO+NAS. There are no formal guarantees on the performance translating to other datasets. The generalization capabilities of solutions obtained using HPO+NAS to other datasets are limited and might even require redoing HPO+NAS on new datasets.

Why can't NAS be performed using only NAS benchmarks as they are efficient?

NAS benchmarks assume a fixed search space and mostly use a single dataset. These might not always generalize to other settings.

NAS benchmarks are efficient for developing new NAS algorithms or for exploring novel architectures with additional constraints, such as low-latency architectures. True NAS requires exploring novel search spaces, and most existing NAS benchmarks are not capable of extrapolating to new model classes. This is a limitation of NAS benchmarks; however, they can be useful in re-exploration of the NAS search spaces yielding novel insights. For instance, NAS benchmark datasets

---

25 Aaron Klein and Frank Hutter, "Tabular Benchmarks for Joint Architecture and Hyperparameter Optimization," *arXiv.org*, May 13, 2019 (*https://arxiv.org/abs/1905.04970*).

26 Mingxing Tan and Quoc V. Le, "EfficientNet: Rethinking Model Scaling for Convolutional Neural Networks," *arXiv.org*, September 11, 2020 (*https://arxiv.org/abs/1905.11946*).

like the EC-NAS dataset included energy consumption to the NAS-Bench-101 dataset. This allows for exploration of inherently energy efficient subspace of the NAS-Bench-101 hypothesis space, as visualized in Figure 5-11. The region to the top left consists of efficient architectures that also yield good performance compared to the top-right region, which incurs a larger energy cost.

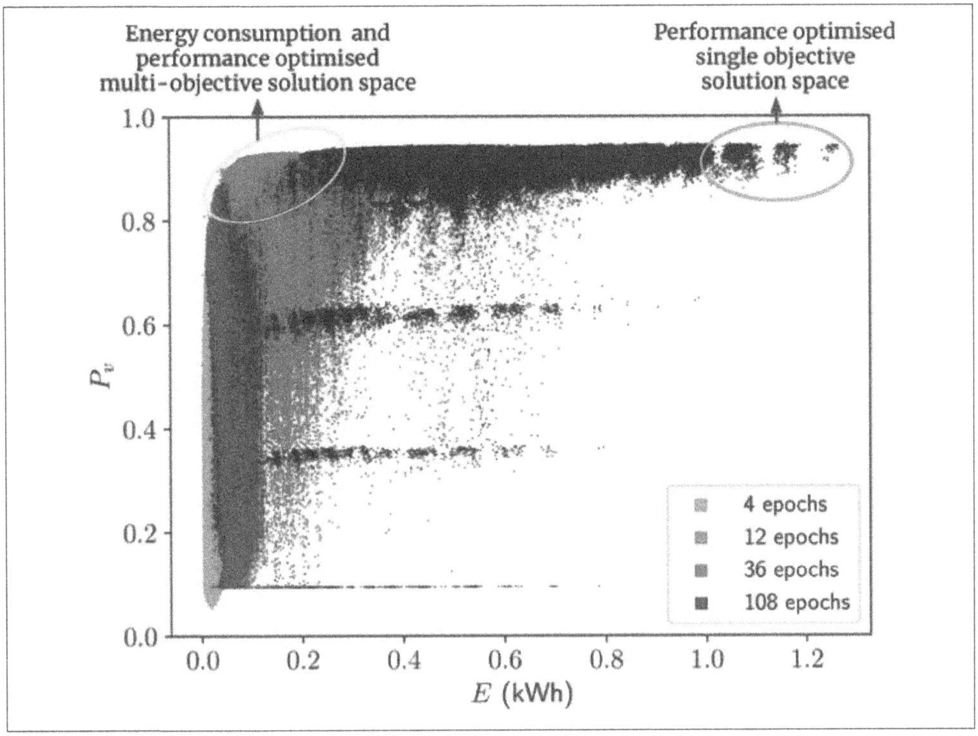

Figure 5-11. The EC-NAS benchmark dataset space. Each point in the plot is a CNN architecture. In total about 1.6 million CNNs are reported in this dataset. (Source: adapted from Pedram Bakhtiarifard et al., "EC-NAS: Energy Consumption Aware Tabular Benchmarks for Neural Architecture Search" (https://doi.org/10.1109/icassp48485.2024.10448303).)

Is performance the only criterion that should be optimized when performing automatic model selection?

Not at all. Joint optimization of multiple objectives that include other factors like latency and energy costs is becoming quite common.

Exploration of NAS spaces to optimize additional dimensions on top of performance is gaining traction in NAS research. To this end, multiobjective optimization methods can be used so that joint optimization of performance and other dimensions can be achieved. While optimizing for latency, hardware considerations, and energy efficiency are studied widely, most recently NAS with fairness objectives are also being considered (see "Resource-Efficient Architectures" on page 175).[27]

How does automatic model selection help improve the sustainability of AI?

Although model selection is expensive, doing it carefully can improve some sustainability aspects of AI.

Automatic model selection has been established to be resource-intensive in this chapter. However, performing NAS can be directed toward discovering inherently efficient neural network architectures, such as the EfficientNet, which when deployed can amortize the one-time NAS resource costs over the lifetime of a deployed model. This can have a positive impact on improving the energy consumption and carbon footprint of ML/AI methods. Further, automatic model selection with joint objectives that include fairness, and robustness, can help improve the social sustainability of AI. Finally, automatic model selection should be treated as one step in improving the sustainability of AI. Other measures presented throughout this book should also be considered.

27 Samuel Dooley et al., "Rethinking Bias Mitigation: Fairer Architectures Make for Fairer Face Recognition," *NIPS '23: Proceedings of the 37th International Conference on Neural Information Processing System* no. 3251 (December 10, 2023): 74366-93 (*https://dl.acm.org/doi/10.5555/3666122.3669373*).

CHAPTER 6
Training Efficiency

In the Indian state of Karnataka, the 12th century Chennakeshava Temple complex features sculptures of deities and epic scenes carved exquisitely in stone (Figure 6-1).[1] The monumental effort required to complete these carvings is similar in some ways to the effort that goes into training modern DL models. Instead of meticulously chiseling away stones, iterative optimization algorithms such as stochastic gradient descent chisel away the trainable parameters of a deep neural network in an iterative manner to create impressive AI models.[2]

Figure 6-1. The stone-carved facade of the temple complex in Belur, India.

1 These *Hoysala* temples are UNESCO World Heritage Sites (*https://oreil.ly/__1Jo*).

2 Researchers who developed the Open Pretrained Transformer (OPT) model published a mind-boggling 114-page log file with all the tricks performed to train this 175-billion parameter model.

In Chapter 5, we explored methods for choosing DL model architecture. Given a specific model architecture, the training process ingests large amounts of training data to obtain models that can be useful for downstream tasks. This training process can be computationally intensive, as models with hundreds of billions of parameters have to work through datasets with as many as a trillion data points (as seen in Chapter 4). Due to these factors, the training compute required is following a mind-boggling trend. According to recent estimates, the compute FLOP required to train DL models has grown four to five times yearly from 2010 to May 2024, as shown in Figure 6-2, for some of the most popular AI models.

In this chapter, we will focus on how DL models are trained—again from the point of view of resource consumption—and identify AI waste (see "AI Waste" on page 53) in this step of the DL pipeline. We will look at methods that offer better trade-offs between performance and resource consumption. These techniques can help reduce computations needed, memory requirements, energy consumption, and carbon footprint of training DL models.

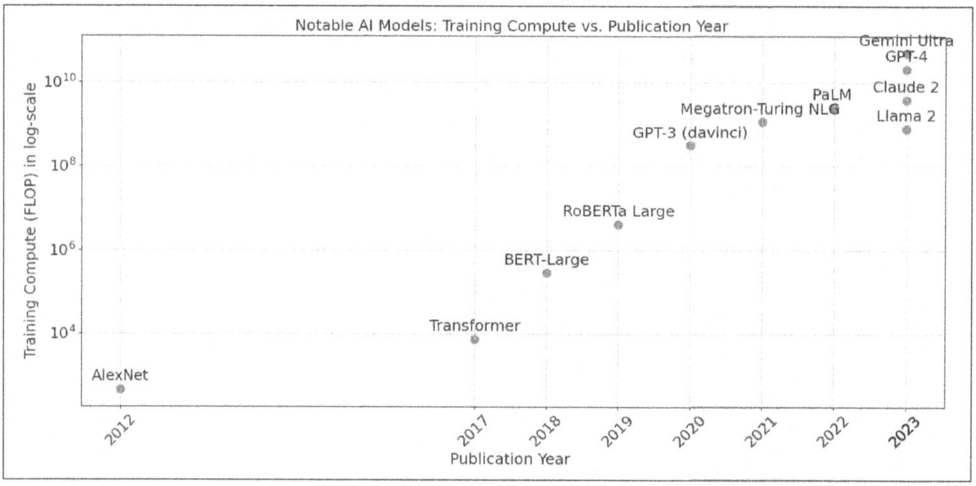

Figure 6-2. Some recent AI models and the corresponding compute (FLOP count) needed for training. (Source: EpochAI data (https://oreil.ly/nDzn7).)

We will start by exploring techniques that allow knowledge recycling from already trained models. Next, I present methods to perform neural network compression under the assumption that compressed networks require fewer resources. Finally, we will look at quantization methods to modulate the number of bits used when training neural networks. All these methods offer different extents of trade-off between performance and resources.

Climate Policy Chatbot

Globally, governments at all levels are developing policies and regulations to mitigate and adapt to climate change. Imagine the value of a chatbot that can parse these documents, consolidate data from different sources, and help with policy formulations. Organizations like Climate Policy Radar (*https://climatepolicyradar.org*) are actively working toward these goals. Figure 6-3 shows the Climate Policy Radar interface you can use to search for relevant policies.

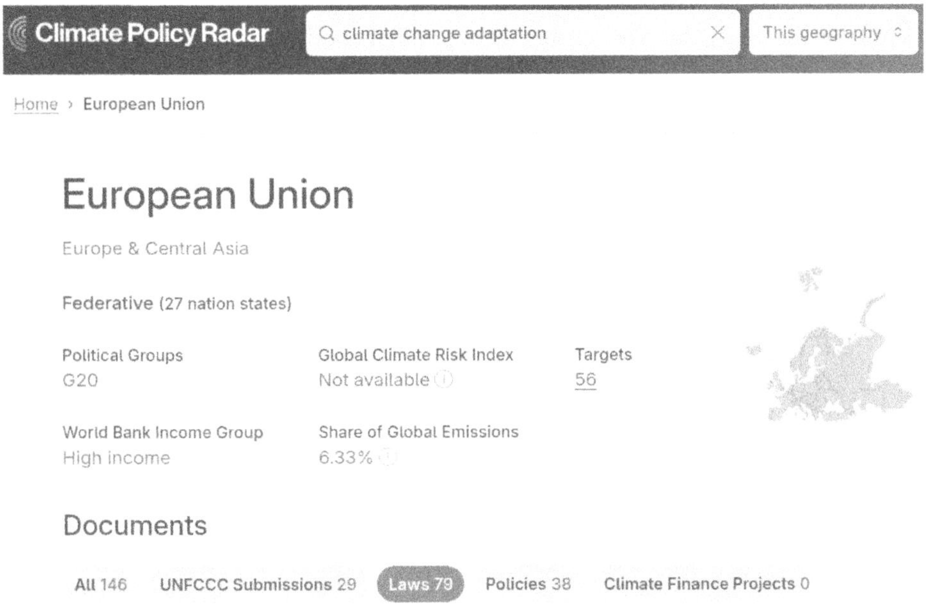

Figure 6-3. Climate Policy Radar's climate policy document explorer.

Building such a chatbot for climate policy is feasible but poses several challenges. These stem primarily from the diversity of data sources, language barriers, and use of actual data sources. As an example throughout this chapter, we will imagine that a small organization with frugal resources desires to develop this chatbot.

Training Costs of AI Models

Consider the task of training a deep neural network in a supervised setting. This consists of predicting the labels for the training data, comparing these predictions with the ground truth labels, computing the prediction error, and adjusting the network parameters to minimize the prediction errors in the next iteration. The computational resources required to train a model can vary depending on the scale of models, number of training data points, nature of the tasks, and quality of performance.

In the simplest settings, the compute required grows with the number of trainable parameters and the amount of data used, as illustrated in Figure 6-2. Using more compute on training models incurs a proportional increase in the energy consumption and the carbon footprint, as these resources are closely related. Estimating the resource costs of training DL models is a challenge due to the lack of standardized tools and the use of hardware platforms that don't allow measurements (see Chapter 3 for an overview of these costs and the associated challenges). Training cost estimates are available, however, for a few of the most popular models, as shown in Figure 6-4.

The costs in Figure 6-4 are for training a handful of AI models. The overall resource costs due to training of all AI models are not easy to estimate due to the scattered nature of AI model development. However, some estimations suggest that the power consumption for training AI models in datacenters was about 0.9GW with a prognosis of growing about 15% in the coming couple of years.[3]

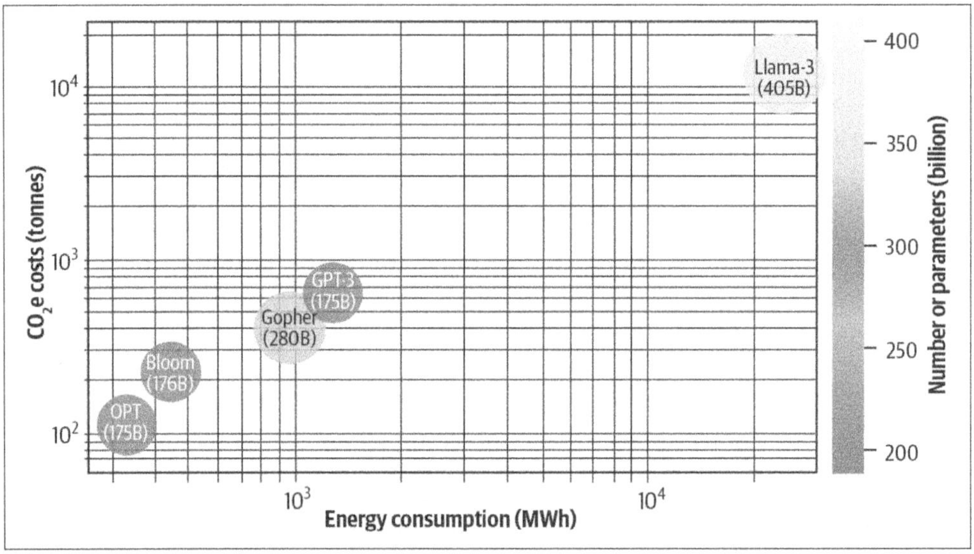

Figure 6-4. Training costs for popular AI models based on the energy consumption reported. The carbon emissions CO_2e are assuming the world average of 481gCO_2e/kWh. For Llama-3 we assume the best reported PUE of 1.1.

3 Victor Avelar et al., "The AI Disruption: Challenges and Guidance for Data Center Design," White Paper 110 Version 2.1 (Schneider Electric Energy Management Research Center, December 3, 2023) (*https://oreil.ly/7T2xu*).

Transfer Learning

We have established by now that training DL models is resource-intensive. From this point of view, the most efficient model is the one that is *not* trained. Of course, randomly initialized models might not be very useful. In this section, instead we will look at techniques that can recycle knowledge from already trained models. These techniques operationalize the concept of *transfer learning*, where models already trained on a dataset can still be useful for new or related datasets.[4]

Pretrained Models

If the task we're interested in is the same as the task on which an existing model has been trained, then we can immediately use pretrained models. All of the resource costs associated with choosing and training models can then be eliminated.

The main challenge in using pretrained models is to find the appropriate model. There are several public repositories where model developers can publish their trained models for others to use, but searching for the best suited model can be difficult. Projects like `timm` offer an easy and standardized interface to accessing computer vision models in PyTorch, which is demonstrated in Example 6-1. Several public repositories host pretrained models. In this example, we will look at the PyTorch Image Models (`timm`) (*https://timm.fast.ai*), which hosts several hundred pretrained models.

Example 6-1. Use of pretrained models in PyTorch

```
# Import timm
from timm import models

# Load all model names available
model_names = models.list_models()
N = len(model_names)
print('Found %d models'%N)

# Load only pretrained models
pretrained = models.list_models(pretrained=True)
M = len(pretrained)
print('%d/%d models are pretrained'%(M,N))

# Load a Pretrained Vision Transformer
model = timm.create_model('vit_base_patch16_224', pretrained=True)
```

4 Stevo Bozinovski, "Reminder of the First Paper on Transfer Learning in Neural Networks, 1976," *Informatica* 44 (September 15, 2020): 291–302 (*https://doi.org/10.31449/inf.v44i3.2828*).

Models are being added and updated on a daily basis. This should result in an output like this providing an overview of available models on `timm`:

```
Found 1657 models
1265/1657 models are pretrained
```

For other domains, there might be no one single source, but platforms like Hugging Face are starting to become the de facto portal for sharing all types of AI models. Model developers can use these platforms to publish and share their models in the spirit of open science. This practice can also have a positive impact on the overall sustainability of AI, as it minimizes wasted effort in repeating training of the same models, on the same datasets.

Sharing and Accessing Pretrained Models

Sharing pretrained models to foster AI development on several platforms is increasingly common. The preprint server *arxiv.org* allows authors to link their papers with official code and datasets. Platforms like Hugging Face (*https://huggingface.co*) collect official and community implementations of different AI methods and host more than one million recent, large-scale AI models. Most of these are also available for the community to download and use.

Fine-Tuning of Pretrained Models

Consider the global tree identification task described in "Curating Datasets Frugally for Global Tree Identification" on page 84. If the initial model is trained on one geographic region, say the African continent, this model might not perform as well on another geographic region without adjustments. This is because the features learned by the model in the initial distribution (over the trees in Africa) might not entirely correspond to the features of the new distribution (over the trees in, say, Asia).

Pretrained models are suitable only if the data on which the model has been trained is from the same distribution as the data we want to use. Pretrained models, in general, cannot handle *domain shift*, wherein the data used to obtain the pretrained model and the new data have different properties.[5]

In cases with domain shift, a pretrained model should be adapted to account for the changes in data distribution. This is achieved by training the model further on the new dataset of interest. This process of customizing a pretrained model on a different dataset is known as *fine-tuning*; it has become standard practice, as it can reduce the amount of data required to train on the new (related) dataset or tasks.

5 Yaroslav Ganin and Victor Lempitsky, "Unsupervised Domain Adaptation by Backpropagation," *arXiv.org*, September 26, 2014 (*https://arxiv.org/abs/1409.7495*).

Understanding Domain Shift

Domain shifts that affect properties of data are inevitable when developing ML models. Any changes in the conditions of the data collection process can introduce domain shift. But, in large-scale AI model development, domain shift could be inevitable as some domains have varying amounts of data. But we would still like to apply the learning from one domain to another.

For instance, pretraining a language model on American English text and using it on British English introduces a small domain shift (difference in spellings of some of the words). The model trained on American English could still yield reasonable performance. However, consider the scenario of training on American English text and using the model on Italian text. We cannot expect the latter case to yield any useful performance. If the domain shift is too drastic, the performance of the pretrained model can potentially be about the same as that of a randomly initialized model.

Fine-tuning a pretrained model on new data can alleviate some of the challenges posed by domain shift. Formally, given a pretrained model $f_{\theta_{PT}}$ and a new dataset $\mathscr{D}_{\text{new}} = \{(x_i, y_i)\}_{i=1}^{N}$, we aim to fine-tune $f_{\theta_{PT}}$ on $\mathscr{D}_{\text{new}}$ resulting in $f_{\theta_{FT}}$.

Fine-tuning models that are pretrained on larger datasets has become standard practice. This can effectively recycle the training already performed on larger datasets by using general features from pretraining and learning only specialized features from the new dataset. Example 6-2 shows the essential steps of saving and loading models. Once a model trained on one dataset is saved, these models can be shared with others who can load them back and fine-tune on new data, thus reducing the AI waste of retraining on larger datasets.

The standard practice for saving and loading standard DL models in PyTorch is to use state dictionaries (`state_dict`), a Python dictionary object that maps each layer to its parameter tensor. It typically contains model parameters for each layer, running statistics (running mean and variance for layers like `batchnorm`).

Example 6-2. Saving and loading models in PyTorch

```
### model class should be defined already
### Instantiate the model
model = SomeModel()

### Save the state dict
torch.save(model.state_dict(), 'model_state_dict.pth')

### Loading a saved model
```

```
# Instantiate the model and load the state dict
model = SomeModel()
model.load_state_dict(torch.load('model_state_dict.pth'))
model.eval()  # Set the model to evaluation mode
```

Transfer Learning for the Climate Policy Chatbot

Using the concepts from Chapter 4, let's assume that the dataset comprising climate policy documents has been curated effectively. Given this dataset, and using principles in Chapter 5, for this task, requiring an LLM is a reasonable choice. How can we then harvest transfer learning ideas discussed so far to develop the climate policy chatbot efficiently?

We could begin with a relevant pretrained, open source model. For example, the Llama-3 family of models would be useful in developing a climate policy chatbot; their existing language understanding would minimize resource usage during the training process.[6]

An organization might select a model like Llama-3-8B parameters or a smaller variant of GPT. Smaller models such as these that have been pretrained on a broad dataset allow for quick deployment with lower computational overhead compared to larger models.

Next, to adapt these general-purpose LLMs to meet the needs of the climate policy chatbot, the organization can fine-tune the chosen pretrained model on the curated dataset of climate policy documents. This targeted fine-tuning allows the model to specialize in the relevant jargon and concepts without the need for extensive computational resources typically required for training from scratch.

In some instances, we might want to resume the training of the model from where we left off instead of training from scratch. This requires storing additional variables—particularly related to the optimizer states—which can also be saved as part of the `state_dict` as shown here:

```
### Instantiate the optimizer
optimizer = torch.optim.SGD(model.parameters(), lr=0.001, momentum=0.9)

### Save optimizer states
torch.save(optimizer.state_dict(), 'optimizer_state_dict.pth')

### Reload optimizer states
optimizer.load_state_dict(torch.load('optimizer_state_dict.pth'))
```

6 Grattafiori et al., "The Llama 3 Herd of Models" (*https://arxiv.org/abs/2407.21783*).

```
### Continue training on new data
model.train()
```

In-Context Learning in LLMs

Consider the sequence $a = 2, b = 3, c = 5, e = ?$ What is the value of e?

Most of us would arrive at the correct solution that $e = 11$ as this the sequence of primes, and we have excluded $d = 7$ resulting in the fifth prime 11. Most recent LLMs can perform tasks like these, even when they have not been explicitly trained to do so. The initial data in the prompt serves as training data for the model to learn from.

While fine-tuning involves additional training of the pretrained model to adapt the model's parameters, LLMs offer an interesting fine-tuning paradigm that does not involve adjusting of the model parameters. This is known as *in-context learning*, where LLMs can adapt to novel tasks without any training, i.e., without any updates to model parameters.

LLMs can learn simple rules from examples shown to them as part of prompts (or in-context). This behavior for LLMs was described already in the GPT-3 paper and has since garnered more interest.[7]

More concretely, in-context learning enables a pretrained LLM model f_F to perform new tasks by utilizing task-specific examples provided as part of the input prompt. This method allows the model to dynamically adapt to different tasks without requiring any updates to its parameters. The following steps outline the process:

1. *Initialization*
   Define the model f_F. Prepare a set of task-specific examples $\mathscr{E} = \{(x_i, y_i)\}_{i=1}^{K}$, where x_i are input examples and y_i are the corresponding outputs. Specify the new input sample x_{new} for which the model needs to predict the output y_{new}.

2. *Input construction*
   Construct the input prompt P for an LLM by concatenating the task-specific examples and the new input sample as follows:

   $$P = [(x_1, y_1), (x_2, y_2), \ldots, (x_K, y_K), (x_{\text{new}}, ?)]$$

   Here, *?* serves as a placeholder for the output that the model will predict.

7 Tom B. Brown et al., "Language Models Are Few-Shot Learners," *arXiv.org*, July 22, 2020 (*https://arxiv.org/abs/2005.14165*).

3. *Inference*

   Provide the constructed prompt P to the LLM f_F. The model processes the prompt and generates the output prediction for the new input:

   $$y_{\text{new}} = f_F(P)$$

4. *Output*

   The predicted output y_{new} for the new input sample x_{new} is obtained, leveraging the context provided by the task-specific examples.

This process enables the LLM to adapt to new tasks dynamically, using in-context learning without the need for parameter updates. The capabilities of LLMs to perform complex tasks learned in-context grow with the scale of LLMs, both in the number of parameters and the amount of data they have been trained on.

> **Can Everything Be Learned In-Context?**
>
> A model trained to perform a task in-context does not remember this training beyond the session because in-context learning relies only on the immediate input, without changing the model's underlying parameters. As each session is independent, any learning that happens in-context disappears at the end of the session. This stateless design in LLMs ensures the model treats each session separately, meaning explicit weight updates are required to make lasting changes in the model, i.e., through additional fine-tuning.
>
> Introducing persistent memory into LLMs so that they can retain information across sessions is an active area of research.

Training Compressed Neural Networks

In "Transfer Learning" on page 147, we explored methods that could recycle knowledge from large, pretrained models using fine-tuning and in-context learning. Relevant pretrained models might not exist in most scenarios; however, these cases then require training of a randomly initialized model on a given dataset.

We will now look into two classes of neural network compression methods, which can reduce AI waste when training models in these settings. The first is based on *pruning*, where neural network parameters that are of low importance (according to some heuristic) are removed during training. The second method is *factorization*, in which large neural network parameter matrices are compressed using low-rank factorizations. Both these methods approximate the neural network using fewer trainable parameters, thus offering better trade-off between resource consumption and performance on downstream tasks.

Neural Network Pruning

Neural network pruning during training is an approach that gradually removes unnecessary parameters as the model learns, leading to a more efficient network by the end of training. This method dynamically identifies and eliminates weights or neurons that contribute little to the model's performance, helping to reduce model complexity without waiting for a full post-training pruning phase.

During training, pruning often uses criteria such as low-weight magnitudes, gradients, or norm-based thresholds to determine which parameters can be removed. Additionally, techniques such as soft pruning may temporarily mask parameters, allowing them to rejoin if they become useful later, providing flexibility and improving accuracy. By pruning progressively, the network structure can be iteratively refined throughout training, resulting in a leaner model that is less computationally demanding while maintaining comparable performance to the unpruned version. Table 6-1 summarizes different pruning methods along with the pruning criteria.

Table 6-1. Summary of popular neural network pruning methods

Pruning method	Pruning criteria	Description	Complexity
Magnitude pruning[a]	Weight magnitude	Removes weights with the smallest absolute values, assuming these contribute least to network output	Low
Gradient-based pruning[b]	Weight gradient	Prunes weights with smaller gradients, assuming they contribute less to loss reduction	Moderate
Structured pruning[c]	Structured elements (e.g., filters, channels)	Removes entire filters, neurons, or channels rather than individual weights, enabling hardware-friendly pruning	High
L1 or L2 norm pruning	Weight norm (L1/L2 corresponding to absolute value or squared magnitude, respectively)	Removes weights with the lowest L1 or L2 norm across channels or layers, assuming these contribute less overall	Moderate
Soft pruning	Weight masking	Masks small weights instead of removing them entirely, allowing potential recovery during training by regrowing pruned connections	Moderate to high
Regularization-based pruning	Regularization (e.g., L1)	Encourages sparsity by adding regularization terms during training to penalize unnecessary weights, indirectly leading to pruning	Moderate to high

[a] Song Han et al., "Learning Both Weights and Connections for Efficient Neural Networks," *arxiv.org*, October 30, 2015 (*https://arxiv.org/abs/1506.02626*).

[b] Yann Le Cunn et al., "Optimal Brain Damage," *NIPS'89: Proceedings of the 3rd International Conference on Neural Information Processing Systems* (January 1, 1989): 598–605 (*https://dl.acm.org/doi/10.5555/2969830.2969903*).

[c] Sajid Anwar et al., "Structured Pruning of Deep Convolutional Neural Networks," *arxiv.org*, December 29, 2015 (*https://arxiv.org/abs/1512.08571*).

Magnitude pruning is a straightforward technique for reducing the size of neural networks by removing weights with the smallest absolute values, based on the assumption that these low-magnitude weights contribute less to the model's output. For example, Figure 6-5 shows the histogram of the magnitude of weights before and after training for ResNet-50, where we observe that a larger chunk of the weights (almost an order of magnitude more) are close to zero. Magnitude pruning removes these low magnitude weights. Performing magnitude pruning during training allows the pruned network to adjust to the changes in the network architecture without drastic degradation in performance. Note that the y-axis is in logarithmic scale.

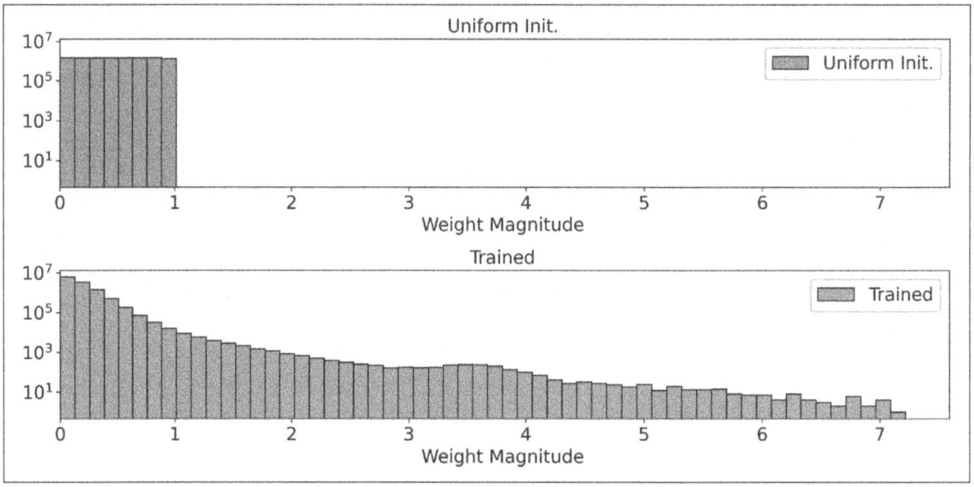

Figure 6-5. ResNet-50 weights at initialization (top) and at convergence (bottom).

Concretely, magnitude pruning during training of a neural network f_θ for N_e epochs by pruning every F_{prune} epochs (how often pruning occurs), to achieve a pruning ratio of r (fraction of parameters to be removed at each pruning step), can be formulated as:

1. *Initialization*

   Define the neural network model f_θ with parameters θ. Specify the training dataset $\mathcal{D} = \{(x_i, y_i)\}_{i=1}^{N}$.

2. *Training with periodic pruning*

   For each epoch $t = 1, 2, \cdots, N_{\text{epochs}}$:

   - Compute the model's predictions for each $x_i \in \mathcal{D}$.
   - Calculate the loss $\mathcal{L}$ (e.g., cross-entropy loss) and compute gradients with respect to θ.
   - Update parameters θ using the optimizer and learning rate η.

- Pruning step (every F_{prune} epochs):
  - Compute the absolute magnitude $|\theta|$ for each parameter in θ.
  - Identify the smallest r-fraction of parameters by magnitude and set them to zero, forming the pruned parameter set θ_{pruned}.
  - Continue training with the pruned parameter set θ_{pruned}, where parameters not pruned retain their values.

3. *Output*

   After training, the pruned model $f_{\theta_{pruned}}$ is obtained, yielding a more efficient network by reducing the number of active parameters.

Magnitude-based pruning methods offer advantages because they are simple and easy to implement, relying only on basic weight magnitude calculations. AI practitioners can apply magnitude pruning during or after training, making it a flexible approach. Magnitude-based pruning compresses models significantly while preserving accuracy, especially when followed by fine-tuning.

Factorized Neural Networks

Neural network weight matrix factorization is a technique aimed at reducing the computational complexity and memory requirements of neural networks by decomposing weight matrices into lower-dimensional representations. This process involves approximating a large weight matrix as a product of smaller matrices, effectively capturing the essential patterns and relationships within the original data while discarding less important information.

Some of the techniques used for data compression in "Data Point Compression" on page 98 are equally useful for compressing neural network weight matrices. For example, consider matrix factorization using low-rank decomposition, as shown in Figure 6-6, where we see that a large matrix of size $K \times D$ is factorized into two smaller matrices of size $K \times R$ and $R \times D$, with $R<<D$. This decomposition can significantly reduce the number of parameters, leading to faster training times and lower resource consumption without a substantial loss in performance. As the elements of these factorized elements can be learned during training, these approximations can be quite useful. Additionally, matrix factorization can help improve generalization by introducing constraints that encourage the model to learn more robust features.

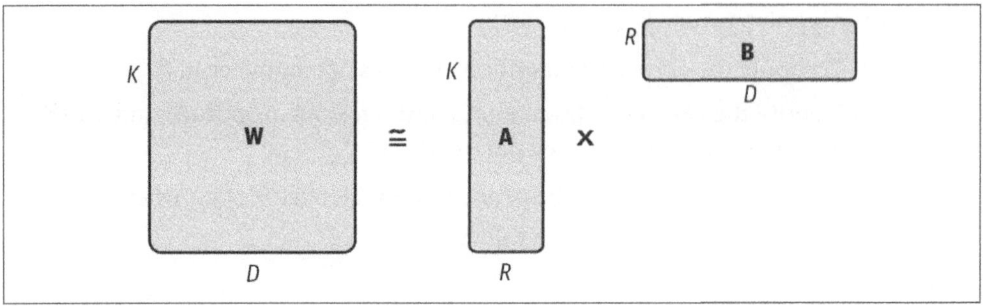

Figure 6-6. Approximation of a large matrix factorized into smaller matrices—basically the outer-product trick in linear algebra.

The rank of the factorization can be treated as a hyperparameter. Figure 6-7 shows the scale of reduction in the number of elements in the original matrix and the factorized matrices for a large matrix. You can learn the efficiency attainable by performing low-rank decomposition in advance; for instance, choosing a rank of 50 results in 85% reduction in the number of elements in this 1,000 × 500 matrix. The effect of this factorization on the performance is not easy to estimate *a priori*, however. Appropriate extent of factorization can be chosen depending on the resources available and/or the performance loss that can be tolerated.

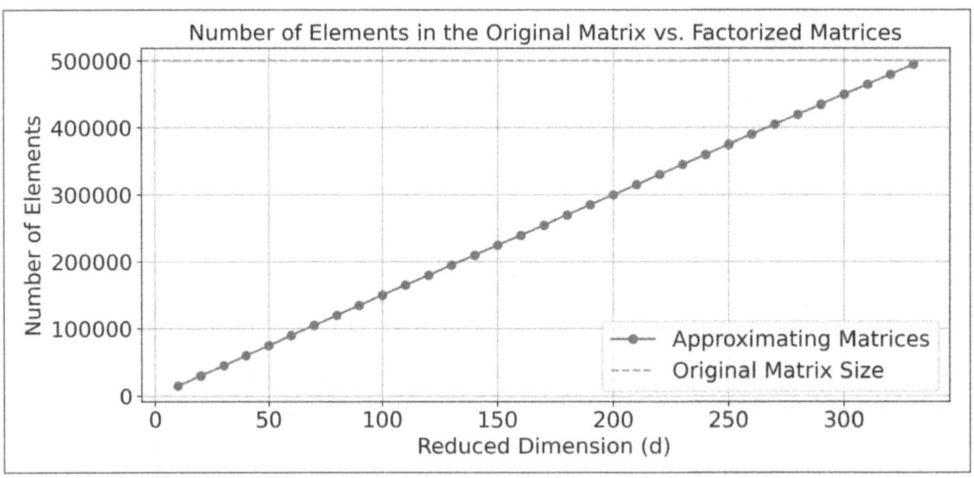

Figure 6-7. A full matrix of size 1,000 × 500 consists of 500,000 elements (dashed line). When the same matrix is factorized using lower rank matrices, the number of elements can be reduced drastically (dotted line).

Many different methods can be used to factorize neural network weights, each offering a trade-off between computational efficiency and expressiveness of the factorized matrices. Table 6-2 provides an overview of some of the commonly used methods.

Table 6-2. Summary of popular neural network weight matrix factorization methods with a brief description of the key idea behind the factorization strategy

Factorization method	Description	Advantages
Singular value decomposition (SVD)[a]	Decomposes a matrix into three components: left singular vectors, singular values, and right singular vectors	Effective at reducing dimensionality and noise
Kronecker factorization[b]	Decomposes weight matrices into Kronecker products, which are particularly efficient for certain types of neural networks	Reduces complexity while retaining higher approximation precision
Low-rank factorization[c]	Approximates a weight matrix as the product of two or more lower-rank matrices, effectively reducing parameter count	Reduces storage and computational complexity
Tensor decomposition[d]	Extends matrix factorization to higher-dimensional tensors, capturing multiway relationships in data	Captures richer patterns in multidimensional data

[a] Gene H. Golub and Charles F. Van Loan, *Matrix Computations*, 4th ed. (Hopkins Press, 2013).

[b] James Martens and Roger Grosse, "Optimizing Neural Networks with Kronecker-Factored Approximate Curvature," *arxiv.org*, June 8, 2020 (*https://arxiv.org/abs/1503.05671*).

[c] Alexander Novikov et al., "Tensorizing Neural Networks," *arxiv.org*, December 20, 2015 (*https://arxiv.org/abs/1509.06569*).

[d] Yuxin Ren et al., "Exploring Extreme Parameter Compression for Pre-trained Language Models," *arxiv.org*, May 20, 2020 (*https://arxiv.org/abs/2205.10036*).

Role of Fine-Tuning When Compressing Neural Networks

Model compression can be carried out with pruning techniques or by factorization of weight matrices. These compressed models have fewer parameters but incur large performance degradation. One of the primary reasons for this degradation in performance of trained models post-compression is the changes to the internal representations. When weights are removed, the internal representations learned during training are changed.

Fine-tuning compressed weights for a few epochs using a subset of the original training data can help recover the degraded performance. If compression destroys the internal representations learned by the model, fine-tuning can help recover these representations.[8]

Factorizing neural networks can have some drawbacks, particularly in terms of increased computations and approximation errors. For instance, SVD is an expensive operation that has $\mathcal{O}(N^3)$ complexity. Furthermore, reducing the model size with factorization also leads to an increase in the number of operations during training and

8 Hallgrimur Thorsteinsson et al., "Adversarial Fine-Tuning of Compressed Neural Networks for Joint Improvement of Robustness and Efficiency," *arXiv.org*, March 14, 2024 (*https://arxiv.org/abs/2403.09441*).

inference. This is due to the introduction of multiple smaller layers or additional operations needed to handle the factorized components, which can offset the expected efficiency gains.

Factorization techniques also result in approximation errors. The factorized representations do not fully capture the complexity of the original model, leading to a loss in performance, especially for complex tasks. These errors arise from the inherent limitations of the factorization methods used, which may not preserve all the nuances of the original weight distributions.

Low-Rank Adaptation of Foundational Models

Low-rank adaptation (LoRA) is a technique designed to fine-tune foundational models efficiently. Instead of updating all parameters of a pretrained model during the fine-tuning process, LoRA introduces low-rank matrices that are added to the original weight matrices during the forward pass. This approach significantly reduces the number of trainable parameters, resulting in faster fine-tuning with lower computational overhead.[9]

By inserting low-rank matrices into specific layers of the model, LoRA effectively captures the necessary adaptations for new tasks without requiring extensive modifications to the original weights. Figure 6-8 illustrates the procedure using a pretrained model with weights W of size $K \times D$, which is adapted with two smaller matrices A,B of rank R. This makes it particularly beneficial for tailoring large foundational models to specific applications while minimizing resource usage.

9 Edward J. Hu et al., "LoRA: Low-Rank Adaptation of Large Language Models," *arXiv.org*, October 16, 2021 (*https://arxiv.org/abs/2106.09685*).

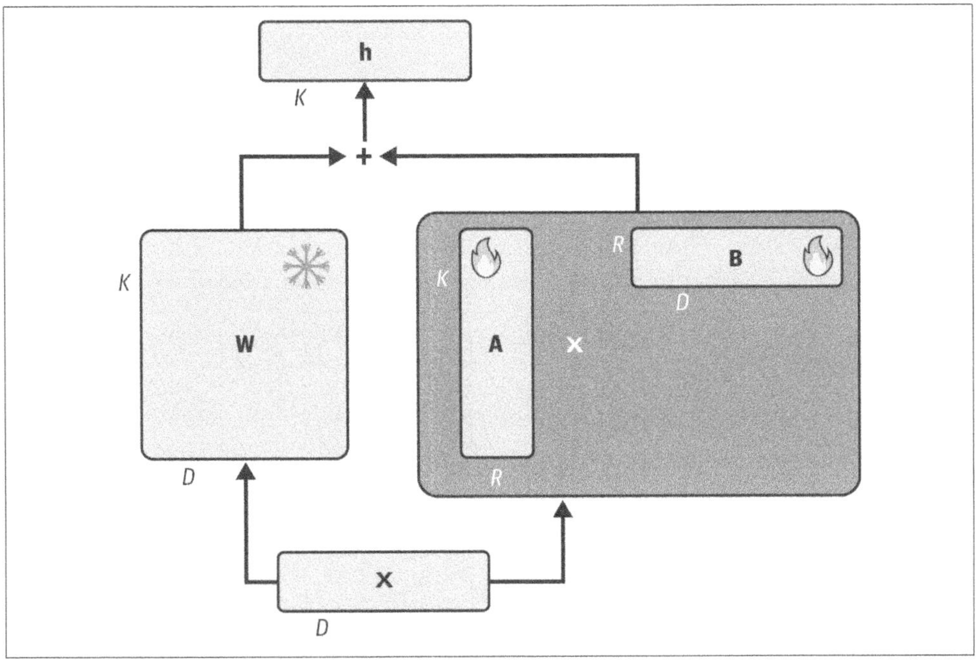

Figure 6-8. The LoRA procedure, which can be used to fine-tune a smaller subset of parameters [A,B] when using a large-scale model with parameters W.

Given a pretrained foundational model f_θ, LoRA adaptors can be to fine-tune this model on the new training dataset $\mathscr{D} = \{(x_i, y_i)\}_{i=1}^{N}$ as follows:

1. *Initialization*
   Specify learning rate η, total number of training epochs N_e , and rank R for the low-rank adaptation.

2. *Set up LoRA modules*
   For each layer ℓ in the model where adaptation is desired:

   - Introduce two low-rank matrices $\mathbf{A}_\ell \in \mathbb{R}^{D \times R}$ and $\mathbf{B}_\ell \in \mathbb{R}^{R \times D}$ that will be used to approximate the weight updates during training, where D is the dimensionality of the layer.
   - Initialize $\mathbf{A}_\ell$ and $\mathbf{B}_\ell$ with small random values.

3. *Training with LoRA*

   For each epoch $t = 1,2,\cdots,N_e$:

   - For each input sample $x_i \in \mathcal{D}$, compute the output for layer ℓ as follows:

   $$f_\ell(x_i) = f_{\mathbf{W}_\ell}(x_i) + A_\ell \cdot B_\ell^T \cdot x_i,$$

     where $f_{\mathbf{W}_\ell}(x_i)$ represents the original output of layer ℓ based on the input x_i with parameters $\mathbf{W}_\ell$. The term $\mathbf{A}_\ell \cdot \mathbf{B}_\ell^T \cdot x_i$ adds the low-rank adaptation based on the input.
   - Calculate the loss $\mathcal{L}$ (e.g., cross-entropy loss) based on the output.
   - Compute gradients with respect to $\mathbf{A}_\ell,\mathbf{B}_\ell$ while keeping the base parameters θ fixed.
   - Update the LoRA parameters $\mathbf{A}_\ell,\mathbf{B}_\ell$ using the optimizer and learning rate η.

4. *Output*

   After training, the adapted model $f_{\theta_{FT}}$ is obtained, utilizing the original parameters θ along with the learned low-rank matrices $\mathbf{A}_\ell$ and $\mathbf{B}_\ell$.

LoRA has become the *de facto* procedure for fine-tuning large foundational models, including LLMs. It has also shown promise in adapting these models to improve robustness and fairness and for alignment tasks wherein a base foundational model is adapted to achieve better performance on other dimensions using specialized LoRA adaptors.

Neural Network Compression or LoRA for the Climate Policy Chatbot?

In developing the climate policy chatbot, choosing between pruning and LoRA for fine-tuning hinges on balancing resource efficiency with domain-specific adaptability.

Pruning reduces the model's size and complexity, making it suitable for deployment on lower-powered devices and ensuring faster response times. However, in this application one can assume that low power is not an essential requirement.

LoRA, on the other hand, provides a task-specific fine-tuning approach that can capture climate policy nuances more effectively. By adapting the model with minimal parameter changes, LoRA fine-tuning could enable the chatbot to generate informed responses to specialized queries without the computational costs of full-model fine-tuning. Additionally, LoRA's efficiency in handling frequent updates allows the model to incorporate emerging climate policies and research without large-scale retraining.

Quantization

So far, this chapter has focused on reducing AI waste during training at a high level using ideas from transfer learning (see "Transfer Learning" on page 147) and model compression methods (see "Training Compressed Neural Networks" on page 152). Now, we will switch gears and explore methods that offer trade-off between performance and resource consumption by adjusting the precision (number of bits) used during training. We will mainly use *quantization* methods to adjust the number of bits used when training a neural network. This includes reducing the precision of training data, neural network weights, gradients, and so on. Many of the quantization ideas are also applicable during inference, which is discussed further in "Post-Training Quantization" on page 182.

Quantization is inherent to all computing as computers are discrete. All real-valued numbers are stored using a certain level of quantization, which is decided by the hardware. The most common quantization used for DL is the 32-bit floating point representation (`FP32`).[10]

Consider the irrational number $\pi \approx 3.14159265358979...$; the `FP32` representation of π is *0 10000000 10010010000111111011011* where the first bit is used for sign, the next 8 bits is for the exponent, and the last 23 bits for the mantissa resulting in $\pi \approx 3.1415927$. In `FP16` it is represented as *0 10000 1001001000*, where the exponent is reduced to using 5 bits and mantissa to 10 bits resulting in $\pi \approx 3.140625$. If we reduce it further to `FP8` with a 4-bit exponent and 3-bit mantissa, we get *0 1000 100*, which results in $\pi \approx 3.25$.[11] As we see, reducing the number of bits has a direct effect on the precision of the variable, in this case the value of π.

When working with lower precision representations, the number of bits used for the exponent and mantissa are modulated (sign is always 1 bit). Figure 6-9 shows these standard schemes and "Post-Training Quantization" on page 182 provides a more in-depth analysis of quantization.

10 Microprocessor Standards Committee, *IEEE Standard for Floating-Point Arithmetic*, (IEEE, July 22, 2019) (*https://oreil.ly/0XsV5*).

11 Paulius Micikevicius et al., "FP8 Formats for Deep Learning," *arXiv.org*, September 29, 2022 (*https://arxiv.org/abs/2209.05433*).

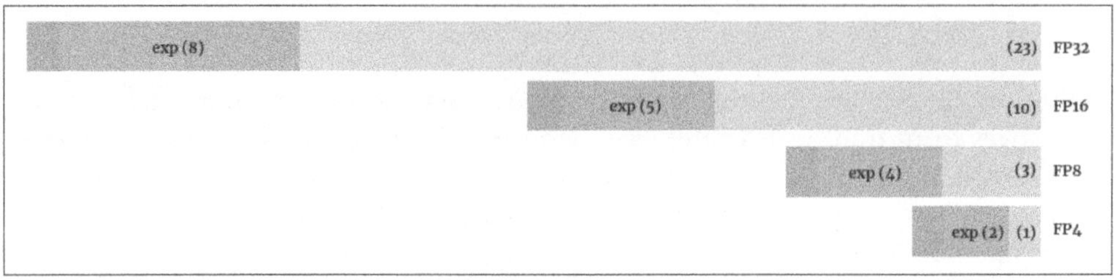

Figure 6-9. Schematic of various floating-point precision representations. While `FP32`, `FP16`, and `FP8` have standardized bit allocation of sign, exponent, and mantissa, `FP4` format can vary between implementations. The first bit is always used for representing the `sign` in all standard floating-point data types.

Low-Precision Training

Modulating the precision of the input data and model parameters during training of a neural network can influence the accuracy of computations, amount of memory required, computational costs, and performance of the learned model. Quantization offers a trade-off between precision of computations (and hence accuracy) and the resources required. In over-parameterized AI models, however, quantization can yield drastic reductions in resources with small performance drops.[12]

Reducing the precision of the data and the model weights can immediately reduce the memory consumption during training. For certain quantization levels, this is well supported in common DL frameworks, as demonstrated in Example 6-3, for reducing the precision to half, which in this case converts all `FP32` data to `FP16`.

Example 6-3. Half-precision training in PyTorch

```
import torch

### Initialize data loader and models as usual ... ###

# Cast the created model to half precision (FP16)
model = model.half()

for i, (inputs, labels) in enumerate(loader_train):
    # Cast the input data and labels into half precision
    inputs = inputs.half()
    labels = labels.half()
```

12 Tim Dettmers and Luke Zettlemoyer, "The Case for 4-bit Precision: K-bit Inference Scaling Laws," *arXiv.org*, February 28, 2023 (*https://arxiv.org/abs/2212.09720*).

Note that even when the model parameters, data, and gradients can be quantized, the arithmetic operations might not be performed in low-precision. Arithmetic operations in low-precision require hardware support, or software adjustments, which might not always be easy or available. `CUDA` kernel adaptations are used to support half precision (`FP16`) in PyTorch, which reduce the memory usage and increase throughput during input-output operations. Figure 6-10 shows the extent of speedup achievable during training due to quantization.

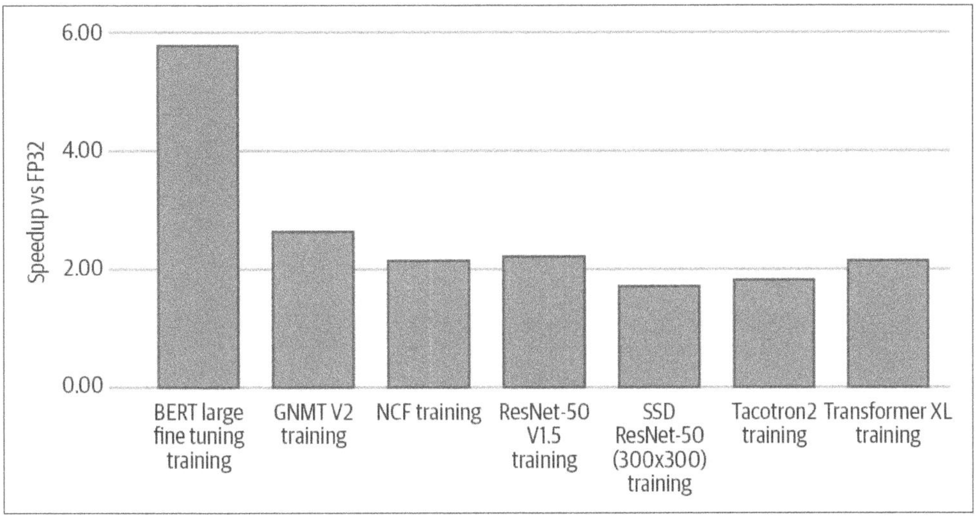

Figure 6-10. Speedup during training when using `FP16` *versus* `FP32` *for various DL models (higher is better) on the same GPU. Across the board, we notice a substantial speedup. (Source adapted from The PyTorch Foundation.)*[13]

Real Quantization Versus Simulated Quantization

Real quantization involves the actual reduction of the data type and bit width of neural network weights and activations during computation, using lower precision formats like `FP8`. This transformation is applied directly in hardware (when supported), making it suitable for deployment on devices with low-precision support, such as mobile and edge hardware.

In contrast, simulated quantization (also known as quantization aware training or QAT) approximates the effects of quantization during model training without changing the actual data type of weights and activations. It simulates the quantization effect by rounding values to lower precision while retaining high-precision storage,

13 Mengdi Huang et al., "Introducing Native PyTorch Automatic Mixed Precision for Faster Training on NVIDIA GPUs," *PyTorch* (blog), July 28, 2020 (*https://oreil.ly/hV_7_*).

typically using FP32. This approach is mainly used during training or testing to prepare models for quantization, allowing for adjustments and optimizations without the need for specific low-precision hardware.

Simulated quantization does not yield any reductions in memory as the data are in fact still stored in original precision. On the contrary, in some instances it might cause an increase in memory consumption and compute.

In some applications, casting all data and model parameters to half precision might result in performance degradation. In these settings, *automatic mixed precision* (AMP) can adjust the precision of data, weights, and gradients, using both full and half precision. This can reduce the negative effects of using half precision. Example 6-4 shows how AMP can be used in PyTorch.

Example 6-4. Implementing AMP in PyTorch

```
import torch
# Creates once at the beginning of training
scaler = torch.cuda.amp.GradScaler()

for data, label in data_iter:
   optimizer.zero_grad()
   # Casts operations to mixed precision
   with torch.cuda.amp.autocast():
      loss = model(data)

   # Scales the loss, and calls backward()
   # to create scaled gradients
   scaler.scale(loss).backward()

   # Unscales gradients and calls
   # or skips optimizer.step()
   scaler.step(optimizer)

   # Updates the scale for next iteration
   scaler.update()
```

Quantizing Optimizer States

During training, some form of gradient-based rules update the model parameters θ. This requires the computation of the gradients of the loss $\mathscr{L}$ with respect to θ at each training iteration t given as $\mathbf{g}_t = \frac{\partial \mathscr{L}}{\partial \theta}$.

In the case of stateful optimizers (see "How to Train Your Model" on page 43 for details) that use momentum-based optimization such as Adam,[14] the first- and second-order statistics of the gradient over time, $\mathbf{M}_t$,$\mathbf{V}_t$, respectively, are also maintained for improved convergence. For a neural network with N parameters, an additional $3 \cdot N$ variables are stored in memory during training. Further, the intermediate activations $\mathbf{H}_\ell$ at layer ℓ are also stored in memory to efficiently perform backpropagation. By default, each individual element in these quantities is stored using `FP32` format.[15]

Figure 6-11 illustrates these quantities in relation to the GPU memory. The trainable parameters use only a fraction of memory. When using stateful optimizers, the first- and second-order statistics of gradients are also stored in memory. Furthermore, the intermediate activations also need to be stored in memory to perform the gradient update.

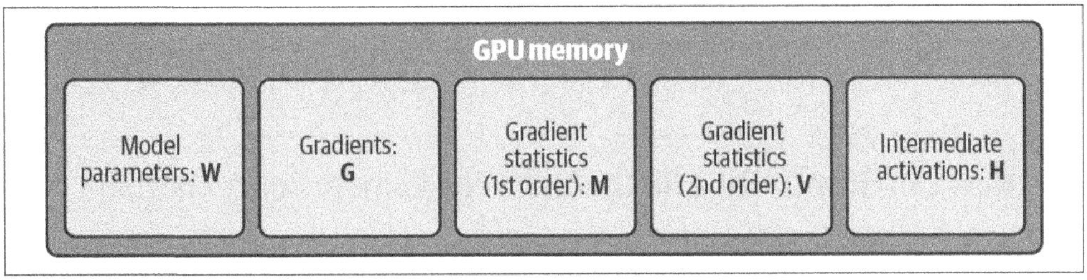

Figure 6-11. GPU memory utilization during training of DL models.

The increased GPU memory consumption due to the optimizer states (which can be three times as much as due to parameters) and the intermediate activation maps have a direct impact on the size of training data batches that can be processed. This can increase training time and/or need for additional GPUs resulting in an overall increase in the resource costs.

Recent 8-bit optimizers can reduce the memory consumption of optimizer states.[16] When using 8-bit optimizers, the optimizer states are quantized to extremely low-precision (`INT8`) before storing them in GPU memory and are dequantized to `FP16` for gradient computations. This has been shown to yield drastic reductions in memory consumption, along with speedup during training and even faster convergence for some models. As with other low-precision operations, quantizing optimizer states

14 Diederik P. Kingma and Jimmy Ba, "Adam: A Method for Stochastic Optimization," *arXiv.org*, January 30, 2017 (*https://arxiv.org/abs/1412.6980*).

15 Raghavendra Selvan et al., "Operating Critical Machine Learning Models in Resource Constrained Regimes," *arxiv.org*, February 4, 2024 (*https://arxiv.org/abs/2303.10181*).

16 Tim Dettmers et al., "8-bit Optimizers via Block-wise Quantization," *arXiv.org*, June 20, 2022 (*https://arxiv.org/abs/2110.02861*).

also causes performance degradation. Example 6-5 shows the use of 8-bit optimizers using the official `bitsandbytes` optimizers.

Example 6-5. One-line code to use 8-bit optimizers like `bitsandbytes` *(https://oreil.ly/Fo5y9)*

```
import bitsandbytes as bnb

### Change the optimizer to BNB
# - optimizer = torch.optim.Adam(...)
optimizer = bnb.optim.Adam8bit(...)
```

Quantization during training can reduce the memory consumption, improve throughput during input-output operations, accelerate training, and result in an overall reduction of the resources required. More recent work has also shown other benefits, such as improved generalization when performing quantization.[17] Furthermore, the degradation in performance due to quantization can be simulated by modelling the quantization error as noise. This is well studied in the literature as QAT.[18]

How Can Quantization Be Useful for the Climate Policy Chatbot?

We have discussed how transfer learning and LoRA-based adaptation can be used to customize an open source LLM to meet the needs of developing a climate policy chatbot. Note that fine-tuning and LoRA both require additional training—either of full network weights or of a fraction of them (in the case of LoRA).

These training procedures require large memory costs. For instance, the Llama-3-8B model can't be generally trained on a GPU with 24GB memory.[19] Quantization strategies discussed in this chapter, especially the quantization of optimizer states to INT8, can alleviate this memory consumption. Furthermore, recent works have also looked at LoRA fine-tuning with quantization.[20]

17 MohammadHossein AskariHemmat et al., "QGen: On the Ability to Generalize in Quantization Aware Training," *arXiv.org*, April 19, 2024 (*https://arxiv.org/abs/2404.11769*).

18 Benoit Jacob et al., "Quantization and Training of Neural Networks for Efficient Integer-Arithmetic-Only Inference," *arXiv.org*, December 15, 2017 (*https://arxiv.org/abs/1712.05877*).

19 Recent works provide additional tricks to LoRA for training large models with fewer resources; see Sebastian Loeschcke et al., "LoQT: Low-Rank Adapters for Quantized Pretraining," *arXiv.org*, November 4, 2024 (*https://arxiv.org/abs/2405.16528*).

20 Tim Dettmers et al., "QLoRA: Efficient Finetuning of Quantized LLMs," *arXiv.org*, May 23, 2023 (*https://arxiv.org/abs/2305.14314*).

These quantization methods can reduce the GPU memory required when training or fine-tuning LLMs and can allow for the development of the climate policy chatbot even on a standalone workstation with a single GPU.

Efficient Training Achieved: What Comes Next?

Training DL models is one of the most resource-intensive steps in the pipeline of developing AI models. In this chapter we have looked at different types of methods that can help improve the training efficiency. Recycling knowledge of pretrained models, fine-tuning models instead of training from scratch, and in-context learning offer high-level optimizations during training. Model compression using neural network compression and quantization offers solutions at the other end of the spectrum by dealing with individual weights or by modulating the number of bits used. A combination of these classes of methods can be used to achieve sustainable training of AI models. What are some additional considerations of these resource efficiencies gained at training?

Are all pretrained models useful?

No. If the domain of the data a model is pretrained on is very different, then it is as good as training a randomly initialized model.

The effectiveness of pretrained models depends on how well their pretraining data aligns with the target domain or task. When there is a significant domain mismatch—such as a model pretrained on general data being applied to a specialized field like medicine or law—the model may perform poorly or even worse than a model trained from scratch, as its learned features might not translate well. In such cases, training a simpler, custom model from scratch can be more efficient and yield better results.

How does one know what data a model has been trained on?

We cannot usually know the training data only from a trained model.

To determine what data a model has been trained on, we usually rely on documentation provided by the model's authors, as the training data itself is not embedded within the model. Open source models often come with detailed disclosures of datasets used, documented in model cards or research papers. However, proprietary models often provide only high-level descriptions due to privacy, security, or competitive considerations.

Model authors have a responsibility to disclose training data sources, biases, and limitations where possible, as these factors affect how the model performs and applies across different domains. Transparency from authors can help users make informed decisions about applying the model responsibly and understanding any limitations in its outputs.

How does one make sure fine-tuned models do not forget their pretraining?

This is an active area of research.

Ensuring that fine-tuned models retain knowledge from their pretraining phase—while also adapting effectively to new tasks—is an active research area. This challenge, often referred to as *catastrophic forgetting*, occurs when a model "forgets" general knowledge learned during pretraining in favor of task-specific information introduced during fine-tuning.[21]

Researchers address this by employing techniques such as regularization methods, which penalize large deviations from pretraining weights, and *progressive learning*, which gradually shifts training from general to specific data. Another strategy is *multitask learning*, where a model is simultaneously fine-tuned on both the new task and samples of pretraining data to balance both types of knowledge. These approaches aim to optimize the fine-tuning process so that the model retains general skills while adapting to new ones, striking a balance between generalization and specialization.

In-context learning seems quite powerful and efficient as we do not fine-tune large models. Are there any other caveats to using it?

It is efficient, but it can solve only simple tasks.

Learning in-context requires a sufficient number of samples to be shown in the prompt. And depending on the complexity of the task being learned in-context, the number of training samples can vary. This introduces an additional hyperparameter (number of samples in the prompt). Furthermore, processing large input prompts can increase the inference time.

Are there other effects to neural network compression than drop in performance?

Yes, it has been shown that compressed models could be affected in other ways, for example, by making them less fair.

Compression techniques, such as pruning and quantization, reduce model size and computational requirements but can also exacerbate bias and fairness issues. Studies have shown that compressed models may retain or even amplify biases present in the original model.[22]

Additionally, compressed models may become more brittle or vulnerable to adversarial attacks, as simplifying the model can make it more predictable or

---

21 James Kirkpatrick et al., "Overcoming Catastrophic Forgetting in Neural Networks," *Proceedings of the National Academy of Sciences* 114, no. 13 (March 14, 2017): 3521–26 (*https://doi.org/10.1073/pnas.1611835114*).

22 Sara Hooker et al., "Characterising Bias in Compressed Models," *arXiv.org*, December 18, 2020 (*https://arxiv.org/abs/2010.03058*).

expose it to exploitative patterns. Therefore, while compression improves efficiency, it also necessitates careful evaluation of these broader impacts on fairness, robustness, and security.

Does quantization always make training efficient?
Only when real quantization is allowed. Simulated quantization can make training less efficient.

Quantization can make training more efficient, but this benefit is typically realized only with real, hardware-supported quantization. Real quantization, where reduced-precision calculations (such as 8-bit or lower) are performed directly on the hardware, can speed up computations and lower memory usage. However, simulated quantization, which mimics quantization effects while still operating at full precision (e.g., `FP32`), often makes training less efficient. Simulated quantization adds overhead by introducing additional computations to mimic lower precision, which can slow down training instead of accelerating it. Therefore, the efficiency gains of quantization largely depend on hardware support for actual low-precision calculations, making it critical for users to consider their hardware capabilities when implementing quantization.

Training is done only once. Why care about its sustainability?
Even single training runs of large models are extremely resource-intensive.

Training large models even once can have a substantial environmental impact due to the vast amounts of energy consumed. The process often involves running thousands of GPUs or TPUs for days, weeks, or even months, which translates to high carbon emissions, especially if powered by nonrenewable energy sources.[23] This intensive resource use raises sustainability concerns, as the carbon footprint of training a single large model can be enormous. Beyond environmental impact, resource-intensive training runs contribute to high financial costs and accessibility issues, as they can limit the ability of smaller organizations and researchers to participate in AI development.

23 Training the Llama-3 family of models emitted 11,390tCO_2e as reported in the model card (*https://oreil.ly/UvTpT*).

CHAPTER 7
Lean Inference

If a tree falls in the forest and no one is around to hear it, does it make a sound? We have all heard this idiom in different settings. For AI practitioners, the related question should be *if a model is developed and no one uses it, what happens to all the resources used in its development?*

All AI models are developed with the hope they will be used extensively. It is not a given that all models will have takers, though. This brings us to a philosophical question on how to allocate resources at the outset when developing any resource-intensive technology.[1] We will discuss this dilemma further in Chapter 9.

In this chapter, we will focus on the resource efficiency and sustainability of AI models at deployment. Technically, using an AI model after training for prediction purposes is known as *inference*. I first present an overview of the inference costs of modern AI models and then look at some effective methods to improve these costs. Many of the methods discussed in Chapter 6 for improving training efficiency, such as quantization and neural network pruning, can also be used to achieve lean inference. In addition, we will consider specialized methods that can accelerate inference of AI models by translating high-level implementations to more efficient, lower-level programming languages such as C++.

1 J Habgood, "The Ethics of Resource Allocation: A Case Study," *Journal of Medical Ethics* 9, no. 1 (March 1, 1983): 21–24 (*https://doi.org/10.1136/jme.9.1.21*).

Lifetime Cost of an AI Model

Consider the inference cost of a large GenAI model, such as Llama-3-405B. Let's assume the energy consumption per prompt is $E_{\text{inference}} = 1Wh$,[2] which does not seem like much by itself. A model such as this is not used only once, however. If the model is used $N_{\text{inference}}$, then the total energy consumption due to the inference phase is $E_{\text{inference}} \cdot N_{\text{inference}}$.

While this calculation captures the energy consumption at the inference stage of the model, we must also account for the model's development costs.

Llama 3.1 Model Card (*https://oreil.ly/m5TNj*) reports the one-time energy consumption of Llama-3-405B to be E_{train} = 23746 million watt hours (MWh). A naive way to determine the developing cost to obtain the lifetime energy consumption of a model is to simply add this one-time cost to the total inference cost:

$$E_{\text{lifetime}} = E_{\text{train}} + E_{\text{inference}} \cdot N_{\text{inference}}$$

The primary argument for developing large-scale AI models is that they are used many times, and the development costs can be *amortized* over the model lifetime. Obtaining the actual inference energy consumption of a particular AI model then should take the amortized training cost into consideration, which is given as:

$$E_{\text{act\_inf}} = E_{\text{train}} / N_{\text{inference}} + E_{\text{inference}}$$

2 This is a reasonable assumption based on the benchmarking reported in the LLM-Perf Leaderboard (*https://oreil.ly/KbphX*).

Training Costs Versus Inference Costs

The one-time training cost of most recent AI models is many times more than than the cost of running the models for prediction. The total energy costs, however, can be drastically skewed depending on several factors (for example, their popularity). For AI models such as the ones behind products like ChatGPT, the training cost can be exorbitant. However, due to their popularity, the scaled-up inference costs might be the main reason for their overall energy consumption.

We don't have accurate estimations as to how the training and inference stages contribute to the energy demands of the AI sector. Some estimations put the overall training energy consumption at only about 20%, with the remainder being attributed to inference costs.[3]

In Figure 7-1 (left side), we analyze different model uptake scenarios by varying the number of inference rns $N_{\text{inference}}$ over the model lifetime. We use $E_{\text{train}} = 23746MWh$ and $E_{\text{inference}} = 1Wh$ (per prompt) for the Llama-3-405B model. The training costs are initially high; however, with increased usage, these costs lower and the inference costs take over. For the Llama-3-405B model, the training and inference costs cross over around $N_{\text{inference}} = 10^5$. The more accurate model of the energy consumption over the model lifetime, E_{lifetime}, takes the amortized training cost into consideration. Figure 7-1 (right side) shows that the crossover between training and inference costs for different uptake extents can change depending on the initial training cost.

3 Avelar et al., "The AI Disruption: Challenges and Guidance for Data Center Design" (*https://oreil.ly/7T2xu*).

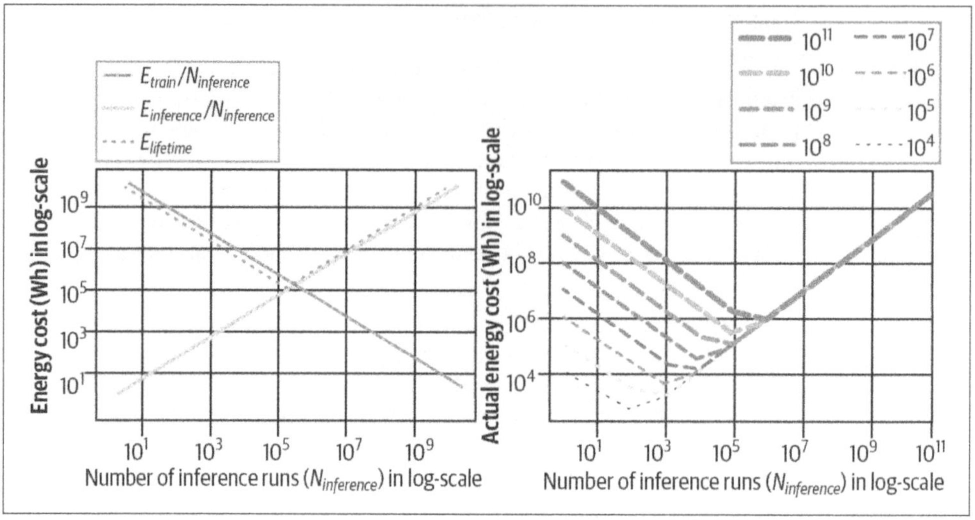

Figure 7-1. Training versus inference energy cost trends over a model's lifetime, where inference costs scale up (left), possibly exceeding the one-time training cost, and lifetime inference costs can easily exceed the one-time training costs (right).

Decentralized AI Dashboard for Disaster Response

Coordinating relief efforts after a natural disaster requires quick and effective responses. But damaged infrastructure can slow things down. In such situations, edge devices like smartphones, traffic cameras, and drones can be leveraged to gather and consolidate data, enabling the monitoring of disaster impacts and planning of relief responses.

An Artificial Intelligence for Disaster Response (AIDR) dashboard can bring together data from edge devices, providing a real-time, interactive map of affected areas, highlighting structural damage, environmental changes, and human distress (see Figure 7-2). The data it stores can send prioritized alerts and help emergency teams, government agencies, and NGOs work together more effectively. AIDR automatically collects and classifies social media posts during humanitarian crises globally.

For such decentralized systems to be most effective, the data analysis should be performed locally on edge devices that handle a wide range of data sources, such as GPS locations, images, text, and sensor readings. Ideally, a powerful but efficient multimodal AI model would be well-suited for this task.

In this chapter, we will explore techniques that can bring complex AI models to low-resource devices. We will use the multimodal AI models on edge devices as the running example to assess the usefulness of the lean inference strategies presented in this chapter.

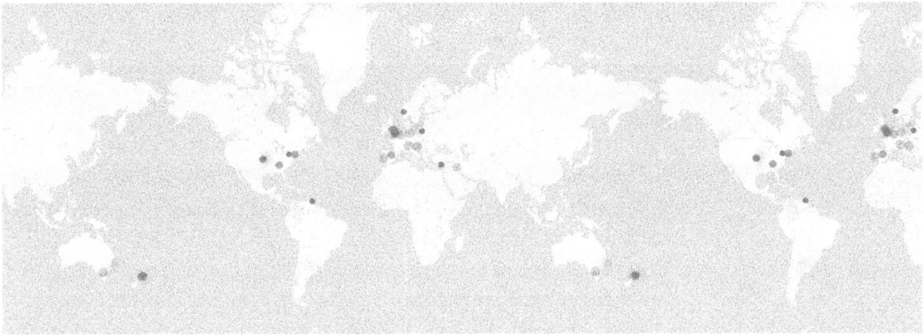

Figure 7-2. The AIDR dashboard (https://aidr.qcri.org).

Achieving Lean Inference

We have seen that for many AI models, the lifetime inference costs can exceed the one-time model development costs. In addition, edge devices often pose resource constraints such as hard power limitations and low latency for real-time applications. Improving the resource efficiency of AI models at inference not only has an impact on their overall sustainability, but can be essential to getting them deployed. In this section, we will look at some widely used techniques to make inference on resource-constrained regimes feasible.

Resource-Efficient Architectures

Obtaining AI models that are resource-efficient from the outset is one way of making them efficient at inference. Developing efficient neural networks often involves this paradigm.

As we have seen in "Neural Architecture Search" on page 129, we can design neural networks as a discrete optimization task using NAS algorithms. NAS aims to maximize the validation performance and, in turn, yield maximally performant models using single-objective optimization. NAS with *multiobjective optimization*, where multiple objectives are jointly optimized, can offer neural network architectures that offer different trade-offs between multiple objectives like accuracy and resource consumption. Table 7-1 lists additional resources that can be included in NAS with multiobjective optimization such as latency, FLOP count, memory, and even energy consumption. We can repurpose many of the NAS algorithms from "Neural Architecture Search" on page 129 with multiobjective optimization to obtain architectures that are resource-constrained.

Table 7-1. Key research publications and the resources they optimize using multiobjective optimization

Method	Resource optimized	Publication
SqueezeNet	Parameters, memory	Forrest N. Iandola et al., "SqueezeNet: AlexNet-Level Accuracy with 50x Fewer Parameters and <0.5MB Model Size," *arxiv.org*, November 4, 2016 (*https://arxiv.org/abs/1602.07360*).
MobileNet	Latency	Andrew G. Howard et al., "MobileNets: Efficient Convolutional Neural Networks for Mobile Vision Applications," *arxiv.org*, April 17, 2017 (*https://arxiv.org/abs/1704.04861*).
EfficientNetf	FLOP count	Mingxing Tan and Quoc V. Le, "EfficientNet: Rethinking Model Scaling for Convolutional Neural Networks," *arxiv.org*, September 11, 2020 (*https://arxiv.org/abs/1905.11946*).
FBNet	Latency	Bichen Wu et al., "FBNet: Hardware-Aware Efficient ConvNet Design via Differentiable Neural Architecture Search," *arxiv.org*, May 24, 2019 (*https://arxiv.org/abs/1812.03443*).
OFA net	MAC, latency	Han Cai et al., "Once-for-All: Train One Network and Specialize It for Efficient Deployment," *arxiv.org*, April 29, 2020 (*https://arxiv.org/abs/1908.09791*).
EC-NAS	Energy	Pedram Bakhtiarifard et al., "EC-NAS: Energy Consumption Aware Tabular Benchmarks for Neural Architecture Search," *arxiv.org*, March 22, 2024 (*https://arxiv.org/abs/2210.06015*).

Resource-aware NAS with Pareto optimization

We can use multiobjective optimization, also known as *Pareto optimization*, to perform NAS that considers resource consumption and accuracy.[4] Compared with single-objective optimization, which yields a single candidate as the solution, Pareto optimization offers a family of solutions. Each solution in this set, known as the *dominant set* or the *Pareto front*, offers different degrees of trade-off between the different objectives.

Of the many techniques to perform multiobjective optimization, random search is a strong baseline when optimizing two to three objectives. Let's work through an example to see how it can be used to optimize two objectives when performing NAS. The final output of any multiobjective optimization procedure is not a single solution but a set of solutions, or the Pareto front.

Consider two objectives in this example: maximizing accuracy (f_1) and minimizing inference energy consumption (f_2). The multiobjective optimization with random search begins by evaluating a few random architectures—say, *A*, *B*, and *C*—to establish an initial Pareto front, meaning none of these architectures is strictly better than the others in both objectives. These initial architectures are shown as blue circles in Figure 7-3 along with their accuracy and energy consumption.

Next, evaluate a new architecture, *D*. Let's say it has 92% accuracy and energy consumption of *70Wh*. While *D* has the highest accuracy compared to the initial Pareto front (consisting of *A*, *B*, and *C*), it also has the highest energy consumption. To

4 Kaisa Miettinen, *Nonlinear Multiobjective Optimization* (Springer Nature, 1998).

determine if *D* can be included in the Pareto front, check if it dominates any existing architectures. Since *D* has better accuracy but worse energy footprint than *A*, *B*, and *C*, it does not dominate any of them. However, because it is also not dominated by any existing architecture because it has the highest accuracy, it is added to the Pareto front depicted as the square in Figure 7-3.

Random search continues by evaluating new architectures and updating the Pareto front based on dominance. Say, in the next sampling, architecture *E* is evaluated and found to have accuracy of 72% and energy consumption of *40Wh*. It's easy to see that *E* is dominated by other architectures in both the objectives, and it doesn't dominate any other architecture in either of the two objectives. So, *E* will not be added to the front, depicted as the triangle in Figure 7-3.

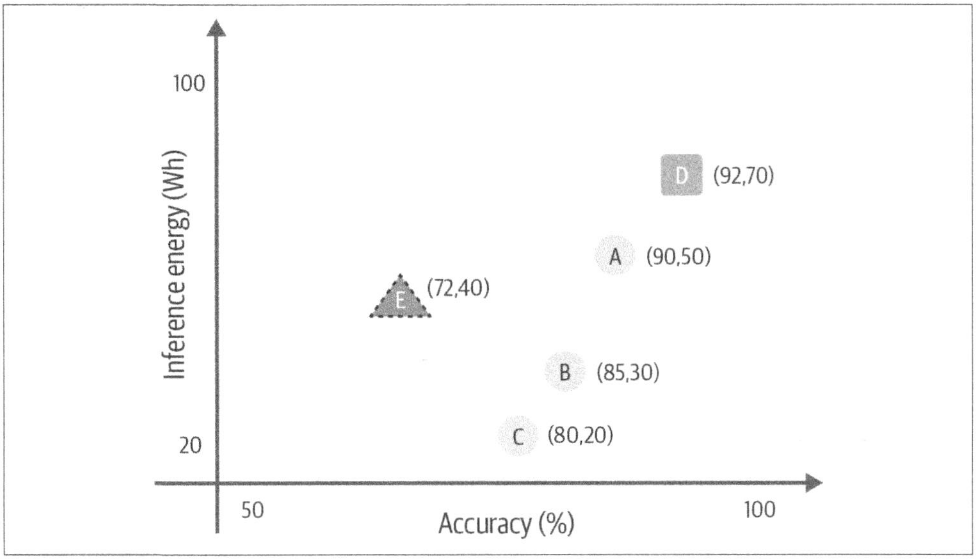

Figure 7-3. Constructing a Pareto front using random search when optimizing multiple objectives for NAS.

This iterative search repeats until a set evaluation limit is reached or the front stabilizes, indicating no significant improvements. In the end, practitioners can choose the solutions from the final Pareto front as each of the architecture offers a unique trade-off.

Knowledge Distillation

In "Dataset Condensation" on page 102, we looked at dataset distillation techniques that capture the characteristics of a large dataset within a smaller dataset. The precursor to dataset condensation or distillation includes methods that distill the knowledge from larger neural networks into smaller neural networks. This procedure is known as *knowledge distillation*,[5] a technique in DL in which a large, pretrained model (often called the *teacher*) transfers its knowledge to a smaller, more compact model (called the *student*). This is particularly useful for deploying DL models on resource-constrained devices, as it allows for a balance between high model accuracy and low computational cost.

The main idea with knowledge distillation is to train the student network to mimic the behavior of the teacher network, rather than learning only from the training data. To achieve this, the student model learns from the "soft targets," which are the predictions of the teacher model. These soft targets contain more nuanced information about class similarities than the "hard targets" or the classification labels in the training data.

Figure 7-4 shows the process of knowledge distillation. The teacher model is pretrained and remains frozen, whereas the student model is updated using two losses: the training loss and the distillation loss. This knowledge distillation process enables smaller models to achieve performance levels that approach those of much larger models, making it a powerful technique for model compression in real-world applications.[6]

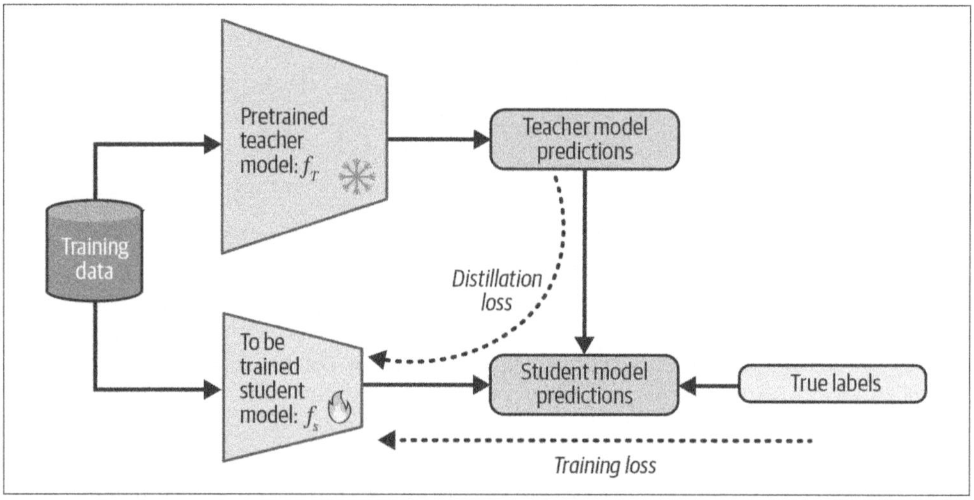

Figure 7-4. Two types of losses (training and distillation) used to adapt the student model parameters.

5 Geoffrey Hinton et al., "Distilling the Knowledge in a Neural Network," *arXiv.org*, March 9, 2015 (*https://arxiv.org/abs/1503.02531*).

6 Yuxin Ren et al., "Exploring Extreme Parameter Compression for Pre-trained Language Models," *arXiv.org*, May 20, 2022 (*https://arxiv.org/abs/2205.10036*).

The purpose of knowledge distillation is to transfer knowledge from a larger, pretrained teacher model f_T to a smaller student model f_S, allowing f_S to achieve comparable performance while being more efficient. This can be performed by the following steps:

1. *Initialization*
   Define the pretrained teacher model f_T and the trainable student model f_S. Let the training dataset be $\mathscr{D} = \{(x_i, y_i)\}_{i=1}^{N}$, where x_i are input samples and y_i are the corresponding labels. Set the temperature parameter τ, the distillation loss weight α, the standard cross-entropy loss function $\mathscr{L}_{\text{CE}}$, and a measure that captures differences between probability densities such as Kullback-Leibler divergence.[7]

2. *Compute soft targets from the teacher model*
   For each input sample x_i, compute the soft logits from the teacher model $z_i^T = f_T(x_i)$ and the softened probabilities (soft targets) $q_i^T = \text{softmax}\left(z_i^T / \tau\right)$.

3. *Training the student model*
   Initialize the parameters of the student model f_S. For each training iteration, sample a mini-batch $\mathscr{B} \subset \mathscr{D}$. For each input sample (x_i, y_i) in the mini-batch $\mathscr{B}$, perform the following steps:

   - Compute the logits from the student model $z_i^S = f_S(x_i)$ and the softened probabilities $q_i^S = \text{softmax}\left(z_i^S / \tau\right)$.
   - Compute the distillation loss $\mathscr{L}_{\text{KD}} = \tau^2 \cdot \text{KL}\left(q_i^T \parallel q_i^S\right)$.
   - Compute the standard cross-entropy loss $\mathscr{L}_{\text{CE}} = \mathscr{L}_{\text{CE}}\left(y_i, \text{softmax}\left(z_i^S\right)\right)$.
   - Compute the total loss $\mathscr{L}_{\text{total}} = \alpha \cdot \mathscr{L}_{\text{KD}} + (1 - \alpha) \cdot \mathscr{L}_{\text{CE}}$.
   - Perform a gradient descent step to update the student model f_S parameters using the total loss $\mathscr{L}_{\text{total}}$.

4. *Output*
   The trained student model f_S is obtained after the completion of the training iterations.

7 S. Kullback and R. A. Leibler, "On Information and Sufficiency," *The Annals of Mathematical Statistics* 22, no. 1 (March 1, 1951): 79–86 (*https://doi.org/10.1214/aoms/1177729694*).

Knowledge distillation results in a student model that has learned the characteristics from a larger model by mimicking the larger model. Distilled models have demonstrated performance that is at par with the original model.[8]

> **Distilling into Efficient Architectures for Decentralized AI Dashboard**
>
> We are after efficient, multimodal models that can be used on edge devices that then feed data into the AIDR dashboard. For many edge devices, we know the hardware limitations *a priori* and can incorporate them as constraints in the multiobjective optimization setup for performing NAS. For instance, we could integrate power or memory limitations into the optimization criterion, drawing on work carried out as part of the hardware-aware NAS literature.[9]
>
> Once we have selected a model with reasonable performance and appropriate hardware requirements using multiobjective NAS, we can use knowledge distillation to further improve the smaller, efficient model. We can then identify a larger model as a teacher model. This teacher model can then be used to update the smaller model that now has the benefits of also distilling knowledge from the more complex model.

Pruning of Trained Models

DL models consist of many more trainable parameters than a given task warrants. From the outset it is not straightforward to design neural networks with the *right* parameter configuration. Concepts like the lottery ticket hypothesis discussed in "Model Selection in the Era of Foundational Models" on page 136 include speculation as to how the optimal, smaller network is *hidden* away inside larger networks.[10]

Neural network compression techniques such as pruning-based methods can reduce the number of parameters of a larger network, resulting in a compressed model, with comparable performance. In "Neural Network Pruning" on page 153, we discussed neural network compression during model training. To compress a trained model, we can use similar concepts based on removing parameters that are of low importance to the downstream performance. This is especially useful when a larger model can be trained, but at inference we cannot use these large models due to resource constraints. Several well-developed methods are available to compress trained models.

8 Victor Sanh et al., "DistilBERT, a Distilled Version of BERT: Smaller, Faster, Cheaper and Lighter," *arXiv.org*, March 1, 2020 (*https://arxiv.org/abs/1910.01108*).

9 Chaojian Li et al., "HW-NAS-Bench:Hardware-Aware Neural Architecture Search Benchmark," *arXiv.org*, March 28, 2025 (*https://arxiv.org/abs/2103.10584*).

10 Jonathan Frankle and Michael Carbin, "The Lottery Ticket Hypothesis: Finding Sparse, Trainable Neural Networks," *arXiv.org*, March 4, 2019 (*https://arxiv.org/abs/1803.03635*).

Example 7-1 showcases the `torch-pruning` package that supports several pruning algorithms.

Example 7-1. Magnitude pruning can be easily applied to any pretrained model, here shown using the `torch_pruning` package

```
import torch
import timm
import torch_pruning as tp

def prune_model(model, example_inputs, amount=0.5):
    # Define the importance criterion based on L1 norm
    importance = tp.importance.MagnitudeImportance(p=1)

    # Create a pruner object
    iterative_steps = 1
    # You can prune your model to the target pruning ratio iteratively.
    pruner = tp.pruner.MagnitudePruner(
            model,
            example_inputs,
            global_pruning=False, # Uniform pruning ratio for all layers.
            importance=importance, # importance criterion for param. selection
            iterative_steps=iterative_steps, # num. of iter. to achieve target ratio
            pruning_ratio=0.5,)
    # Apply the pruning
    pruner.step()
    return model

# Example input tensor for the ResNet50 model
example_inputs = torch.randn(1, 3, 224, 224)
# Load a pretrained ResNet50 model from Timm
model = timm.create_model('resnet50', pretrained=True)
nParam = sum(p.numel() for p in model.parameters() if p.requires_grad)
print("Number of parameters in base model:%.2fM"%(nParam/1e6))

# Prune the model
pruned_model = prune_model(model, example_inputs, amount=0.5)
nParam = sum(p.numel() for p in pruned_model.parameters() if p.requires_grad)
print("Number of parameters in pruned model:%.2fM"%(nParam/1e6))
```

This should result in the following output:

```
Number of parameters in base model:25.56M
Number of parameters in pruned model:6.41M
```

Importance of Fine-Tuning After Pruning

Neural network pruning removes weights or groups of weights of low importance to the downstream task. The standard ways the parameter importance is determined are based on the magnitude or some property of the weights (see Table 6-1 for a more complete list). Removing weights or groups of weights doesn't account for the correlative effects they might have on other parts of the neural network. So, in almost all cases, performing a few epochs of fine-tuning after pruning is highly recommended so that the pruned model can adjust the changes to its new network topology.

Post-Training Quantization

Converting continuous physical quantities into discrete, digital representations is achieved using quantization.[11] Consider the grayscale, which spans all hues of gray from black to white. If we only use 1 bit, then all the grayscales are binned into $2^1 = 2$ buckets (either black or white). Increasing the number of bits used can increase the resolution of how the grayscale is represented. Using 8 bits yields $2^8 = 256$ levels, and the transition from black to white through all the grays almost becomes indiscernible, as shown in Figure 7-5. Similarly, we can modulate the precision of quantities such as weights and activations in AI models to reduce the AI waste (see "AI Waste" on page 53).

In "Quantization" on page 161, we have seen how quantization can be used to modulate the precision of weights, activation, and optimizer states, which can result in reduced memory, compute, and other resources consumed during model training. Several of these techniques are equally applicable also at inference; quantizing neural networks weights after training is known as *post-training quantization* (PTQ).[12]

Quantization and dequantization requires two parameters: the scale and zero-point values as discussed in "Quantization" on page 161. These parameters can be precomputed during training or learned during model execution, resulting in the two variants of PTQ, which are discussed next.

11 B.M. Oliver et al., "The Philosophy of PCM," in *Proceedings of the IRE* 36 no. 11 (1948): 1324–331 (*https://oreil.ly/uNCXC*).

12 Raghuraman Krishnamoorthi et al., "Introduction to Quantization on PyTorch," *PyTorch* (blog), March 26, 2020 (*https://oreil.ly/LX4aQ*).

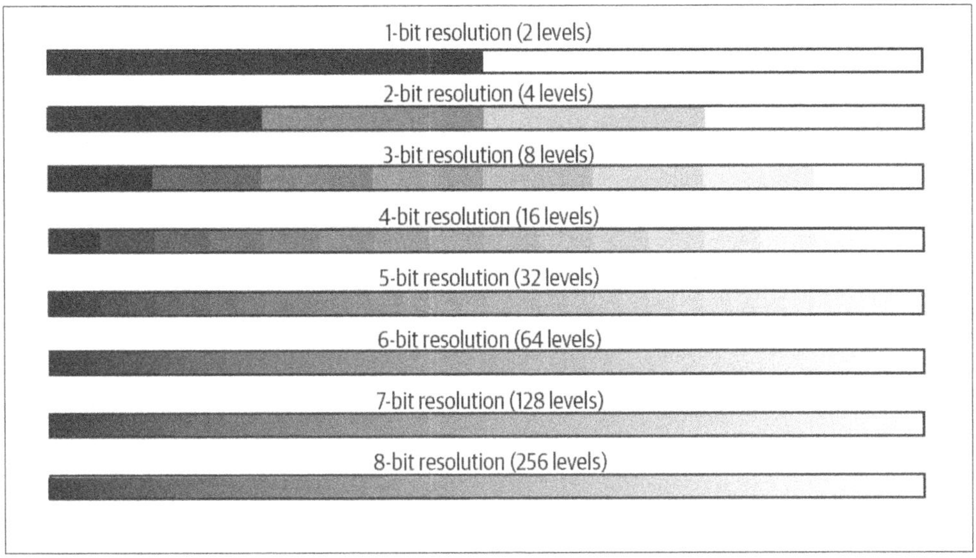

Figure 7-5. The effect quantization on the resolution of grayscale colors when using 1 bit (2 levels) to 8 bit (256 levels).

Static quantization

Static quantization involves converting a pretrained floating-point model to a lower precision model (typically INT8 or INT4) using calibration with a representative dataset. The scale s maps the floating-point range $[\alpha_{min}, \alpha_{max}]$ to the integer range [0,255] (for INT8 quantization). The zero-point z aligns the floating-point value *0* with an integer value:

1. *Initialization*

   Let f_{FP32} be the pretrained model with `FP32` weights and activations and $\mathcal{D}_{\mathrm{cal}}$ be the calibration dataset.

2. *Calibration*

   Do the following for each input $\mathbf{x} \in \mathcal{D}_{\mathrm{cal}}$:

   a. Perform a forward pass through f_{FP32} to collect statistics about activations:

   $$\mathbf{y} = f_{\mathrm{FP32}}(\mathbf{x})$$

   b. Collect the minimum and maximum values for each layer's activations $\mathbf{a}$:

   $$\alpha_{\mathrm{min}}, \alpha_{\mathrm{max}} = \min(\mathbf{a}), \max(\mathbf{a})$$

3. *Calculate scale and zero-point*

   For each layer ℓ, compute the scale s_ℓ and zero-point z_ℓ for both weights and activations:

   a. $s_\ell = \frac{\alpha_{\text{max}} - \alpha_{\text{min}}}{2^b - 1}$ where b is the bit-width (e.g., $b = 8$ for INT8).

   b. $z_\ell = \text{round}\left(\frac{0 - \alpha_{\text{min}}}{s_\ell}\right)$

4. *Quantize weights and activations*

   For each weight w in layer ℓ:

$$w_q = \text{round}\left(\frac{w}{s_{w,\ell}}\right) + z_{w,\ell}$$

   where $s_{w,\ell}$ and $z_{w,\ell}$ are the scale and zero-point for weights.

   For each activation a in layer ℓ:

$$a_q = \text{round}\left(\frac{a}{s_{a,\ell}}\right) + z_{a,\ell}$$

   where $s_{a,\ell}$ and $z_{a,\ell}$ are the scale and zero-point for activations.

5. *Output quantized model*

   Replace floating-point operations in f_{FP32} with their quantized counterparts using the quantized weights and activations. The model after quantization is represented as f_{INT8}.

Finally, the quantized model f_{INT8} is ready for inference, utilizing integer arithmetic for improved efficiency.

Dynamic quantization

Dynamic quantization, on the other hand, quantizes the weights of a pretrained neural network to a lower precision (e.g., INT8) *during inference*. Unlike static quantization, dynamic quantization does not require a calibration dataset; instead, the quantization parameters are computed dynamically during inference based on the range of weights and activations encountered. The key difference lies in how the scaling and zero-point are determined only during the forward pass and not via a separate calibration phase.

Dynamic quantization is useful for reducing the size and speeding up the inference of neural networks without needing a separate calibration dataset. The key advantage is that the quantization parameters are computed during inference, allowing for a more flexible and lightweight approach. Example 7-2 shows the procedure to perform dynamic quantization natively in PyTorch.

Example 7-2. Example showing dynamic quantization of a pretrained model.

```
import timm
import torch
import torch.quantization

def check_model_disk_space(model, file_path='temp_model.pth'):
    # Save the model to disk
    torch.save(model.state_dict(), file_path)
    # Get the size of the file in megabytes
    file_size = os.path.getsize(file_path) / (1024*1024)
    return file_size

# Load a pretrained ResNet50 model from Timm
model = timm.create_model('vit_base_patch16_224', pretrained=True)
nParam = sum(p.numel() for p in model.parameters() if p.requires_grad)
print("Number of parameters in base model:%.2fM"%(nParam/1e6))
model_size=check_model_disk_space(model)
print(f"Model size on disk: {model_size:.2f} MB")

model_dynamic_quantized = torch.quantization.quantize_dynamic(
    model, qconfig_spec={torch.nn.Linear}, dtype=torch.qint8
)
model_size=check_model_disk_space(model_dynamic_quantized)
print(f"Quantized model size on disk: {model_size:.2f} MB")
```

The quantized model should have smaller disk space. For this example, it should output the following:

```
Model size on disk: 330.28 MB
Quantized model size on disk: 85.12 MB
```

Compressed Neural Networks for the Decentralized AI Dashboard

In our running example of developing multimodal models that can run on end-point devices like smartphones, we have seen how NAS can be used to obtain efficient architectures, which can then be updated further using knowledge distillation.

Power primarily from batteries on end-point devices like smartphones or drones is a critical resource following a disaster. DL models can drain power on these devices with even limited usage. So, compressing them further using model pruning and quantization can reduce the power consumption.

Extreme pruning (removal of >90% weights) and low-precision quantization (down to INT2) can reduce the overall resource consumption, at the cost of performance. As we envision a dashboard that will aggregate information from many end-point devices, the degradation in performance can be alleviated by ensembling the data from multiple users.

Deploying Models

ML/AI developers often need to learn and maintain proficiency in multiple frameworks, duplicating efforts and increasing the development time. Models may need to be rewritten or converted to be compatible with different frameworks, leading to inefficiencies and potential performance inconsistencies. Additionally, managing dependencies and ensuring compatibility across frameworks can strain computational and human resources, ultimately slowing down the overall progress in model development and deployment.

The ML/AI development ecosystem is rich with several platforms that offer comprehensive frameworks. While the most popular platforms are PyTorch and TensorFlow, Figure 7-6 shows several other frameworks. Each of these frameworks offers unique features tailored to different aspects of model development and deployment. However, this diversity can lead to significant resource consumption issues.

Figure 7-6. Several ML/AI frameworks to develop DL models. (Source: onnx.ai (https://oreil.ly/QmqZD).)

Cross-Platform Models

Some efforts have focused on developing common platforms where models can be translated seamlessly between frameworks to avoid duplicate development. *Open Neural Network Exchange* (ONNX) (*https://onnx.ai/about.html*) is one such open source format for representing DL models.

ONNX facilitates interoperability and allows models to be transferred between different frameworks and environments. The ONNX format was developed by a consortium to enable developers to use the best tools for their needs without being locked into a specific ecosystem. Technically, the ONNX format is a rich graph representation of a neural network consisting of nodes with neural network elements including attributes, weight tensors, and directed edges between these nodes, as shown in Figure 7-7 for the Inception network.

ONNX supports optimized inference and hardware acceleration across diverse platforms, ensuring consistent performance and efficient resource usage. Backed by major industry players, ONNX enjoys broad adoption and extensive tooling, further streamlining model development and deployment. Example 7-3 shows the steps to convert a PyTorch model into ONNX format and load an ONNX model created from other platforms into PyTorch.

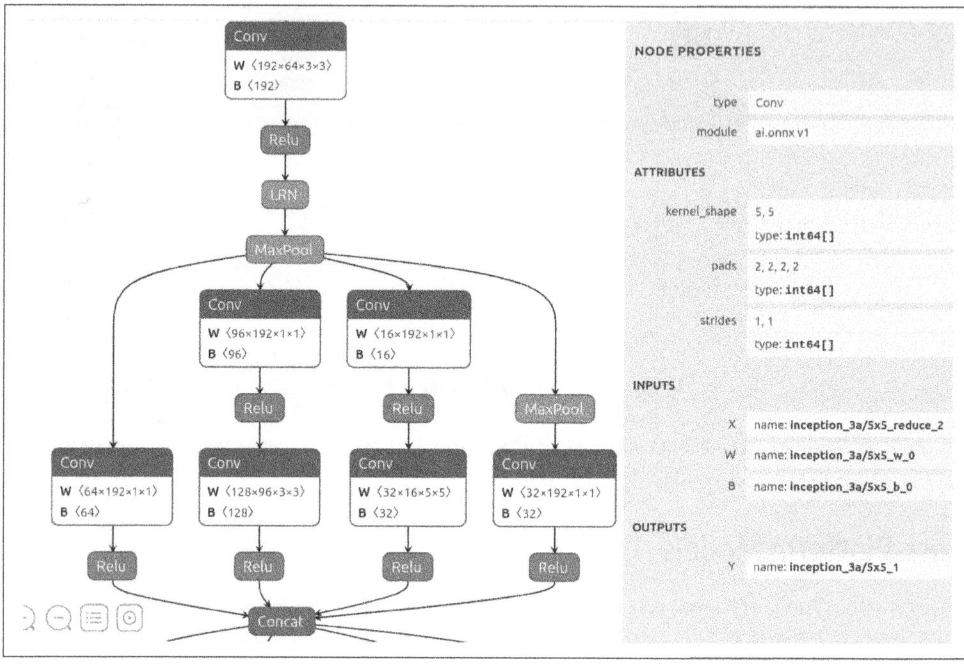

Figure 7-7. Inception model in ONNX format using netron.app (https://oreil.ly/fVioY) showing some of the layers and their attributes as well as options to inspect the elements.

Example 7-3. Conversion of PyTorch model into ONNX format

```
import torch
import torchvision.models as models

# Load a pretrained model or your custom model
model = models.resnet18(pretrained=True)
model.eval()  # Set the model to evaluation mode
# Create a dummy input tensor of the correct shape
dummy_input = torch.randn(1, 3, 224, 224)
# Export the model
torch.onnx.export(model, dummy_input, "resnet18.onnx", \
                verbose=True, input_names=['input'], output_names=['output'])
```

The saved ONNX model can be loaded and run within `ONNX-Runtime`, which is a common platform that is agnostic to all other platforms, as shown in Figure 7-6:

```
import onnx
import onnxruntime as ort
import numpy as np

# Load the ONNX model
onnx_model = onnx.load("resnet18.onnx")
onnx.checker.check_model(onnx_model)
```

```
# Run inference with ONNX Runtime
ort_session = ort.InferenceSession("resnet18.onnx")
# Run the model
outputs = ort_session.run(None, {"input": dummy_input})
```

The more useful scenario is interoperability. The ONNX model saved from PyTorch can now be loaded into TensorFlow if needed. This requires additional packages like `onnx-tf` to be installed:

```
from onnx_tf.backend import prepare
import tensorflow as tf

# Load the ONNX model
onnx_model = onnx.load("path/to/your/resnet18.onnx")
# Convert ONNX model to TensorFlow model
tf_rep = prepare(onnx_model)
# Export the TensorFlow model to a SavedModel directory
tf_rep.export_graph("tensorflow_model")
# Load the TensorFlow model
model = tf.saved_model.load("tensorflow_model")
```

In summary, platforms like ONNX enhance resource efficiency by promoting interoperability, reducing redundancy, saving development time and costs, optimizing deployment, and leveraging extensive community support. This makes it a valuable asset for multiframework model development and deployment.

> **ONNX and Resource Efficiency**
>
> The ONNX format enhances resource efficiency by providing a standardized model representation, facilitating interoperability between different frameworks. This reduces AI waste as models can be trained in one framework and deployed in another without retraining. It saves development time and costs, allowing developers to focus on model improvements rather than managing multiple framework-specific versions.
>
> Already a vast variety of ONNX models are curated by the community in the ONNX Model Zoo (*https://onnx.ai/models*), promoting recycling of models developed in different platforms.

Inference Beyond Python

In the age-old battle of programming languages, Python seems to have emerged as the winner when it comes to the development of AI. Python is widely used due to its ease of use, readability, and vast ecosystem of libraries and frameworks like the ones shown in Figure 7-6. It allows for rapid prototyping, which is crucial for research and development. Python is also a high-level programming language, whose syntax is simple, making it highly accessible to data scientists and engineers. Python can also easily incorporate other low-level languages such as C++ to accelerate certain operations, and this capability of orchestrating across other languages has been essential in bridging performance and ease of use for Python-based DL frameworks. However, Python is *interpreted* and relatively slow compared to *compiled* languages, which can be a drawback in performance-critical applications. It also has higher memory consumption, which can be limiting in resource-constrained environments.

A low-level language like C++, on the other hand, is a high-performance language, offering fine-grained control over system resources and memory management. It's ideal for deployment in production environments, especially where low latency and high throughput are crucial, such as in embedded systems or large-scale applications. C++ also allows for optimization at a low level, making it well-suited for performance-critical tasks. However, C++ has a steeper learning curve, with more complex syntax and concepts like manual memory management. It also lacks the high-level libraries that Python offers for ML, making development slower and more challenging for tasks like model training and experimentation.

The efficiency (or lack thereof) of high-level languages is also reflected in their energy consumption. In Figure 7-8 (top), the energy consumption for a suite of standard programming tasks is benchmarked for different programming languages.[13] The energy consumption values are normalized with respect to the lowest value. Figure 7-8 (bottom) shows the popularity of these languages in 2023, based on the number of GitHub pushes (*https://oreil.ly/YoklV*). As expected, Python is the most popular language and one of the most energy-intensive languages. Low-level languages such as C++ are highly energy efficient but not as popular. The trade-off between performance and ease of use is a significant factor in the overall sustainability of AI.

13 Rui Pereira et al., "Ranking Programming Languages by Energy Efficiency," *Science of Computer Programming* 205 (January 15, 2021) (*https://doi.org/10.1016/j.scico.2021.102609*).

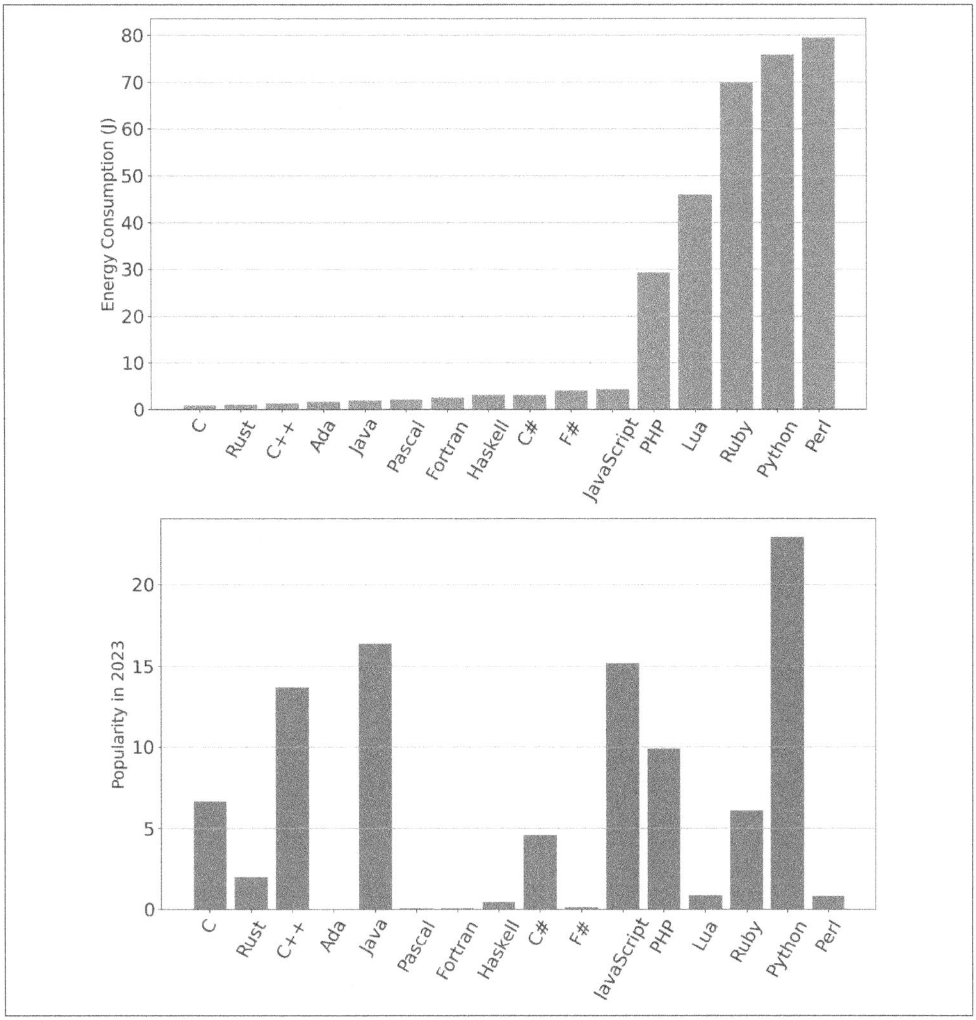

Figure 7-8. Energy consumption of different programming languages (top) and their popularity in 2023 (bottom) for three standard programming tasks (accessing random sequences, traversing binary trees, and generating random DNA sequences). (Source: based on the results in Pereira et al. "Ranking Programming Languages by Energy Efficiency" [2021].)

AI Model Inference in Low-Level Languages

As established in the previous section, developing ML/AI models is easier in high-level languages, particularly Python. Popular DL frameworks such as TensorFlow and PyTorch provide excellent support for model training and evaluation, but they often rely on dynamic computation and memory allocation, which can be slow for inference. Converting DL models to C++ can significantly accelerate inference times. Furthermore, C++ models can run on a wide range of hardware platforms, including older hardware, embedded systems, and low-power devices. This means they can be used with hardware that is energy-bound and, in many cases, using "obsolete" hardware.

Several tools can translate Python-based DL models into low-level languages. ONNX, which we have already seen in "Cross-Platform Models" on page 187, is one. ONNX Runtime offers acceleration of DL models by converting them to low-level languages like C++. This offers a balance between ease of use during development, which can be carried out in Python and for efficient inference by converting the models into low-level languages. Specific libraries such as TensorRT (*https://oreil.ly/2Bjam*) pack several acceleration techniques discussed in this chapter to improve the inference speed of models.

Example 7-4 shows a PyTorch model converted to ONNX and then to TensorRT, which uses C++ under the hood.

Example 7-4. Exporting ONNX model into TensorRT format

```
trtexec --onnx=resnet50_pytorch.onnx --saveEngine=resnet_engine_pytorch.trt
```

Running models from the TensorRT format and benchmarking them are shown in the online notebook for this chapter.

Native Edge Hardware Support for the Decentralized AI Dashboard

In Figure 7-2, we are hoping to run powerful yet efficient multimodal models on smartphones, drones, and other end-point devices. To this point, we have shown efficient architecture, knowledge distillation, pruning, and quantization, to be useful in reducing the resource consumption.

While these are useful, the final models still need specialized runtime environments like PyTorch, ONNX Runtime, or TensorRT. Setting these up on end-point devices might be cumbersome, or even infeasible.

Converting these compressed models into C++ that is natively supported by edge devices might be one way of deploying these models without requiring additional requirements.

Serving Foundational Models in C++

Many projects have attempted to accelerate inference of foundational models by porting the models to C++. The TensorRT framework in Example 7-4 is for general-purpose DL models. To include additional transformer-specific features, projects such as TensorRT-LLM (*https://oreil.ly/Ui3XP*) and ExecuTorch (*https://oreil.ly/zdCn9*) are under development.

The most widely used framework to convert LLMs and other transformer-based models to C++ is the llama.cpp project, which provides accelerated models based on the GGML library (*https://huggingface.co/ggml-org*). This project converts LLMs and other foundational models into a custom format (.gguf) and is able to run these compiled models within the llama.cpp runtime environment, which is easily installable for *nix machines. Once the runtime is installed, setting up a fairly large LLM on a laptop with few resources can be done as follows:

```
llama-cli -m models/meta-llama-3.1-8b-instruct-q4_0.gguf -cnv
```

Converting LLMs and foundational models to low-level languages like C++ will be crucial in reducing their exorbitant resource requirements. Projects like llama.cpp have demonstrated that nonspecialized hardware such as standard CPUs with frugal memory and compute are able to run these models. While this improves access to these advanced AI models, the projects can also repurpose what is considered to be old and obsolete hardware. This can have a significant impact on the overall environmental sustainability of AI.

Inference Is Lean: What Comes Next?

We started this chapter by pondering about the resources used to develop AI models when they are not deployed for further use. This is still a difficult question to answer. Under the assumption that all models are equally likely to be used, we focused on quantifying the energy consumption and carbon footprint of AI models at deployment.

We also looked at several methods that can reduce the AI waste when models are deployed, resulting in leaner inference costs. Methods like hardware-aware NAS and knowledge distillation are techniques to obtain efficient models at the design level. We then zoomed in one level and looked at methods that adjust the number of weights or the number of bits used when models are deployed. These techniques can reduce the latency, memory consumption, energy consumption, and corresponding carbon footprint of the inference stage.

Finally, we explored methods to translate models developed using high-level frameworks into C++ for wider deployment. Combining these methods can help us achieve lean inference. All these techniques do not make the inference step holistically sustainable, however, and leave some open areas to be addressed. We grapple with some open questions:

When does inference energy consumption take over model development costs?
: *There is no clear answer to this question as it depends on how much a model is used after development.*

  Some estimates currently predict that about 80% of the total energy consumption in datacenters is for the inference stage, and only 20% is used for development.[14]

  This estimation, however, is skewed due to the survivorship bias. Companies only deploy successful models at scale, in large datacenters. The development cost of all the models that did not make the cut are not accounted for.

If C++ is more efficient, shouldn't all AI/ML always use it??
: *Yes, ideally this would make it more efficient but the rate of progress in AI would not have been the same.*

  As shown in Figure 7-8, C++ is one of the most (energy) efficient languages; however, it's not widely used in developing AI models. This is primarily due to the lack of easy-to-use development frameworks that are natively in C++. This is on top of the complexity of programming in low-level languages such as C++, which can be a big hurdle for data scientists.

  The current approaches that use Python-based frameworks for development and then optimize it for C++ deployment offer a good trade-off between access and resource efficiency.

  This being said, we could also argue that the easy access to model development can be sometimes wasteful. If developers had to spend a lot of time and effort carefully developing models, we might have less AI waste in C++ at the expense of slow progress.

Is wider access not at odds with improving environmental sustainability?
: *Yes, this is one of the paradoxes of arguing for efficiency. However, this could improve overall sustainability of AI.*

  The primary objective of this chapter was to make inference leaner, so that powerful AI models could be used by more users even on their end-point devices. By making models more efficient, there is more use of these models, with net increase in the resource consumption. This is known as the Jevons Paradox or the rebound effect, which was touched upon in "Resource Efficiency and Climate Awareness" on page 56.

---

14 Victor Avelar et al., "The AI Disruption: Challenges and Guidance for Data Center Design," Schneider Electric (Schneider Electric, October 13, 2023) (*https://oreil.ly/KkOH_*).

Seen only from the resource consumption point of view, making AI models more efficient has a negative effect on environmental sustainability of AI. However, this could have a positive effect on the overall sustainability of AI, which then includes social sustainability. By improving access, AI methods are democratized further, which can improve participation of diverse communities instead of a monolithic AI that caters only to a small global population, particularly from the Global North.[15]

15 Nur Ahmed and Muntasir Wahed, "The De-democratization of AI: Deep Learning and the Compute Divide in Artificial Intelligence Research," *arXiv.org*, October 22, 2020 (***https://arxiv.org/abs/2010.15581***).

CHAPTER 8

Hardware Considerations

The term *cloud computing* evokes an ethereal impression of blue skies with scattered patches of white clouds. In reality, cloud computing happens in industrial datacenters that are typically housed in brutalist concrete buildings embodying massive material resource consumption (see Figure 8-1).[1] Within each center, hundreds of dense racks house thousands of humming CPUs and GPUs that must be cooled either by powerful fans or by liquid cooling systems.

The current class of GenAI models relies on cloud computing to function. The actual scale, capacity, and cost of these datacenters for AI use is not always known. However, some predictions estimate a threefold increase in capacity by 2030, fueled primarily by AI-related demands.[2]

Consider the case of Meta AI Research's planned 2GW+ datacenter that, according to CEO Mark Zuckerberg (*https://oreil.ly/Ue3Xx*), "would cover a significant part of Manhattan," bringing more than 1.3 million GPUs online. Powering datacenters at this scale requires vast amounts of electricity, sometimes sourced from dedicated power plants. The International Energy Agency (IEA) (*https://oreil.ly/rBeuB*) estimates that by 2026, datacenters will use approximately 800TWh worldwide, almost 4% of the total global electricity demand.

1 Kate Crawford, *The Atlas of AI* (Yale University Press, 2021).

2 Bhargs Srivathsan et al., "AI Power: Expanding Data Center Capacity to Meet Growing Demand," *McKinsey & Company*, October 29, 2024 (*https://oreil.ly/Gxq6h*).

Figure 8-1. A datacenter as imagined by the text-to-image generative model DALL-E introduced by Aditya Ramesh et al. in "Zero-Shot Text-to-Image Generation" (https://arxiv.org/abs/2102.12092).

Throughout this book we have established that AI is computationally intensive and that algorithmic choices can improve the efficiency of data use (Chapter 4), model selection (Chapter 5), model training (Chapter 6), and model deployment (Chapter 7). A common layer of optimization to improve efficiency at each step is hardware. In this chapter, we will look at the material basis and the climate impact of the hardware used to develop and implement AI models. We will explore hardware optimization strategies that can help us further the goals of achieving sustainable AI. In particular, we will focus on optimizing hardware configuration and utilization at multiple levels: distributed clusters, single accelerators, and custom hardware. Each of these levels poses different types of challenges and offers varying degrees of control and gains.

Underutilization of energy-intensive hardware is another form of AI waste (see "AI Waste" on page 53), which will be the focus of this chapter. I will demonstrate several utilities that can improve the overall efficiency of hardware usage in AI. As distributed clusters housed in large-scale datacenters comprising hardware accelerators are primarily used to develop and deploy AI models, any efficiency improvements to this infrastructure can influence the overall environmental impact of AI.

Energy Consumption As a Proxy for Climate Impact

Energy consumption in itself is not a direct measure of environmental impact. This book and most discourses on the topic use the growing energy consumption of datacenters as a proxy for broader environmental impacts. As described in Chapter 3, quantifying energy consumption is easier than the carbon emissions and correlates extremely well with the operational carbon emissions and portions of embodied emissions.

Environmental Cost of AI Hardware

In Chapter 3, we tried to estimate the carbon footprint of AI (see "Carbon Footprint of AI Models" on page 68) by focusing primarily on the carbon emissions from the energy consumption at different stages of an AI model lifecycle. Those incurred during the manufacturing of the hardware itself are a component of *embodied emissions*, which we describe next.

Embodied Emissions

Embodied emissions capture the carbon footprint associated with manufacturing, transporting, and assembling AI hardware. These emissions are locked in before a single AI model runs, yet they contribute significantly to AI's overall environmental impact.

One of the most carbon-intensive components of AI hardware is the GPU, or other AI accelerator chip, which requires advanced semiconductor fabrication. Modern chip manufacturing is an extraordinarily precise process that demands vast amounts of energy and specialized materials. The extraction and refinement of these materials add further carbon costs. AI chips rely on silicon, copper, cobalt, tantalum, gold, and other rare earth elements, all of which require energy-intensive mining and processing. Producing just 1kg of refined silicon can require up to 100kWh of electricity, with additional emissions from metallurgical purification, which can require up to 2500kWh/kg of refined silicon.[3] Furthermore, the semiconductor manufacturing process is also a major emitter of more potent GHGs such as perfluorinated compounds (PFCs), which have thousands of times the warming effect of CO_2 (see "Carbon Footprint of AI Models" on page 68 for more on GHGs).

Given that large-scale AI training clusters can house tens of thousands of GPUs, the embodied emissions from the chips alone can be significant. These emissions grow

3 Eric D. Williams et al., "The 1.7 Kilogram Microchip: Energy and Material Use in the Production of Semiconductor Devices," *Environmental Science & Technology* 36, no. 24 (October 25, 2002): 5504 -10 (*https://doi.org/10.1021/es025643o*).

even larger when accounting for the manufacturing of networking equipment, storage infrastructure, and cooling systems.

The hyperscale datacenters that house the AI hardware carry their own substantial embodied emissions. Constructing a GW datacenter can result in additional emissions, largely due to the use of concrete, steel, and glass—all highly energy-intensive materials. The cooling infrastructure required to dissipate the enormous heat generated by AI workloads further adds to the carbon burden, with immersion cooling tanks, introducing additional manufacturing emissions.

Estimating Embodied Emissions of a Datacenter

Operational emissions, which stem from energy consumption, are relatively straightforward to calculate versus embodied emissions. The difficulty in estimating embodied emissions stems from both a lack of transparency and complexities in tracking them across a datacenter's lifecycle.

Bux et al. assessed the environmental impact of a datacenter located in Italy using a prototypical datacenter that spans $865m^2$ with a compute capacity of 5 million watts (MW) and a lifespan of 10 years.[4] According to their study, the estimated GWP of the datacenter was $677,724tCO_2e$ with a cumulative energy consumption of 558,894MWh and an annual emission factor of 925kg/MWh per year.

The GWP of such a single datacenter is about the same as the annual carbon footprint of 125,000 Italians using an estimate of $5.3tCO_2e$ per capita emissions.[5]

E-Waste

The Global E-waste Monitor (*https://globalewaste.org*) reports that in 2022, a record 62 billion kg of e-waste was generated across sectors, which amounts to about 7.8kg per capita. Of this, only 22% of e-waste was formally recycled. Figure 8-2 shows the historical trends of scale of e-waste that is being generated compared to the extent of documented recycling. These estimations were for all sectors; the specific estimations for the datacenter industry and for AI are unknown.

4 Christian Bux et al., "A Critical Analysis of Global Warming Potential of Data Centers in the Digital Era," *The International Journal of Life Cycle Assessment*, January 6, 2025 (*https://doi.org/10.1007/s11367-024-02419-2*).

5 Hannah Ritchie et al., "CO_2 and Greenhouse Gas Emissions," *OurWorldinData.org*, 2023 (*https://oreil.ly/o2agx*).

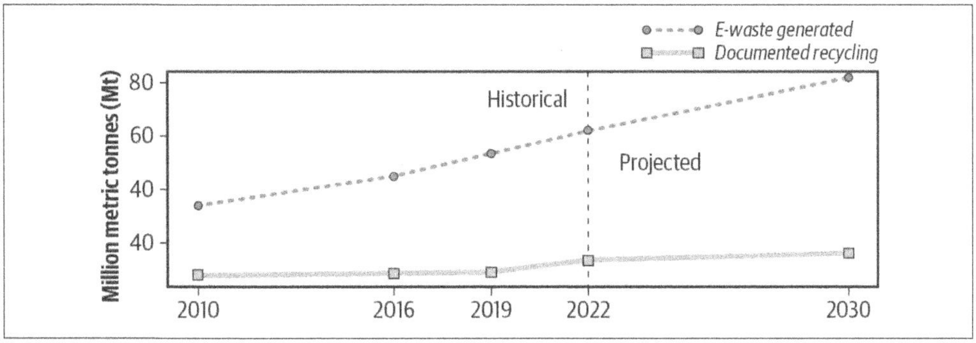

Figure 8-2. Trends of e-waste generated and documented extent of e-waste recycling. (Source: data from E-Waste Monitor (https://ewastemonitor.info).)

The rapid expansion of AI datacenters could contribute significantly to the growing e-waste crisis, as outdated servers, GPUs, and storage devices are frequently replaced to keep up with increasing computational demands. These discarded electronic components contain hazardous materials like lead, mercury, and cadmium, which can leach into soil and water if improperly disposed of, posing serious environmental and health risks. Estimations project that the e-waste due to AI could contribute to as much as 11% to the total global e-waste by 2030.[6] Without robust recycling programs and sustainable design practices, the AI industry's e-waste footprint will continue to escalate, amplifying its adverse environmental impact.

Server Refresh Cycles Versus Efficiency

Should AI datacenters prioritize longevity or efficiency when it comes to hardware refresh cycles? Keeping older servers running can delay the embodied emissions of manufacturing new ones, reduces e-waste, and saves upfront investment costs. However, aging hardware consumes more energy per computation, making AI workloads increasingly inefficient and expensive over time.

On the flip side, upgrading to newer servers with better performance-per-watt, can cut energy use by 30% to 50%, lowering operational emissions, but at the cost of increased manufacturing and disposal impacts. If powered by carbon-intensive grids, energy savings may not justify the carbon cost of frequent upgrades. But in renewable-powered datacenters, newer, more efficient hardware could provide net environmental benefits.

6 Peng Wang et al., "E-waste Challenges of Generative Artificial Intelligence," *Nature Computational Science* 4 (October 28, 2024): 818–23 (*https://doi.org/10.1038/s43588-024-00712-6*).

> Dealing with server refresh cycles to strike the right trade-off between continuing to use existing hardware and replacing them with new ones is not straightforward.[7] Some might argue for a systems-thinking approach to tackling this conundrum (see "Systems Thinking" on page 261 for more).[8]

Hardware Scaling Laws of AI

Through empirical experiments, Kaplan and colleagues observed the test loss of transformer-based language models over seven orders of magnitude and found that it follows a clean power law in each of three resources: trainable parameters (N), data tokens (D), and training compute (C).[9] These experimentally driven trends are loosely dubbed as the *scaling laws*, which are shown in Figure 8-3. Note how the test loss goes down with the exponential increase in compute, dataset size, and number of parameters.

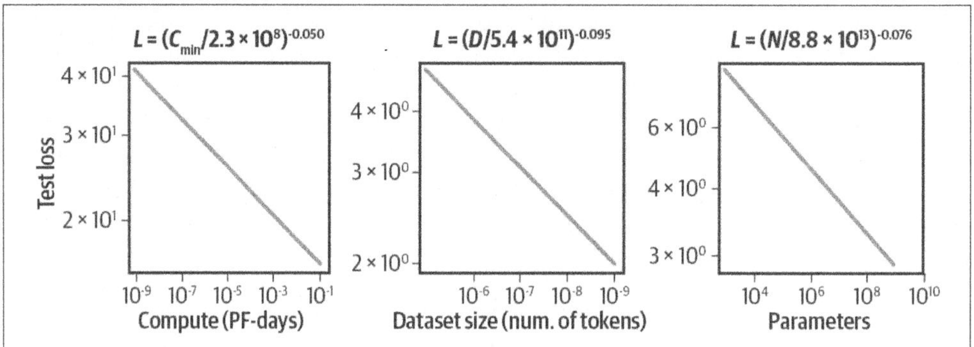

Figure 8-3. Empirical scaling laws for transformer-based large language models. Note that both axes are in log-scale. (Source: reproduced from the empirical equations provided in Kaplan et al. (https://arxiv.org/abs/2001.08361).)

These empirical scaling laws focus on the proportion of data to computing power necessary for advancing GenAI models. These insights have guided recent progress in the field. Before these observations, some of the hardware scaling laws emerging from the semiconductor industry had already predicted how the compute capacity would

7 Rabih Bashroush, "A Comprehensive Reasoning Framework for Hardware Refresh in Data Centers," in *IEEE Transactions on Sustainable Computing* 3, no. 4 (2018): 209–20 (*https://doi.org/10.1109/tsusc.2018.2795465*).

8 Dustin Wright et al., "Efficiency Is Not Enough: A Critical Perspective of Environmentally Sustainable AI," *Communications of the ACM* 68, no. 7 (June 26, 2025): 62–69 (*https://doi.org/10.1145/3724500*).

9 Jared Kaplan et al., "Scaling Laws for Neural Language Models," *arXiv.org*, January 23, 2020 (*https://arxiv.org/abs/2001.08361*).

grow. We briefly examine these laws to understand their potential impact on the future of AI.

Moore's law is an empirical observation stating that the number of transistors on a microchip doubles every 1.5 to 2 years, leading to the exponential growth in computational power.[10] This principle has driven the scaling of compute performance for decades. Now, however, it is encountering physical constraints due to effects like quantum tunneling and power density issues, leading to the speculation that Moore's law is dead.[11]

Koomey's law, on the other hand, observes that the energy required per computation halves every 1.57 years, reducing power requirements despite increasing compute loads.[12] However, *Landauer's principle* theoretically limits this exponential gain in efficiency. According to this principle, the fundamental energy cost for erasing a bit of information is $E_{min} = 10^{-21}$ J at room temperature, which constrains further improvements in energy efficiency. Traditional scaling thus becomes infeasible.[13]

Initially, Moore's law drove compute growth, with Koomey's law ensuring power efficiency. As current silicon scaling slows and Koomey's efficiency gains saturate at Landauer's limit, power constraints begin to dominate.

Some argue that in the post-Moore era, new paradigms like reversible computing, quantum architectures, neuromorphic chips, and photonic logic are required to sustain efficiency and performance growth beyond classical limits.[14] These technologies are either nascent or nonexistent, so scaling up the compute required for AI has primarily relied on parallelism. In this context, parallelism is achieved using *distributed computing*, which involves orchestrating clusters of several GPUs to work on the same task. Figure 6-2 captures this exponential compute growth for AI model training, a development that has benefited from the gains in compute efficiency afforded by Moore's law and Koomey's law and has been further enhanced by distributed computing.

10 Gordon E. Moore, "Cramming More Components onto Integrated Circuits," *Electronics*, 38, no. 8 (April 19, 1965).

11 Nick Zhang, "Moore's Law Is Dead, Long Live Moore's Law!" *arxiv.org*, May 27, 2022 (*https://arxiv.org/abs/2205.15011*).

12 Jonathan Koomey et al., "Implications of Historical Trends in the Electrical Efficiency of Computing," in *IEEE Annals of the History of Computing* 33, no. 3 (2011): 46–54 (*https://doi.org/10.1109/MAHC.2010.28*).

13 R. Landauer, "Irreversibility and Heat Generation in the Computing Process," *IBM Journal of Research and Development* 5, no. 3 (July 1, 1961): 183–91 (*https://doi.org/10.1147/rd.53.0183*).

14 Alexis De Vos, *Reversible Computing: Fundamentals, Quantum Computing, and Applications* (Wiley, 2010).

AI for Radiotherapy Under Resource Constraints

Developing AI segmentation tools for radiotherapy often appears straightforward in a research environment. A team can train large models on multi-GPU clusters using curated datasets, fast storage, and abundant computational resources. But the moment those models are prepared for deployment in underresourced clinical settings, the assumptions begin to break down.[15] Figure 8-4 shows a typical workflow with AI models.

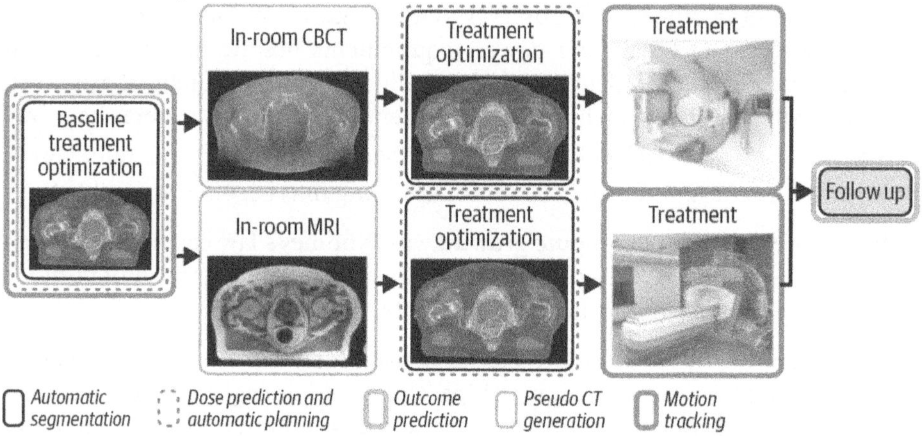

Figure 8-4. AI can accelerate clinical workflows related to radiotherapy. (Source: adapted from Guillaume Landry et al. (https://doi.org/10.1259/bjro.20230030).)

Workstations in clinics are typically outdated, with only a few GB of RAM, no GPU, older operating systems, and highly restricted software environments. Installing new software can risk breaking regulatory compliance or voiding vendor support. Cloud-based inference is rarely an option, since patient data can't easily leave the premises and network connectivity is often unreliable. Running the model locally, under these conditions, becomes a significant technical challenge.

This scenario highlights the deeper question of how to use hardware efficiently. In the sections that follow, we will use this as a motivating example to explore how AI systems can be developed and deployed with a full awareness of hardware limitations, so they remain usable where they are needed most.

15 Raghavendra Selvan et al., "Operating Critical Machine Learning Models in Resource Constrained Regimes," in *Lecture Notes in Computer Science*, (Springer Nature, 2024): 325–35 (*https://doi.org/10.1007/978-3-031-47425-5_29*).

The Alchemy of Creating AI

The capabilities we attribute to AI stem not only from advanced algorithms but also from raw computing power, high-speed storage, advanced networking, and sophisticated cooling systems working tirelessly behind the scenes. Figure 8-5 presents a high-level overview of a GPU compute cluster that is essential for creating AI models. A typical setup includes CPUs, GPUs, storage infrastructure (disks, DRAM), networking fabric (CPU-GPU communication, GPU-GPU communication), and cooling infrastructure. Each of these components contributes to the overall resource cost of developing AI:

Logic processing
: The "thinking" part of AI is powered by specialized processors like GPUs, TPUs, and custom accelerators, designed to handle massive parallel computations. NVIDIA's H100 GPU (*https://oreil.ly/kSRLr*), for instance, delivers 60 TFLOPs of FP64 compute and over 1,000 TFLOPs of AI-focused FP8 performance. These chips rely on ultra-fast memory with more than 3TB/s bandwidth, to feed data-hungry AI models. Without this raw power, modern large-scale models like Llama-3 would not be possible.

Storage infrastructure
: AI models consume and generate enormous amounts of data, far beyond what traditional storage solutions can handle efficiently. Training a model like Llama-3 requires processing datasets in the PB range. High-speed disks with read speeds exceeding 7 GB/s, along with distributed storage systems such as Ceph (*https://ceph.io/en*) or Lustre (*https://lustre.org*) ensure rapid data retrieval. A single AI training run can involve tens of exabytes of data movement, meaning that storage speed and scalability are just as critical as raw compute.

Networking fabric
: AI training does not happen on a single machine but scales across entire clusters, requiring ultra-fast, low-latency networks. High-performance AI clusters rely on InfiniBand-type connectivity, offering speeds up to 400GB/s per link with microsecond-level latency.[16] NVIDIA's NVLink enables 900GB/s of direct GPU-to-GPU bandwidth, essential for synchronizing massive AI models across thousands of accelerators.[17] Without this kind of interconnect, large AI models would take weeks or even months to train.

---

16 Gregory F. Pfister, "Aspects of the InfiniBand(tm) Architecture," in 2013 IEEE International Conference on Cluster Computing (CLUSTER), Newport Beach, CA, 2001, 369 (*https://doi.ieeecomputersociety.org/10.1109/CLUSTR.2001.960002*).

17 Rick Merritt, "What Is NVLink?," *NVIDIA* (blog), March 6, 2023 (*https://oreil.ly/6KIhP*).

Cooling infrastructure
: The sheer computational intensity of developing and running AI models on datacenters generates immense heat, demanding cutting-edge cooling solutions. Liquid cooling solutions, including direct-to-chip cooling and immersion cooling, reduce thermal constraints and improve energy efficiency. Some hyperscale AI datacenters even recycle heat for district heating systems.

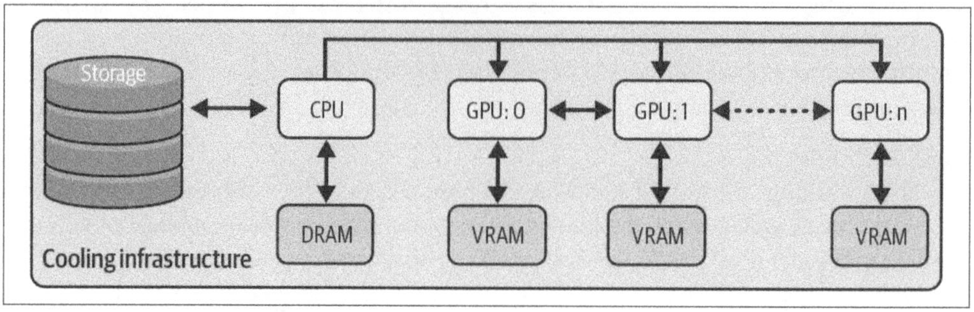

Figure 8-5. Schematic overview of a distributed system commonly used in developing AI models.

Improving the Resource Efficiency of AI Hardware

AI/ML practitioners have significant control over algorithmic choices that influence the efficiency and sustainability of AI models, as previous chapters explored. However, when considering hardware, the level of direct influence shifts away from purely algorithmic decisions to a more constrained set of optimizations. While software-driven choices offer flexibility, opportunities to improve the resource efficiency of ML/AI through hardware are more limited and often require different approaches.

Despite these constraints, there are still effective strategies to improve the resource efficiency of AI through hardware optimization. These strategies primarily focus on maximizing hardware utilization and optimizing system configurations, rather than relying only on more efficient algorithms. In this section, we'll explore optimization techniques at three key hardware levels: at the distributed/cluster level, where we will look at techniques to improve resource allocation and workload scheduling; at the single-device or accelerator-level, where better sharing of GPUs between jobs can reduce waste; and at the customized hardware level, where purpose-built chips can deliver high efficiency for specific AI tasks.

Cluster-Level Optimization

Distributed computing, with its large-scale compute clusters of thousands of GPUs coordinated by powerful CPUs (as depicted in Figure 8-5), has been pivotal in enabling current AI models. However, studies have reported that these distributed computing platforms often suffer from inefficient usage. This inefficiency stems from improper parallelization of jobs, job scheduling, or suboptimal hardware configurations. Figure 8-6 shows these variations in energy efficiency of the top 500 supercomputers, globally. The difference in the energy efficiency of these supercomputers spans two orders of magnitude.

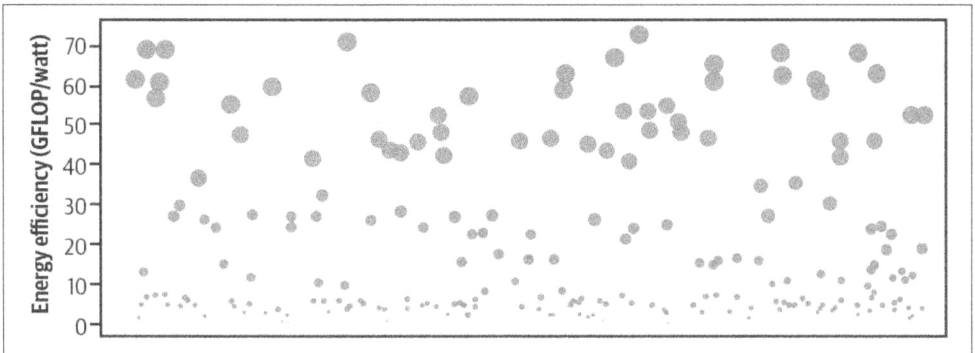

Figure 8-6. Energy efficiency of the top 500 supercomputers globally with marker sizes shown in proportion to their energy efficiency measured in GFLOPs/watt. Random indices are assigned on the x-axis for better visualization. (Source: Green500) (https://oreil.ly/zmWCM).

Green scheduling

The *green scheduling* strategy shifts compute jobs to times or places when the electricity used by a cluster comes from lower-carbon sources.[18] While the total amount of energy consumed for a task stays roughly the same, the carbon emissions can vary significantly depending on the energy mix of the grid (see "Carbon Footprint of AI Models" on page 68). A job run during the night, when wind power is abundant, can produce far fewer carbon emissions than the same job run during the day when fossil fuels dominate the energy mixture. By aligning workloads with these cleaner periods, operators can reduce emissions without changing the underlying hardware or software.

Green scheduling introduces a trade-off between carbon emissions and latency by delaying a job to wait for cleaner energy. Some tasks, such as model training, can tolerate this delay. Others, like real-time inference or user-facing applications, require immediate responses. Green scheduling works best when it can identify which jobs are flexible and which are not, balancing lower emissions with acceptable response times. Figure 8-7 illustrates the trade-off offered by green scheduling on the carbon emissions as a function of latency.

---

18 Íñigo Goiri et al., "GreenSlot: Scheduling Energy Consumption in Green Datacenters," *SC '11: Proceedings of 2011 International Conference for High Performance Computing, Networking, Storage and Analysis*, November 12, 2011, 1–11 (*https://doi.org/10.1145/2063384.2063411*).

Fluctuations in the instantaneous carbon intensity and the corresponding electricity price variations are shown on the left of Figure 8-7. Modulating when computations are performed can yield considerable reductions in the aggregate carbon footprint (and also cost). On the right of Figure 8-7, the reduction in the carbon emissions for a job that requires 24 hours to complete is shown. If the carbon emissions due to instantaneous execution is 100%, scheduling can yield up to 50% reduction for the same compute job executed at latency.

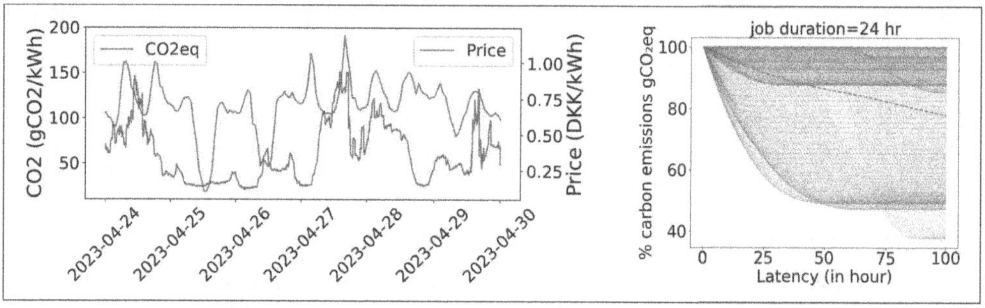

Figure 8-7. The trade-off of green scheduling.

Green Scheduling and Cluster Idling

What happens when the cluster remains idle while waiting for low-carbon energy? Even when they're not actively computing, servers still draw power to maintain memory, keep disks active, and run background processes. Extended idle time reduces the overall efficiency of the compute infrastructure and can offset some of the carbon savings. Hardware ages and can be deprecated whether it is in use or not. If expensive components sit idle too often, their environmental cost from manufacturing (embodied emissions) is spread across fewer productive jobs, making the entire operation less sustainable. More advanced green scheduling strategies try to also take this into account by including additional penalty terms for cluster idling.

A well-designed green scheduling policy needs to balance three goals: reducing carbon emissions, maintaining reasonable job latency, and keeping hardware effectively utilized. The aim is to run jobs when energy is cleanest without leaving machines idle for too long or compromising performance.[19]

19 Ana Radovanovic et al., "Carbon-Aware Computing for Datacenters," *arXiv.org*, June 11, 2021 (*https://arxiv.org/abs/2106.11750*).

Parallelism in AI workloads

Parallelism in AI is fundamentally different from traditional parallel computing, primarily because of the distinct computational characteristics of DL models. Unlike traditional parallel computing, where tasks often operate independently, AI workloads involve highly interdependent operations. These include large-scale computations that have sequential dependencies such as gradient updates during training and that demand significant communication overhead. Addressing these challenges requires specialized strategies, such as *data parallelism*, where batches of data can be processed in different instances of the same model running on multiple GPUs. Other strategies include *pipeline parallelism*, which stages computations across GPUs to minimize idle time, and *model parallelism*, which distributes layers or parameters of a model across GPUs efficiently (see Figure 8-8). Using multiple GPUs can enhance the data-intensive and model-intensive portions of processing.

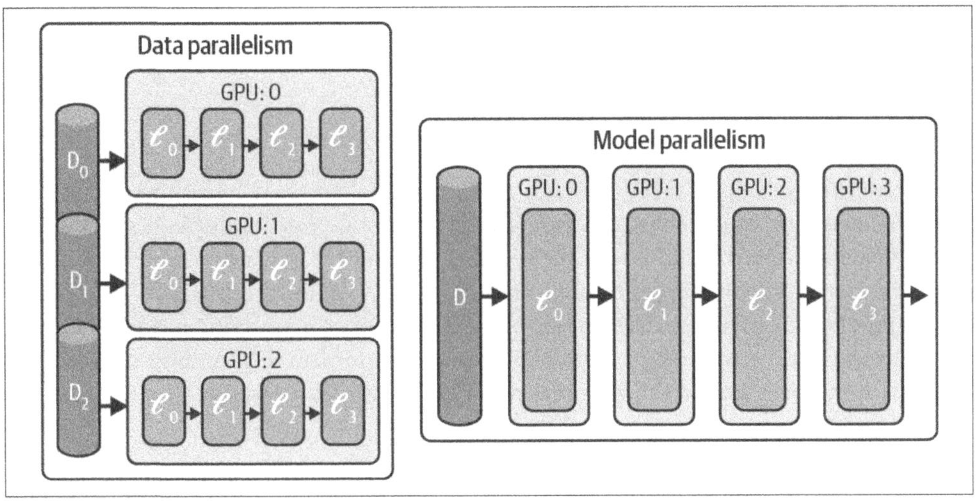

Figure 8-8. Data and model parallelism techniques.

Data parallelism involves splitting a dataset into smaller batches, which are then processed in parallel across multiple devices or cores. During model training, for example, each device holds a copy of the model and computes the forward and backward passes independently for its assigned data subset. Afterward, the gradients (or updates) from each device are synchronized and averaged to update the shared model. This method is well-suited for models that can be replicated across multiple devices without modifying the structure of the model itself. Example 8-1 shows the procedure to enable data parallelism in PyTorch.

Example 8-1. Enabling data parallelism in PyTorch is straightforward if multiple GPUs are available for training

```
import torch
import torch.nn as nn

# Check if GPUs are available and move the model to GPU(s)
if torch.cuda.is_available():
    model = model.cuda()  # Move model to GPU
    model = nn.DataParallel(model)
    # Wrap model with DataParallel for multi-GPU support

# Continue with normal training...
```

Model parallelism is another popular parallelism method where a (usually large) DL model is divided into smaller components and run on separate devices or threads. A model can be split into two components, for example, each running on a dedicated GPU, allowing for efficient utilization of both devices. We next look at a specific type of model parallelism known as model sharding.

Model sharding

Model sharding is a specialized form of model parallelism that partitions the model into smaller units, called shards, which are distributed across multiple devices. Each shard typically contains a subset of the model's parameters or tensors, enabling better memory management and computational efficiency. While the broader concept of model parallelism involves distributing various model components, model sharding focuses specifically on the distribution of model parameters. Depending on how the model is split, there are two common approaches to model sharding:

Layer-wise sharding
: In this method, the model is divided by layers. Each GPU manages a subset of layers, as shown in Figure 8-8 (right). Communication occurs between GPUs as activations are passed from one layer to another during the forward pass, and gradients are synchronized in the backward pass.

Parameter-wise sharding
: This approach involves distributing the model parameters (e.g., weights) across multiple devices. Each GPU holds a portion of the parameters for each layer. This is particularly useful for models with large parameter sets, as it ensures no device is overloaded with memory demands.

As with other parallelism approaches, sharding incurs communication overhead, as GPUs must frequently exchange intermediate activations and gradients during model parallelism. Example 8-2 shows the procedure to obtain model shards of the ResNet-18 model in PyTorch.

Example 8-2. Basic PyTorch code to save the ResNet-18 model into shards of 10MB and reloading the original model from these shards

```
import torch, os

def shard_model(model, shard_dir="model_shards", shard_size_mb=10):
    os.makedirs(shard_dir, exist_ok=True)  # Directory to store shards
    # Init. shard list and tracking variables
    tensors, size, shards = model.state_dict(), 0, [{}]
    limit = shard_size_mb * 1024 * 1024 # Convert MB to bytes

    for k, v in tensors.items(): # Calculate tensor size in bytes
        v = v.cpu()
        v_size = v.element_size() * v.numel()
        if size + v_size > limit: # If shard is full, start a new one
            shards.append({})
            size = 0
        shards[-1][k] = v
        size += v_size

    # Save shards as separate file
    [torch.save(shard, f"{shard_dir}/shard_{i}.pth") \
    for i, shard in enumerate(shards)]
    return len(shards)

def reload_model(model, shard_dir="model_shards"):
    # Load each shard in order
    state_dict = {k: v for f in sorted(os.listdir(shard_dir))
                  for k, v in torch.load(f"{shard_dir}/{f}", \
                  map_location="cpu").items()}
    model.load_state_dict(state_dict) # Load parameters into model
    return model

# Example Usage
if __name__ == "__main__":
    from torchvision.models import resnet18
    num_shards = shard_model(resnet18(pretrained=True))  # Shard model
    print('Model saved into %d shards'%num_shards)
    model_reloaded = reload_model(resnet18())  # Reload model
    print('Reloaded the model from shards!')
```

This should result in the model shards stored in `SHARD_DIR`:

```
Model saved into 6 shards
Reloaded the model from shards!
```

Pipeline parallelism is a technique where the training or inference process is broken down into smaller stages, each stage running in parallel on a separate device or thread. Consider the case of deploying an LLM, where the inference process involves multiple stages, such as tokenization, embedding, attention, and output generation. In a pipeline parallelism approach, each of these stages can be run in parallel on separate devices (such as any available CPU, GPU, and TPU resources), reducing the overall computational load and minimizing idle time on specific compute resources. Implementing pipeline parallelism involves specific choices on where to split the model pipeline. This can be done in PyTorch by wrapping the pipeline steps within the `nn.Seqential()` class and wrapping it in the `torch.distributed.pipeline` functionalities (see Example 8-3).

Example 8-3. A simple case for chunking an MLP into two chunks for using two GPUs

```
import torch
import torch.nn as nn
from torch.distributed.pipeline.sync import Pipe

# Define two sequential stages of simple MLP model
class Stage1(nn.Module):
    def __init__(self):
        super(Stage1, self).__init__()
        self.fc1 = nn.Linear(784, 128)
    def forward(self, x):
        return torch.relu(self.fc1(x))

class Stage2(nn.Module):
    def __init__(self):
        super(Stage2, self).__init__()
        self.fc2 = nn.Linear(128, 10)
    def forward(self, x):
        return self.fc2(x)

# Use Pipe to wrap the model and enable pipeline parallelism
def get_pipeline_model():
    model = nn.Sequential(Stage1(), Stage2())
    return Pipe(model,
                devices=[torch.device('cuda:0'), torch.device('cuda:1')],
                chunks=2)
# Resume normal training ...
```

Parallelism to the Rescue in AI for Radiotherapy Task

The first step of the task in "AI for Radiotherapy Under Resource Constraints" on page 204 is to develop a powerful segmentation model that can be used in radiotherapy workflows. The model can be developed at a different location with few more resources than where they are to be deployed. Training large-scale foundation models for radiotherapy segmentation is computationally intensive, especially with large 3D medical datasets that require high memory and careful preprocessing. A university research center typically has access to a small, diverse GPU cluster comprising a mix of V100s, A100s, and even older cards, and faces real challenges in scaling these workloads efficiently.

We can tackle these limitations to some extent using parallelism strategies. Data parallelism can be used to distribute batches of medical images across GPUs, enabling higher throughput when the model fits on each device. But for larger models that exceed memory limits, model parallelism splits the network itself across GPUs, allowing training of architectures that would not otherwise fit on a single GPU. When GPU capacities differ, pipeline parallelism stages the model across devices, letting batches of data flow to balance memory and keeping all hardware engaged.

By combining these parallelism strategies, even a modest cluster can train large-scale segmentation models efficiently.

Accelerator-Level Optimization

Because access to large-scale datacenters for AI model development and deployment is limited,[20] most researchers and ML practitioners rely on standalone GPUs as their primary hardware accelerators. Typically, these setups encompass one or two GPU cards housed in a desktop cabinet with fan-based cooling systems that inadvertently may also serve as room heaters. Maximizing the use of these is essential for enhancing resource efficiency and sustainability. Techniques such as effective workload scheduling on GPUs to use them to the maximum (GPU collocation) and optimizing power consumption can help reduce the AI waste due to the underutilization of the hardware.

GPUs: The Accidental Workhorse of AI

Originally designed in the 1990s to accelerate graphics rendering for video games and 3D applications, GPUs offload complex visual computations from CPUs. These early GPUs were optimized for parallel processing, excelling at executing the same operation on many data points simultaneously.

In the early 2000s, the computational power of GPUs began to catch the attention of researchers beyond the graphics community, particularly in scientific computing. As GPUs were inherently proficient at parallel tasks, they became instrumental in simulations, cryptography, and weather modeling. This expansion of applications led to the development of general-purpose GPU (GPGPU) computing. In 2006, NVIDIA launched CUDA, a model that enabled developers to program GPUs for tasks far beyond graphics.

20 Ahmed and Wahed, "The De-democratization of AI: Deep Learning and the Compute Divide in Artificial Intelligence Research" (*https://arxiv.org/abs/2010.15581*).

But it wasn't until the late 2000s and early 2010s that GPUs truly found their unexpected role as the workhorse of AI. With the rise of DL, AI researchers quickly realized that the training of neural networks could be accelerated using GPUs.[21] And today, NVIDIA is a trillion-dollar company riding on the back of this accidental workhorse of AI.[22]

GPU collocation

Many DL tasks that require GPU resources do not fully utilize all available compute cores, memory bandwidth, or execution units, resulting in wasted capacity and overall underutilization of these resources. Estimates show that in datacenters *only about half* the GPU capacity is used.[23] This can be improved using techniques like *GPU collocation*, the practice of efficiently sharing GPU resources. It addresses this inefficiency by allowing multiple workloads, processes, or instances, which enables multiple workloads to efficiently share a single GPU. Note that the better GPU utilization offered by collocation can sometimes result in slower overall runtimes for the jobs being run.

NVIDIA GPUs offer several methods for collocation, each with different levels of resource sharing, memory separation, and execution overhead. The three primary approaches are multistream execution, multiprocess service, and multi-instance GPU. Figure 8-9 illustrates these approaches, demonstrating how three different DL jobs can be executed on the same GPU.

Multistream execution allows a single process to manage multiple CUDA streams,[24] enabling concurrent execution of independent kernels and memory transfers. Since all streams share the same memory space, there is no memory isolation between them. This method is particularly effective for maximizing GPU utilization within a single application by overlapping computation and data movement. However, resource sharing is limited to what the CUDA scheduler allows within the process. Multistream execution is native to most recent NVIDIA GPUs and is used when multiple jobs are run on the same GPU.

Multiprocess service (MPS) is a user-space service that allows multiple CUDA processes to share a single GPU more efficiently. Unlike traditional multiprocess execu-

21 Rajat Raina et al., "Large-Scale Deep Unsupervised Learning Using Graphics Processors," in *Proceedings of the 26th International Conference on Machine Learning*, Montreal, Canada, 2009 (*https://oreil.ly/zG3SG*).

22 Michael Cusumano, "NVIDIA at the Center of the GenAI Ecosystem—For Now," *Communications of the ACM* 67, no. 1 (2023): 33–35 (*https://doi.org/10.1145/3631537*).

23 Myeongjae Jeon et al., "Analysis of Large-Scale Multi-Tenant GPU Clusters for DNN Training Workloads," in 2019 USENIX Annual Technical Conference, Renton, WA, July 2019 (*https://oreil.ly/QE889*).

24 A CUDA stream is a sequence of operations that execute on GPU.

tion, where GPU contexts are switched between processes, MPS merges process-level streams, reducing the overhead associated with context switching. This leads to improved GPU occupancy and better resource utilization across multiple workloads. However, like multistream execution, MPS also does not provide strict memory separation, as all processes still share the same GPU memory space. It is particularly useful for high-performance computing (HPC) workloads that require multiple cooperating processes to execute efficiently on a single GPU. Example 8-4 shows the simple sequence of steps required to enable MPS on NVIDIA GPUs.

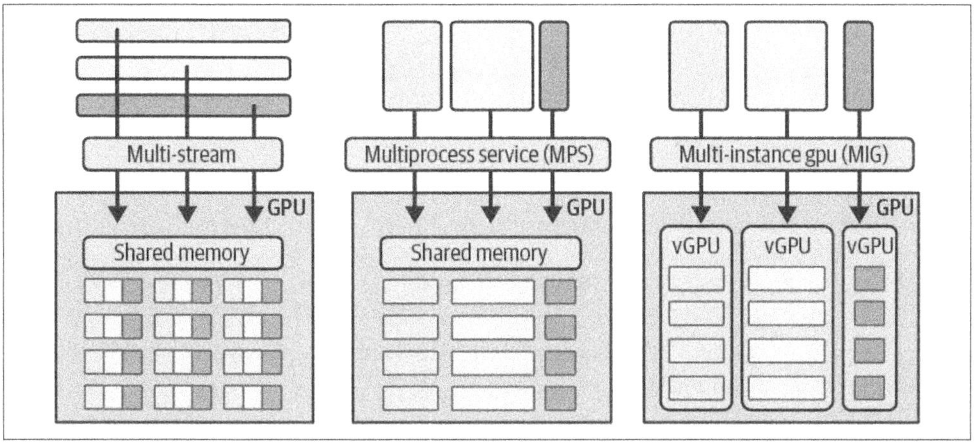

Figure 8-9. Multistream execution, multiprocess service, and multi-instance GPU collocation strategies. (Source: adapted from Ties Robroek [2024] (https://oreil.ly/RogMl).)

Example 8-4. Enabling MPS using NVIDIA utilities can be done using the `nvidia-cuda-mps-control` daemon

```
nvidia-cuda-mps-control -d                    # Enable MPS
CUDA_VISIBLE_DEVICES=0 python my_script.py    # Submit job to GPU
echo quit | nvidia-cuda-mps-control           # Disable MPS
```

When multiple jobs are being run, the MPS daemon should schedule them concurrently to maximize GPU utilization. We can verify this using the `nvidia-smi` utility in a bash terminal.

Multi-instance GPU (MIG) offers hardware-level partitioning of a GPU, allowing multiple workloads to run in isolated instances. This is a relatively recent feature available on NVIDIA A100, H100, and other newer GPUs. MIG ensures that each instance has dedicated memory, compute cores, and cache, preventing interference between workloads. Unlike multistream and MPS, which share resources dynamically, MIG guarantees strict separation, making it ideal for cloud computing, virtualization, and multitenant environments where predictable performance and security are critical. Example 8-5 shows how to set up multiple virtual GPUs using the MIG features of NVIDIA using `nvidia-smi`.

Example 8-5. Setting up multiple virtual GPUs (vGPUs) using MIG on the more recent NVIDIA GPUs

```
sudo nvidia-smi -i 0 -mig 1      # Enable MIG

nvidia-smi -i 0                  # Verify if MIG is enabled

nvidia-smi mig -lgip             # Check available vGPU profiles
```

This should show available GPU partitions, such as:

```
+---------------------------------------------------------------+
| GPU  ID | Profile ID | Name            | Memory  | CUDA Cores  |
+---------------------------------------------------------------+
| 0       | 19         | 1g.5gb          | 5 GB    | 1280        |
| 0       | 14         | 2g.10gb         | 10 GB   | 2560        |
| 0       | 9          | 3g.20gb         | 20 GB   | 5120        |
+---------------------------------------------------------------+
```

As an example, to create 3 vGPUs with 20GB, 10GB, and 5GB separation, the following configuration should work:

```
sudo nvidia-smi mig -i 0 -cgi 9 -C  # 20GB instance
sudo nvidia-smi mig -i 0 -cgi 14 -C # 10GB instance
sudo nvidia-smi mig -i 0 -cgi 19 -C # 5GB instance
```

The three vGPUs allocated using MIG can be accessed as three separate GPUs and jobs can be assigned to each of them using the `CUDA_VISIBLE_DEVICES` environment variable.

By using these GPU collocation techniques, multiple processes or tasks can run concurrently, maximizing GPU utilization, improving throughput, and reducing idle time.[25] This is particularly critical in HPC, AI, and cloud environments, where GPU resources are expensive and need to be used as efficiently as possible. Table 8-1 summarizes of the three GPU collocation strategies.

---

25 Ties Robroek et al., "An Analysis of Collocation on GPUs for Deep Learning Training," EuroMLSys '24: Proceedings of the 4th Workshop on Machine Learning and Systems, (April 19, 2024): 81–90 (*https://doi.org/10.1145/3642970.3655827*).

Table 8-1. Summary of GPU collocation strategies, primarily implemented for NVIDIA GPUs

Feature	Multistream	MPS	MIG
Scope	Single process	Multiple processes	Multiple isolated instances
Memory separation	No (shared memory space)	No (shared memory space)	Yes (each instance has dedicated memory)
Compute resource sharing	Yes (shared across streams)	Yes (shared across processes)	No (each instance has dedicated compute resources)
Execution overhead	Low (within the same process)	Moderate (service manages execution)	Low (hardware partitioning)
Concurrency control	Software (CUDA streams)	MPS daemon controls scheduling	Hardware-enforced isolation
Use case	Overlapping computation and memory transfers	Reducing GPU context switching for multiprocess workloads	Secure multitenant GPU sharing
Ideal workloads	Single-process, multikernel applications	HPC, multiprocess AI workloads	Cloud, virtualization, containerized applications
Isolation level	Low (same memory, shared resources)	Medium (some scheduling control)	High (hardware-enforced separation)
Kernel scheduling	CUDA stream prioritization	MPS scheduler	Independent per instance

Dynamic voltage frequency scaling

The intensity of workload on CPUs or GPUs varies with time depending on the operations being performed. For example, data transfer between disk and memory is a CPU-intensive task, during which the GPU could be idling. This is all the more aggravated if no parallelism (see "Parallelism in AI workloads" on page 209) or collocation (see "GPU collocation" on page 214) are used. In situations like these, when the logic elements are idling, the power draw can be reduced by *modulating* the voltage frequency. This can result in significant energy savings.

Dynamic voltage and frequency scaling (DVFS) is the most widely used method to reduce the overall energy consumption that dynamically adjusts a processor's voltage V and clock frequency f in response to workload demands.[26] Since the dynamic power consumption P is proportional to $V^2 \cdot f$, reducing voltage has a quadratic impact on power savings, while frequency scaling provides finer control over performance and efficiency.

26 Zhenheng Tang et al., "The Impact of GPU DVFS on the Energy and Performance of Deep Learning: An Empirical Study," *arXiv.org*, May 27, 2019 (*https://arxiv.org/abs/1905.11012*).

Figure 8-10 shows the total energy consumption of a processor if it draws constant power compared to the energy consumed in response to the fluctuations in workload. We see that, without DVFS, the total energy consumption due to constant power draw of 50W for 100 minutes is $50 \cdot 100/60 = 416.67$Wh, and with the scaling shown in the figure it is reduced to 113.21Wh.

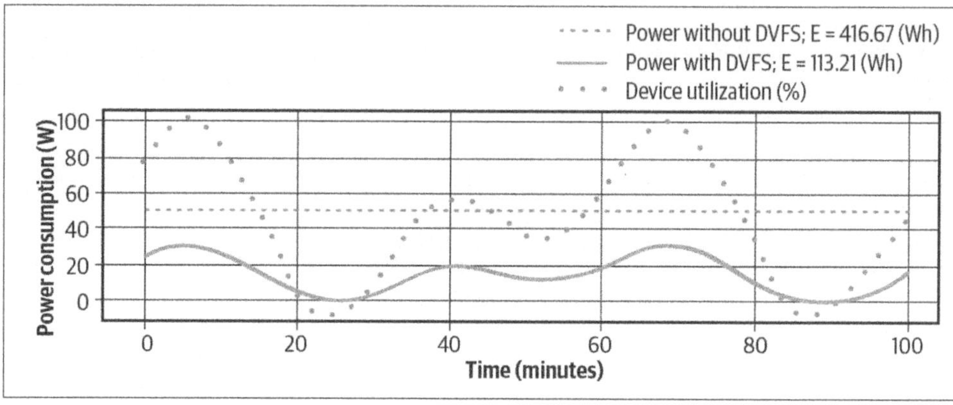

Figure 8-10. DVFS and its impact on power consumption when tasked with a workload that has variable GPU utilization assuming a maximum thermal power draw (TDP) of 100W.

One of the primary benefits of DVFS is power efficiency, particularly in battery-powered devices. By lowering both V and f during idle or low-load periods, energy consumption is significantly reduced, leading to extended battery life. For instance, a smartphone processor running at 2.5GHz under high load can dynamically scale down to 800MHz when idle, minimizing unnecessary power drain.

Beyond power savings, DVFS also plays a critical role in thermal management. High processor frequencies generate more heat, which can lead to thermal throttling and reduced hardware lifespan. By adjusting V and f dynamically, DVFS ensures that the temperature remains within safe operating limits, thereby improving system reliability. A laptop experiencing excessive heat, for example, can reduce processor voltage and frequency to cool down without requiring active cooling measures.

DVFS for Cluster-Level Optimization

DVFS can also be used in cloud computing and server environments, as DVFS enables efficient resource utilization by scaling performance up during peak loads and reducing frequency during off-peak hours, thereby lowering power consumption.

By dynamically allocating computational resources, cloud platforms can adjust processing power based on real-time demand. This reduces operational costs and enhances energy efficiency, contributing to more sustainable computing.[27] Companies like Google, AWS, and Microsoft Azure use DVFS in their server farms to minimize power consumption while maintaining service quality.

DVFS can sometimes increase the latency of jobs when the processors have to switch from low frequency/voltage settings to higher values due to a sudden increase in workload. Advanced scheduling algorithms are continually being developed to reduce such latency.[28] Overall, DVFS is a fundamental technique for balancing performance, power efficiency, and thermal constraints, while incurring some additional latency.

Squeezing Everything Out of a GPU for the AI in Radiotherapy Task

Returning to the "AI for Radiotherapy Under Resource Constraints" on page 204, when developing segmentation models on a limited GPU cluster, every watt and every compute cycle counts. Large 3D medical datasets demand high memory and compute, but many stages of training, like validation, data augmentation, or patch-wise inference, do not fully saturate the GPU. Instead of letting that capacity go unused, GPU collocation can be used to run multiple lightweight tasks side-by-side, increasing GPU utilization, reducing total runtime, and improving overall hardware efficiency.

At the same time, DVFS can be used to cut energy usage during lower-demand phases. When the GPU is not fully loaded, DVFS reduces clock speeds and voltage, trimming power consumption without slowing down the job in any meaningful way.

A combination of parallelism, collocation, and DVFS translates to faster iteration, lower energy bills, and a more carbon efficient path toward training clinically viable AI models.

---

27 Chia-Ming Wu et al., "A Green Energy-efficient Scheduling Algorithm Using the DVFS Technique for Cloud Datacenters," *Future Generation Computer Systems* 37 (July 14, 2014): 141–47 (*https://doi.org/10.1016/j.future.2013.06.009*).

28 Zhuo Tang et al., "An Energy-Efficient Task Scheduling Algorithm in DVFS-enabled Cloud Environment," *Journal of Grid Computing* 14, no. 1 (2016): 55–74 (*https://doi.org/10.1007/s10723-015-9334-y*).

Custom Hardware Optimization

While GPUs have evolved to become the accidental workhorse of AI, without further optimization the energy consumption of executing instructions on GPUs can be quite high. At the first level, software optimization with specialized CUDA kernels can already yield considerable improvements in the energy cost per instruction on GPUs. Figure 8-11 shows the instruction-level energy consumption for different NVIDIA GPUs with and without CUDA optimization. For some instructions (like division), the energy cost without software optimization is about five times more compared to when executed after optimization. While tricks like these are specific to NVIDIA hardware, similar optimizations can be performed on all hardware accelerators.

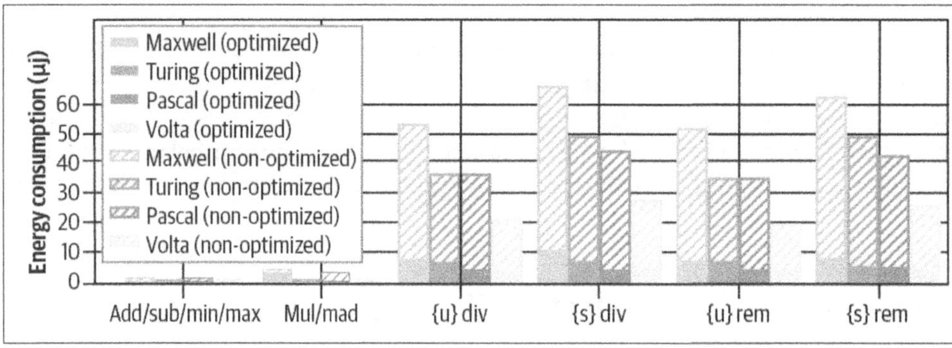

Figure 8-11. Energy cost for executing some of the NVIDIA instructions across different generations of NVIDIA GPUs. (Source: data derived from Yehia Arafa et al. [2020] (https://arxiv.org/abs/2002.07795).)

Hardware-optimized software

Frameworks like PyTorch and TensorFlow offer high-level functionalities that work across a broad spectrum of hardware and as a result can be suboptimal for a specific piece of hardware, as shown in Figure 8-11. Hardware-optimized software is designed to take full advantage of specific hardware architectures, maximizing performance and efficiency. This optimization can involve low-level programming techniques, parallelization, vectorization, memory hierarchy tuning, and specialized instruction sets. By aligning software execution with the underlying hardware capabilities, applications can achieve significant speedups, reduced power consumption, and improved scalability.

One approach to hardware optimization is leveraging specialized compilers that translate high-level code into machine instructions optimized for a particular architecture. A prime example is NVIDIA's NVCC (NVIDIA CUDA Compiler), which is designed for CUDA-enabled GPUs. NVCC compiles CUDA C/C++ code into GPU-executable binaries, optimizing memory access patterns, thread execution, and instruction scheduling to maximize parallel throughput.

By utilizing NVCC, developers can write high-performance applications that exploit the massively parallel processing power of modern GPUs. A simple NVCC optimization example is shown in Example 8-6.

Example 8-6. Demonstration of a custom CUDA kernel that implements the `relu` operation for speedup in an NVIDIA GPU using NVCC

```
extern "C" __global__ void relu_cuda(float* x, float* y, int N) {
    int idx = blockIdx.x * blockDim.x + threadIdx.x;
    if (idx < N) {
        y[idx] = fmaxf(0.0, x[idx]);
    }
}
```

Compile the CUDA kernel using NVCC into a shared library object `relu_kernel.so`:

```
nvcc -O3 -use_fast_math -arch=sm_75 -shared -Xcompiler \
-fPIC relu_kernel.cu -o relu_kernel.so
```

Benchmark the speed-up with this custom kernel specialized for the GPU being used, compared to the standard PyTorch function:

```
import torch, time, ctypes

# Load compiled CUDA kernel
relu_cuda = ctypes.CDLL("./relu_kernel.so")

# Define wrapper function
def relu_optimized(x):
    N = x.numel()
    y = torch.empty_like(x)
    threads_per_block = 256
    blocks_per_grid = (N + threads_per_block - 1) // threads_per_block
    relu_cuda.relu_cuda(x.data_ptr(), y.data_ptr(), N)
    return y

# Test optimized CUDA function
x_cuda = torch.randn(100000, device="cuda")

# PyTorch ReLU
start = time.time()
for _ in range(1000):
    y = torch.relu(x_cuda)
torch.cuda.synchronize()
torch_time = time.time()-start
print("PyTorch ReLU Time:%.4f s"%torch_time)

# Custom CUDA ReLU
start = time.time()
for _ in range(1000):
    y = relu_optimized(x_cuda)
```

```
torch.cuda.synchronize()
cuda_time = time.time()-start
print("Custom CUDA ReLU Time:%.4f s"%cuda_time)
print("Speed-up factor: %.2f"%(torch_time/cuda_time))
```

Depending on the GPU being used, the speed-up can be different, with a result similar to this:

```
PyTorch ReLU Time:0.0112 s
Custom CUDA ReLU Time:0.0018
Speed-up of 6.26
```

Optimizing a simple operation like `relu` in Example 8-6 already shows a considerable speedup. Broader optimization across other operations can also yield similar performance gains, as shown in Figure 8-11.

Neural processing units

Neural processing units (NPUs) are purpose-built hardware for accelerating neural network operations. They incorporate highly specialized units optimized for the mathematical operations prevalent in DL models, such as matrix multiplications, convolutions, and activations. Unlike the general-purpose cores of GPUs, NPUs typically feature dedicated processing blocks for these operations, often utilizing specialized accelerators to handle tensor-based computations. These blocks are tailored to efficiently perform the computations involved in training and inference, with minimal overhead.

NPUs often also feature a memory hierarchy tailored for ML workloads, with substantial emphasis on *processing in memory* to minimize data transfer latency. These memory architectures are designed to accommodate the smaller, frequently accessed datasets used in AI operations, thus optimizing the overall processing time by reducing reliance on external memory. The ability to locally store intermediate tensors and results is crucial for improving both performance and energy efficiency.[29]

29 Paul Delestrac et al., "Analyzing GPU Energy Consumption in Data Movement and Storage," 2024 IEEE 35th International Conference on Application-specific Systems, Architectures and Processors (ASAP), Hong Kong, Hong Kong, July 2024, 143–51 (*https://doi.org/10.1109/asap61560.2024.00038*).

While GPUs remain dominant for training DL models, NPUs are rapidly becoming the popular solution for AI inference, offering better energy efficiency and faster execution tailored to the needs of modern AI applications. Google's TPUs are some of the most popular NPUs that currently power Google's AI datacenters.

Deploying Models in Clinical Workflow for AI in Radiotherapy

Deploying large radiotherapy segmentation models into real clinical settings means adapting them for resource-constrained hardware, which oftentimes are old CPUs with limited memory and strict regulatory controls. These systems cannot run large, dynamic models as is.

The first step is to compress and quantize them using techniques like model pruning and low-precision quantization, discussed in Chapter 7. This cuts memory use and speeds up inference, making deployment on minimal hardware feasible.

When legacy NVIDIA GPUs are present, use of tools like NVCC becomes critical. By compiling custom CUDA kernels ahead of time, rather than relying on high-overhead frameworks, developers can produce efficient, deterministic binaries tailored to the clinic's exact hardware. This avoids runtime errors, ensures reproducibility, and meets strict clinical requirements.

Together, compression and custom compilers can turn high-end research models into lean, reliable tools that actually work where they are needed in real radiotherapy clinics.

Hardware Optimized: What Comes Next?

Hardware manufacturing significantly impacts the environment through the materials used and the energy consumed through the lifecycle of products. Optimizing hardware usage is one way of reducing the AI waste and hence improving the overall efficiency and sustainability of AI hardware.

This chapter has explored various methods to improve hardware utilization at different levels. First, at the cluster or datacenter level, using parallelism strategies that can use the compute resources better by orchestrating data, model, and pipeline parallelism. Second, we focused on improving the utilization of AI accelerators like GPUs using workload scheduling techniques like collocation or DVFS, and using hardware optimized software using specialized compilers like NVCC. Furthermore, customized accelerators like NPUs can yield better resource efficiency as they are designed for AI operations.

These tools and techniques offer trade-offs between resource efficiency and performance gains. They also come with some caveats and limitations:

Are customized AI chips more sustainable than general-purpose ones?

Not always. The lifecycle of developing a new chip can be more resource-intensive if the net gains of using such specialized hardware are limited.

Customized AI chips can be more efficient in specific tasks, reducing power consumption and improving performance compared to general-purpose chips. However, their sustainability depends on the full lifecycle, including design, manufacturing, and eventual disposal. Developing a specialized chip requires significant resources, from raw materials to fabrication and testing, which can offset potential energy savings if the chip's advantages are marginal or if it becomes obsolete quickly. In contrast, general-purpose chips may have longer usability across different applications, reducing electronic waste. Therefore, the sustainability of customized AI chips is context-dependent and not inherently superior.

Should one always switch to using recent, efficient hardware compared to older, less-efficient hardware?

Again, not always. The sunken cost of already used resources in older hardware should be justified.

Upgrading to newer, more efficient hardware can reduce energy consumption and improve performance, but the sustainability benefits must be weighed against the environmental cost of producing new devices. Older hardware has already incurred its resource and manufacturing footprint, meaning discarding it prematurely contributes to electronic waste and negates the benefits of its full lifecycle use. If the older hardware still meets performance needs and can be maintained, continuing its use may be the more sustainable choice. The decision should balance efficiency gains with the environmental impact of production, disposal, and resource consumption.

Are there other environmental effects due to AI hardware, beyond emissions and e-waste?

Broader environmental effects due to hardware manufacturing can have considerable impact on different aspects of the environment.

Operational and embodied emissions account for the energy consumed during the usage and manufacturing of hardware. Figure 4-1 shows the GHG emissions across the lifecycle of storage devices; a similar attribution can also be made for AI computational hardware such as GPUs. The environmental impact of hardware can extend beyond these emissions, as we have already seen with e-waste. Beyond these aspects, AI datacenters exert significant environmental pressures through water consumption,[30] extractive mining processes, and end-of-life waste.[31] These broader environmental effects due to AI hardware are difficult to reliably quantify due to the complications in performing *lifecycle assessment* (LCA) of hardware manufacturing, usage, and disposal. Regulatory compliance and standardized reporting can improve the accounting of these broader environmental effects, which can have considerable impact on the sustainability of AI.

30 Pengfei Li et al., "Making AI Less 'Thirsty': Uncovering and Addressing the Secret Water Footprint of AI Models," *arXiv.org*, March 26, 2025 (*https://arxiv.org/abs/2304.03271*).

31 Lynn H. Kaack et al., "Aligning Artificial Intelligence With Climate Change Mitigation," *Nature Climate Change* 12, no. 6 (2022): 518–27 (*https://doi.org/10.1038/s41558-022-01377-7*).

CHAPTER 9

A Recipe for Sustainable AI

In the 1990s, many systems stored dates using two digits for the year—"97" for 1997, "99" for 1999, and so on—to save memory and simplify string handling. This worked fine until the year 2000 approached. Suddenly, "00" could mean 1900 or 2000, and countless systems risked malfunctioning or crashing because they could not disambiguate the century. This led to the global frenzy known as the *Y2K bug*.[1]

In the scramble to patch systems before the millennium, developers used various stopgap fixes. One such hack involved adding a "Y2K compliance" flag or setting arbitrary rules to interpret dates—like assuming any year less than 20 meant 2000—2019, and any year 20 or higher meant 1920—1999. The code might look like this:

```
def interpret_year(year):
    if year < 20:
        return 2000 + year
    else:
        return 1900 + year
```

And next to it, developers would often write comments like:

```
# Temporary Y2K fix. Remove by 2010.
```

Of course, 2010 came and went, but the code remained. No one was sure what systems depended on this logic. Removing it could have subtle effects—date misinterpretations, billing errors, archival failures—so it stayed. Teams eventually became too afraid to touch it. In some legacy banking and insurance systems, versions of this logic persisted for decades.

1 Capers Jones, *The Year 2000 Software Problem: Quantifying the Costs and Assessing the Consequences*, (ACM Press/Addison-Wesley, 1997).

This is a textbook case of *technical debt* in software engineering,[2] the implicit cost of choosing an easy or limited solution now instead of a better approach that would take more effort. While shortcuts are sometimes necessary, they accrue penalties over time. Technical debts make future changes more difficult, introduce fragility, and often demand costly solutions down the line. In other words, *technical debt trades long-term maintainability for short-term speed.*

In this chapter, I will introduce the *environmental debt of AI* as a concept similar to the technical debt of software. It will be useful in thinking about the downstream environmental costs of making short-sighted design choices when building AI solutions. I present different components that pay into the environmental debt: transparency, data, algorithmic and infrastructure debts. Drawing on the concepts from systems engineering, I'll also introduce *green MLOps* as one way to overcome these costly environmental debts of AI, arguing for a holistic framework that can embed sustainability as a design constraint rather than an afterthought.

Technical Debt of Machine Learning

Unlike conventional software systems, ML systems are deeply entangled with data, models, experiments, and infrastructure—all of which are constantly shifting. This leads to a proliferation of hidden dependencies and interlocking components that are notoriously difficult to untangle. D. Sculley et al. at Google documented this phenomenon in "Hidden Technical Debt in Machine Learning Systems" (*https://dl.acm.org/doi/abs/10.5555/2969442.2969519*). They argue that in ML pipelines, only a small fraction of the system consists of actual model code as Figure 9-1 shows, where the ML code is only a small portion of the larger framework, as the rest is glue code, data pipelines, configuration, monitoring, orchestration, and other supporting infrastructure. All of these components can accumulate technical debt—seemingly small compromises that can have large detrimental effects down the line.

Generally in ML/AI systems, feedback loops between model outputs and future training data can create complex, emergent behaviors that are difficult to debug. For instance, data dependencies can harden into assumptions that break silently as data distributions shift (see "Fine-Tuning of Pretrained Models" on page 148). Models trained under one set of constraints may become brittle or inapplicable when deployed in production environments with different failure modes or latency constraints.

This is why the technical debt in ML is not just about code complexity—it is about the fragility introduced by dynamic data, stochastic processes, and rapidly evolving

2 Ward Cunningham, "The WyCash Portfolio Management System," ACM SIGPLAN OOPS Messenger 4, no. 2 (December 1, 1992): 29–30 (*https://doi.org/10.1145/157710.157715*).

tooling, which are inherent to these systems. It can manifest in brittle feature engineering code, untracked data dependencies, underdocumented experiments, or models that are difficult to reproduce or interpret—which are unfortunately pervasive.[3] Over time, this debt slows down iteration, introduces risk, and limits the system's adaptability.

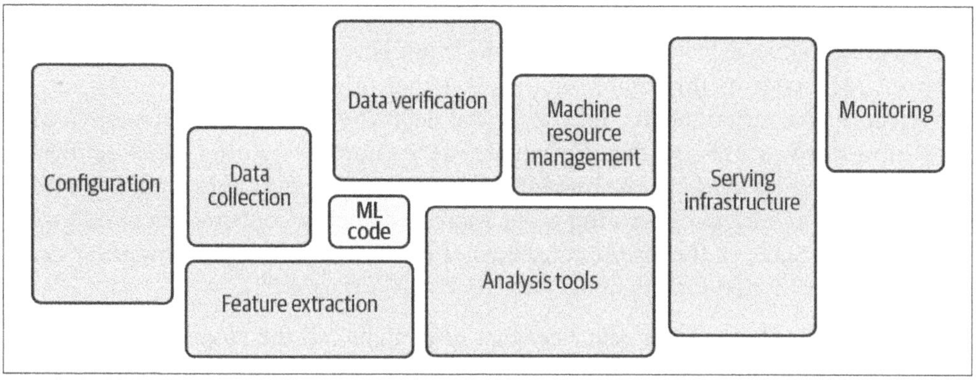

Figure 9-1. Hidden technical debt of ML; various components supporting the ML code can be only a small portion of an AI system. (Source: adapted from Sculley et al. [2015] (https://dl.acm.org/doi/abs/10.5555/2969442.2969519).)

Technical Debt in the Global Tree Identification System

Consider the AI system for global tree identification discussed in "Curating Datasets Frugally for Global Tree Identification" on page 84. If the model is trained on high-resolution images from a specific region—say, sub-Saharan Africa—internally, the model may be relying not just on the presence of tree canopies but also on context cues like soil color, lighting patterns, or seasonal artifacts. But these internal dependencies are opaque. Once deployed in a new region—say, Southeast Asia—the model can fail silently, mistaking shadows or crops for trees. Users relying on the count to make policy or funding decisions are now operating on faulty data, and they may not immediately know it.

This is one example of the hidden technical debt manifested as data debt in AI systems, which Sculley et al. detail in their paper (*https://dl.acm.org/doi/abs/10.5555/2969442.2969519*).

3 Sayash Kapoor and Arvind Narayanan, "Leakage and the Reproducibility Crisis in ML-Based Science," *arXiv.org*, July 14, 2022 (*https://arxiv.org/abs/2207.07048*).

Environmental Debt of AI

Technical debt of ML is a useful concept to understand the hidden costs of short-term decisions when designing and developing complex AI systems. If we reimagine this concept of technical debt using the lens of sustainability, we arrive at the concept of *environmental debt.*

The environmental debt of AI refers to the cumulative ecological burden incurred due to AI/ML systems through design choices that prioritize scale, performance, or convenience over sustainability. Like technical debt, environmental debt is often hidden—embedded in massive data hoarding, energy-hungry training runs, inefficient model architectures, and opaque infrastructure choices—and its consequences unfold over time through higher operating costs, increased energy consumption, and growing emissions. Some of the visible consequence of environmental debt manifest as AI waste addressed in previous chapters (see "AI Waste" on page 53).

At the root of environmental debt lies what one might call the *abundance mindset*—the implicit assumption that compute, storage, data, and energy are effectively limitless. This mindset has shaped much of modern ML: training ever-larger models under the logic of scaling laws;[4] storing "everything" because storage is cheap, resulting in dark data;[5] relying on brute-force search over optimization; and deploying models with little regard for their inference footprint. The abundance mindset externalizes environmental costs and locks systems into wasteful paths by the sole focus on arbitrary performance metrics not rooted in resource costs (see "Quantifying Resource Consumption of AI" on page 57).

In contrast, I have argued for a *frugal mindset* throughout the book, asking practitioners to focus on reducing AI waste.[6] This encourages more transparent reporting (Chapter 3), smarter data curation (Chapter 4), Pareto optimal models (Chapter 5), efficient training (Chapter 6), leaner models at deployment (Chapter 7), and overall deliberate choices aimed at minimizing the environmental impact of AI systems. The frugal mindset recognizes that environmental debt, if not consciously avoided or repaid, will return in the form of climate-related costs due to AI systems.

4 Jared Kaplan et al., "Scaling Laws for Neural Language Models," *arXiv.org*, January 23, 2020 (*https://arxiv.org/abs/2001.08361*).

5 P. Bryan Heidorn, "Shedding Light on the Dark Data in the Long Tail of Science," *Library Trends* 57, no. 2 (September 1, 2008): 280–99 (*https://doi.org/10.1353/lib.0.0036*).

6 Works like Evchenko et al. (*https://arxiv.org/abs/2111.03731*) discuss efficient ML practices under the umbrella term *frugal machine learning*. While they don't explicitly deal with environmental debts, the broader appeal on making ML more frugal is meaningful and aligns with the message in this chapter.

> **Abundance Mindset and Frugal Mindset in Llama-3 Versus DeepSeek-V3**
>
> LLaMA-3.1, a 405-billion parameter model developed by Meta (*https://oreil.ly/Exlu1*), trained over 30.84 million GPU hours. In contrast, DeepSeek-V3 (*https://arxiv.org/abs/2412.19437*), a similarly scaled mixture-of-experts model with 671 billion parameters, was trained using just 2.8 million GPU hours. The DeepSeek team was forced into this constraint not by choice but by necessity: export controls barred their access to cutting-edge NVIDIA GPUs, leaving them to work with older, less efficient hardware. This imposed extreme resource constraints that resulted in a staggering 90% reduction in compute for comparable performance across several benchmark tasks. While environmental sustainability was not the driving motivation behind this frugal mindset, the outcome is a compelling demonstration of what can be achieved when abundance mindset is not the norm.

Lapses in taking sustainability considerations at different stages in the AI system lifecycle can introduce different debts that contribute to the environmental debt. We will discuss some of these debts next: transparency, data, algorithmic, and infrastructure.

Transparency Debt

When ML practitioners do not report the environmental debt of AI systems, they create *transparency debt*—because environmental costs do not go away just because no one tracks them.[7] Skipping the measurement or disclosure of energy usage, carbon emissions, or hardware demands might seem harmless at first, especially in a culture that rewards speed and accuracy above all else.[8] But this lack of transparency builds systemic fragility. Just like undocumented code, hidden environmental impacts become technical liabilities. They make it harder to benchmark progress, adapt to regulatory changes like the EU AI Act, or defend sustainability claims with any credibility. Fixing them later usually means costly redesigns, firefighting compliance issues, or watching your stack crumble under scrutiny.

Data Debt

Data debt arises when vast amounts of data are collected, stored, or processed without critical evaluation of their necessity, quality, or long-term cost. On the surface, this might look like due diligence—"collect everything, just in case"—but it

7 Marcin Spoczynski et al., "Atlas: A Framework for ML Lifecycle Provenance and Transparency," *arXiv.org*, May 14, 2025 (*https://arxiv.org/abs/2502.19567*).

8 Raghavendra Selvan et al., "PePR: Performance per Resource Unit as a Metric to Promote Small-Scale Deep Learning in Medical Image Analysis," *arXiv.org*, December 5, 2024 (*https://arxiv.org/abs/2403.12562*).

quickly becomes an ecological and operational burden. Every bit of data has a cost as we have seen in Chapter 4 as data relies on physical infrastructure that consumes electricity, requires cooling, and demands long-term maintenance.

Data debt is a critical but often overlooked source of environmental debt in AI systems. When engineers rely on poorly labeled, inconsistent, or redundant datasets, they trigger inefficient workflows—retraining models unnecessarily, consuming excess compute, and inflating storage demands. These practices drive up energy use, emissions, and hardware wear, not because the models are inherently inefficient, but because the data pipeline lacks discipline. Each wasted GPU hour or redundant data operation adds to the system's environmental footprint.

Other Elements of Environmental Debt

Continuing along the lifecycle of an AI model, one can also identify *algorithmic debt*, which is the environmental cost incurred when practitioners choose inefficient or overpowered models in the short term—either because they take less design effort or simply because they are trendy. These decisions inflate compute time, energy use, and carbon footprint down the line as these choices persist across the model lifecycle (see Chapter 5).

Similarly, *infrastructure debt* is the environmental cost of building AI systems on inefficient or outdated hardware, architectures, or deployment setups. It shows up in wasted energy, underutilized resources, and high operational overhead—like running models on the wrong compute tier, ignoring load balancing, or failing to optimize for energy efficiency. This debt accumulates quietly and is hard to unwind, locking in waste across the system lifecycle (as discussed in Chapter 8).

Environmental Debts Are Not Easy to Measure

Environmental debt arises from structural inefficiencies embedded across the AI pipeline—ones that standard metrics miss. In the global tree identification model (discussed in Chapter 4), this could include redundant satellite data (data debt), inefficient algorithms chosen for marginal accuracy gains (algorithmic debt), or poorly optimized deployment on generic infrastructure (infrastructure debt). These decisions quietly inflate energy use and emissions over time, even if the immediate environmental cost looks acceptable. Because these costs are buried in pipeline design and system choices, this debt accumulates invisibly, making the model far less sustainable than it appears.

Operationalizing Sustainable AI

Environmental debt of AI is a useful notion to think about the climate impact of AI systems across their lifecycle. These debts can be mitigated to some extent at each step of the lifecycle using the techniques presented in the previous chapters. However, these debts accumulate across the different stages of the AI model lifecycle, and it requires a systemic view of these complex systems to effectively address them.

This brings us to the question: how are AI systems even operationalized in the first place? Once we identify the processes that operationalize AI systems, we can holistically embed sustainability considerations into their lifecycles. In this section, we will tackle these challenges using concepts from software engineering—particularly DevOps and MLOps—resulting in green MLOps, which aims to achieve sustainability as a design constraint and not a post-hoc appendage when operationalizing AI systems.

MLOps

In classical software engineering, developers introduced *DevOps* to address the inefficiencies between software development and IT operations. They aimed to deliver software faster and more reliably by automating processes, fostering collaboration, and incorporating continuous feedback, all to reduce the overall technical debt that is accrued in software systems.

In the DevOps model, developers treat code as deterministic: once they write and test software, they expect it to behave predictably—unless they change the code itself. They focus primarily on system integration, deployment automation, environment consistency, and incident response. Two of the core principles of DevOps are *continuous integration* (CI), which means frequently merging code with automated builds and tests, and *continuous testing* (CT), which runs automated tests continuously to ensure quality throughout the pipeline. The code determinism and principles like CI and CT have led to establishing the International Standards Organization (ISO) standard for DevOps more easily.[9]

If we turn toward ML, the classic DevOps principle—rooted in determinism—does not hold well. This has given rise to MLOps, which adapts DevOps principles into the ML domain. Definitions of MLOps typically fall into three categories: vendor-driven narratives shaped by tooling constraints, framework-specific models like Google's maturity levels rooted in particular engineering cultures,[10] and informal lists of

9 "ISO/IEC/IEEE 32675:2022: Information Technology—DevOps—Building Reliable and Secure Systems Including Application Build, Package and Deployment" (2022).

10 Jarek Kazmierczak et al., "MLOps: Continuous Delivery and Automation Pipelines in Machine Learning," Google Cloud, August 28, 2024 (*https://oreil.ly/WBmAr*).

disconnected practices such as versioning or monitoring. While each element has merit, their aggregation lacks the coherence of a true conceptual framework that could perhaps lead to a standard.

Given all this vagueness, we'll use the definition from the MLOps special-interest group Continuous Delivery Foundation (*https://oreil.ly/Ir_91*) that best matches the scope of MLOps in this book:

> An optimal MLOps experience [as] one where Machine Learning assets are treated consistently with all other software assets within a CI/CD environment. Machine learning models can be deployed alongside the services that wrap them and the services that consume them as part of a unified release process.

This definition is formalized into three MLOps phases: design, model development, and operations. Figure 9-2 shows the interdependency of these phases in the MLOps pipeline and briefly describes the individual steps within each phase.

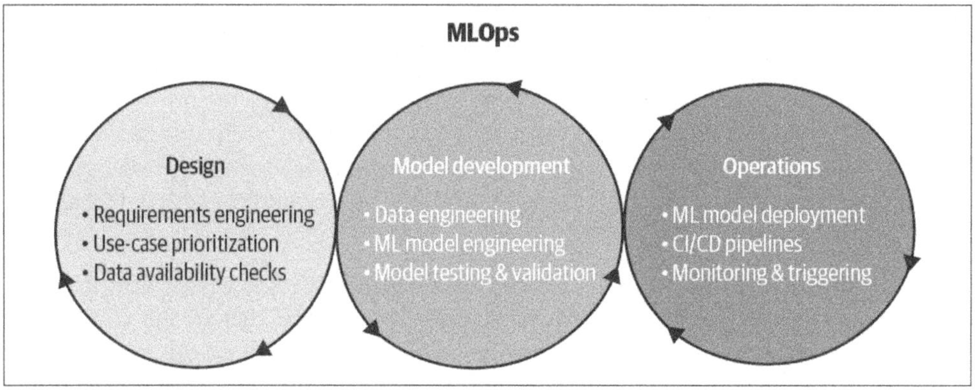

Figure 9-2. The design, model development, and operations MLOps phases. (Source: adapted from INNOQ (https://oreil.ly/Ir_91), License: CC BY 4.0. Modified to include MLOps concepts.)

In the design phase, teams define the ML problem, map out data flows, and formulate the pipeline. They decide on data sources, annotation strategies, infrastructure components, and integration points with downstream systems. This phase sets the groundwork for the entire ML lifecycle.

During the model development phase, practitioners process data, engineer features, train models, and evaluate their performance. They track experiments, version datasets and code, and ensure the reproducibility of results. This phase transforms abstract goals into validated, deployable models.

In the operations phase, teams deploy models into production environments, monitor their behavior, and maintain their performance over time. They detect drift, retrain models as needed, and respond to infrastructure failures or data issues. This phase keeps models functional and reliable under real-world conditions.

By actively connecting these phases through automated workflows and shared observability, MLOps enables teams to iterate quickly, scale reliably, and maintain control over complex ML systems. Table 9-1 summarizes these three phases in MLOps.

Table 9-1. Standard MLOps phase steps

MLOps phase	MLOps step	Description
Design	Requirements engineering	Define system goals, constraints, performance metrics, and non-functional requirements.
	Use-case prioritization	Select ML problems based on feasibility, usefulness, and business value.
	Data availability checks	Assess whether suitable, sufficient, and usable data exists for the target problem.
Model development	Data engineering	Collect, clean, and pipeline data for modeling; includes transformation and feature design.
	ML model engineering	Build and train models, tune hyperparameters, and optimize for accuracy/performance.
	Model testing & validation	Evaluate models on held-out data; test robustness, generalization, and fairness.
Operations	Model deployment	Push models into production—batch, online, or edge. Ensure availability and scalability.
	CI/CD pipelines	Automate model building, testing, and release cycles for frequent updates.
	Monitoring	Track model performance, data drift, system health, and trigger updates or rollbacks.

This formulation avoids the trap of reducing MLOps to tooling, while also grounding it in operational realities. It provides a conceptual backbone around which practices, roles, and infrastructure can be coherently aligned.

Green MLOps

To move ML toward a more sustainable path, we need to rethink how we approach MLOps by shifting the focus from pure performance and scalability to efficiency and resource awareness. We can begin to define what a practical, actionable form of green MLOps looks like by considering sustainability within the MLOps paradigm. This does not entail simply adding sustainability as a side concern—it is about integrating it directly into how we build and maintain ML systems.

I propose three phases of green MLOps in this book (see Figure 9-3):

Design
: Green MLOps defines success by including environmental limits alongside accuracy, latency, and reliability. It treats emissions budgets, compute thresholds, and deployment locality as part of requirements engineering. It defines responsible project scoping by prioritizing use cases that maximize real-world benefit per unit of energy, and it anchors data strategy in minimization—reusing, filtering, and curating data to avoid excess.

Model development
: Green MLOps defines modeling as an optimization over both performance and environmental cost. It specifies model engineering practices that favor smaller architectures, efficient fine-tuning (like adapters or quantization), and selective retraining. It redefines evaluation by incorporating metrics like energy per inference, training emissions, and hardware utilization—treating energy efficiency as core to model quality.

Operations
: Green MLOps defines deployment strategy in terms of carbon and compute efficiency. It mandates infrastructure choices that reduce emissions—such as low-carbon regions or adaptive scaling—and it embeds environmental logging into CI/CD and monitoring workflows. It defines model maintenance as a lifecycle responsibility, where systems must justify their ongoing energy cost or face decommissioning.

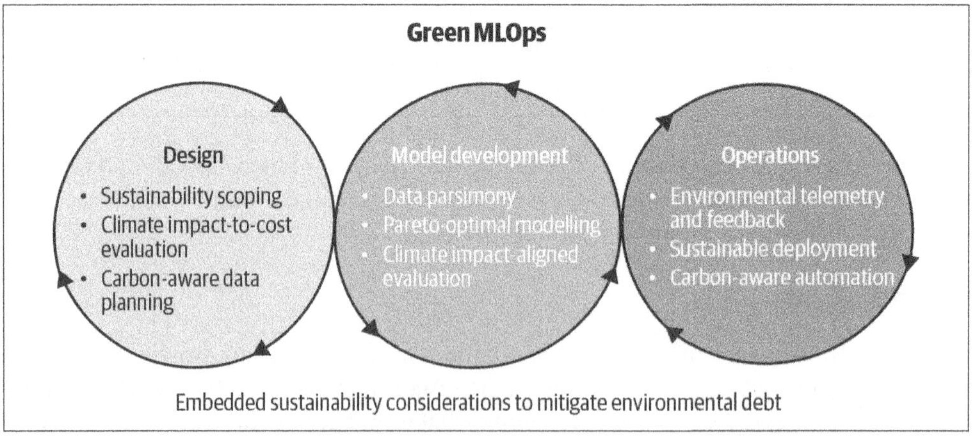

Figure 9-3. Green MLops as a reimagination of MLOps that is rooted in climate awareness. Embedding sustainability considerations into each of the steps of MLOps requires conscious choices in each step, as shown in this overview.

Altogether, green MLOps aspires toward a professional standard: to treat sustainability as a technical and ethical obligation, shaping ML systems that serve their purpose without exhausting the ecosystems they aim to protect. Table 9-2 summarizes the steps within the three green MLOps phases.

Table 9-2. Steps of the green MLOps phases

Green MLOps phase	Green MLOps step	Description
Design	Sustainability scoping	Add energy/emission limits, lifecycle cost targets, and sustainability KPIs.
	Climate impact-to-cost evaluation	Prioritize use cases with high utility relative to energy and compute cost.
	Carbon-aware data planning	Select minimal, high-value datasets to reduce storage, duplication, and preparation cost.
Model development	Data parsimony	Reduce unnecessary preprocessing; design for reuse and minimize pipeline waste.
	Pareto-optimal modeling	Select models with optimal accuracy–energy trade-offs; use distillation, sparsity.
	Climate impact-aligned evaluation	Track energy per inference/training run; evaluate sustainability alongside accuracy.
Operations	Environmental telemetry and feedback	Log energy usage, hardware efficiency, and footprint; inform retraining/retirement.
	Sustainable deployment	Deploy models in low-emission regions, on efficient hardware, with adaptive scaling.
	Carbon-aware automation	Deploy models in low-emission regions, on efficient hardware, with adaptive scaling.

Climate Policy Chatbot Developed Using Green MLOps

We previously looked at the climate policy chatbot in "Climate Policy Chatbot" on page 145. How can we use the green MLOps principles to build this climate policy chatbot such that sustainability is embedded from design to deployment.

In the design phase, instead of defaulting to massive LLMs, we can define emissions limits, explore lightweight models, and curate only high-value climate data. This trims data debt from the start.

During model development, we can avoid brute-force fine-tuning by applying efficient adapters (e.g., LoRA), using smaller domain-adapted models, and evaluating not just accuracy, but energy per inference and training emissions. Every modeling choice is benchmarked against its environmental cost.

In operations, we can deploy the chatbot in low-carbon datacenters, scale infrastructure intelligently, and automate updates only when necessary. Real-time telemetry tracks energy usage and helps flag inefficiencies for retraining or decommissioning.

By following this green MLOps approach, the chatbot's environmental impact stays aligned with its climate mission—proving that building AI for sustainability can itself be sustainable.

Green MLOps in Practice

While the green MLOps framework offers a principled vision for sustainable AI, translating these principles into everyday engineering practice remains difficult—largely due to a lack of mature tools, standards, and institutional scaffolding.

Take Carbontracker (*https://carbontracker.info*),[11] for example: a Python package that estimates the energy consumption and carbon emissions of training DL models (also see "Carbon Footprint of AI Models" on page 68). It represents an important step forward, making it technically feasible to monitor emissions from ML workloads. But even with Carbontracker, integration into mainstream ML pipelines like TensorFlow, PyTorch Lightning, or CI/CD frameworks is limited. Most teams do not embed such tools in their development workflows, and platform support for environmental telemetry is practically nonexistent.

Worse still, there is no standard requirement—from either regulators or industry—for reporting emissions data alongside accuracy or latency. Models are evaluated in terms of performance, not footprint. Tools like Carbontracker exist in isolation, unsupported by broader guidelines on when, where, or how to use them. There is no shared framework to help engineers trade off model improvements against emissions costs, nor is there institutional incentive to make low-carbon choices when speed or performance dominates metrics.

As a result, even when sustainability tools are available, they remain underused—either because teams don't know about them or because their use adds friction without organizational recognition. Closing this gap requires more than better tooling; it demands clear standards, built-in support in ML platforms, and a cultural shift that treats emissions as a core engineering metric, not a peripheral concern.

To turn green MLOps from principle into practice, we need a robust set of tools, frameworks, and standards that embed environmental responsibility into the core of ML development. Some initial efforts in this regard are introduced next.

11 Anthony et al., "CarbonTracker: Tracking and Predicting the Carbon Footprint of Training Deep Learning Models" (*https://arxiv.org/abs/2007.03051*).

Model Cards

Model cards provide a structured way for practitioners to document the properties, intended uses, and limitations of ML models. Researchers originally designed them to promote transparency around fairness, accuracy, and dataset provenance, but the field must now expand their scope to include environmental accountability.[12]

By embedding resource consumption metrics such as training energy, carbon emissions, hardware details, and energy source mix into model cards, developers can make the environmental costs of ML systems both visible and comparable. This added transparency allows engineers, policymakers, and users to evaluate models not just by their outputs but by the environmental impact of producing those outputs.

Within green MLOps, model cards play a central role in exposing hidden environmental debt. They standardize the disclosure of emissions, support energy efficiency benchmarking across model iterations, and guide decisions about model reuse, retraining, or retirement. As more teams adopt sustainability-augmented model cards, the field moves closer to treating environmental performance as a core evaluation metric—on par with accuracy or speed.

Platforms like Hugging Face offer tools for writing standard model cards. Figure 9-4 shows an example with multiple relevant fields written using the Hugging Face model cards tool (*https://oreil.ly/Fi8Pv*). Model cards consist of multiple standardized reporting fields that can improve transparency and help the goals of green MLOps.

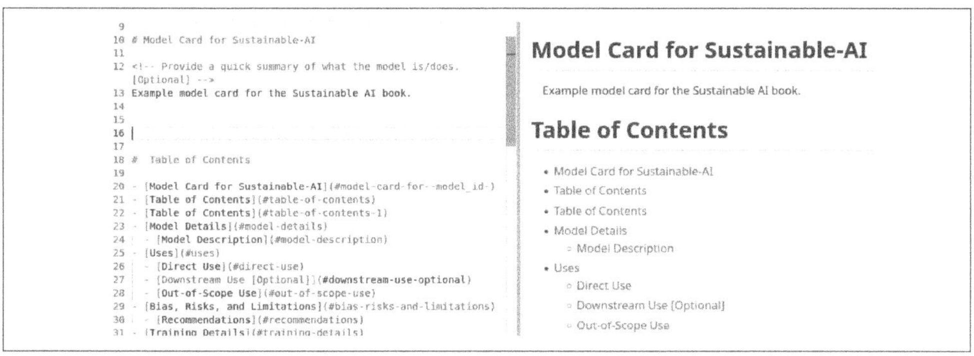

Figure 9-4. Model card example written using the Hugging Face model card tool.

12 Margaret Mitchell et al., "Model Cards for Model Reporting," in *FAT* '19: Proceedings of the Conference on Fairness, Accountability, and Transparency*, (January 9, 2019): 220–29 (*https://doi.org/10.1145/3287560.3287596*).

Self-reporting platforms tools like ML CO_2 Impact Calculator (*https://mlco2.github.io/impact*) or platforms like HCI GenAI CO_2ST Calculator (*https://hcico2st.com*), which are more specialized for human computer interface–specific ML (see Figure 9-5), can also be used to generate standardized environmental impact reports.[13]

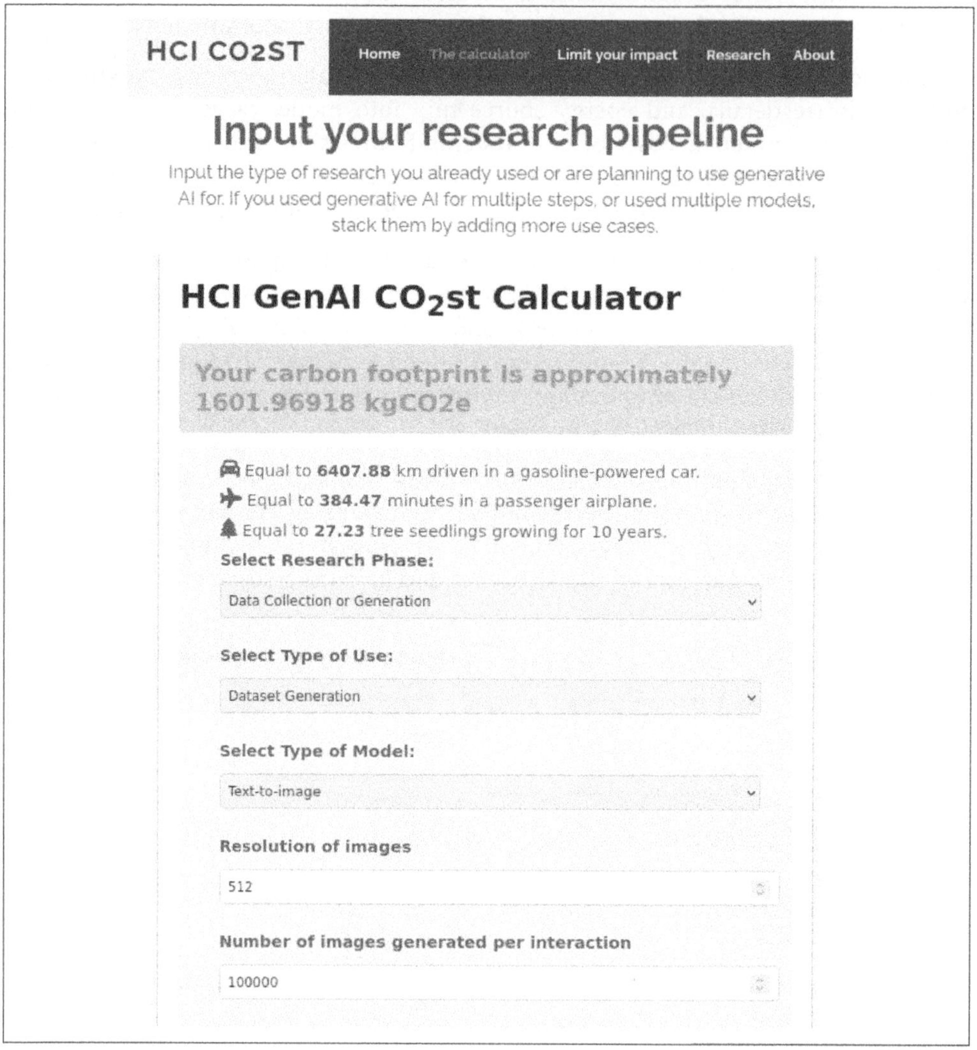

Figure 9-5. Self-reporting platform HCI GenAI CO_2ST Calculator (https://hcico2st.com).

13 Nanna Inie et al., "How CO2STLY Is CHI? The Carbon Footprint of Generative AI in HCI Research and What We Should Do About It," in *CHI '25: Proceedings of the 2025 CHI Conference on Human Factors in Computing Systems* no. 206 (April 24, 2025): 1–29 (*https://doi.org/10.1145/3706598.3714227*).

Energy Ratings

Energy ratings for ML take the idea of energy scores a step further—they not only quantify energy use but classify it into standardized tiers or labels that communicate efficiency in a more accessible, comparative form. Think of them like Energy Star labels for appliances or fuel economy ratings for cars: they turn complex technical data into a shorthand that signals environmental impact to both technical and nontechnical stakeholders.[14]

In practice, an energy rating system for ML could categorize models (or even full pipelines) based on total energy consumption, emissions per prediction, or energy-to-performance ratio. A model that achieves high accuracy with minimal energy could earn a top-tier rating, while models that consume excessive resources without proportional performance gains would fall lower on the scale.[15]

But today, no universal framework for ML energy ratings exists. We lack shared baselines for what "A-rated" energy performance means, and most research papers and products still omit environmental metrics entirely. Some early work, like the Carbon Efficiency Score from Hugging Face, moves in this direction, but these efforts remain fragmented and nonstandardized.

Figure 9-6 shows several image generative models sorted based on the Energy Score rating according to the AI Energy Score rating (*https://oreil.ly/5fD6b*). Expanding such leaderboards across the AI ecosystem needs more concerted efforts. As with the appliance energy labels, a five-star rating is supposed to be more energy efficient than a one-star model.

14 Stephen Wiel and James E. McMahon, "Energy-Efficiency Labels and Standards: A Guidebook for Appliances, Equipment, and Lighting," *Collaborative Labeling and Appliance Standards Program (CLASP)*, February 16, 2001 (*https://doi.org/10.2172/836221*).

15 Raphael Fischer et al., "Energy Efficiency Considerations for Popular AI Benchmarks," *arXiv.org*, April 17, 2023 (*https://arxiv.org/abs/2304.08359*).

AI Energy Score

Model	Provider	GPU Energy (Wh)	Score
distilgp2	distilbert	1.31	★★★★★
opt-125m	facebook	1.94	★★★★★
gp2	openai-community	2.15	★★★★★
openai-gpt	openai-community	2.70	★★★★★
gpt2-medium	openai-community	3.96	★★★★★
OLMo-1B-hf	allenai	5.59	★★★★★
gpt2-large	openai-community	6.12	★★★★★

Figure 9-6. The Hugging Face energy score leaderboard for image generative models.

Orchestration Frameworks

Orchestration frameworks are software systems that automate the management, scheduling, and coordination of complex ML workflows across compute infrastructure. They handle tasks like launching training jobs, managing dependencies, scaling resources, and monitoring performance. These are the closest implementations of MLOps principles as tools. Frameworks like Kubernetes (*https://kubernetes.io*), Ray (*https://www.ray.io*), and Airflow (*https://airflow.apache.org*) are some of the popular orchestration frameworks that manage compute resources, parallelization, and workflow automation.

These orchestration frameworks can play a foundational role in green MLOps because they govern how ML workloads are scheduled, scaled, and executed—decisions that directly shape environmental impact. Currently, most frameworks treat compute as fungible, with little regard for environmental considerations.

To align these systems with sustainability goals, orchestration frameworks must become climate-aware. That means, for example, incorporating real-time data about carbon intensity from energy grids and using it to make smarter decisions. A framework might delay nonurgent training jobs until cleaner energy is available, route workloads to datacenters powered by renewables, or dynamically scale down resources during carbon peaks (see "Green scheduling" on page 207). It could also prioritize model variants or pipeline steps that are more energy efficient, based on telemetry and historical metrics. Furthermore, they do not generally expose APIs for emissions tracking, lack hooks for energy-aware scheduling policies, and rarely surface sustainability metrics in UIs.

To shift this, orchestration frameworks need to adopt sustainability as a first-class concern—just like reproducibility, security, scalability, or uptime. Doing so would enable infrastructure-level alignment with green MLOps, turning every design decision into a chance to reduce emissions and conserve resources. This in effect can bring the green MLOps principles into practice.

Sustainable AI Operationalized: What Comes Next?

In this chapter, we formalized the concept of environmental debt, drawing upon parallels with the technical debts that accumulate in software systems due to shortsighted decisions. Environmental debts can accrue in every stage in the lifecycle of AI systems. Alleviating these environmental debts might not be effective when the debts at each stage are considered in isolation.

We have seen how concepts from MLOps can be extended to include sustainability by design to arrive at the green MLOps framework. Embedding climate awareness and resource awareness in every step of the model design, development, and operations phases is important to reduce the environmental debt and in achieving more sustainable AI.

When it comes to the principles of green MLOps, the gap between theory and practice is stark. Tools like model cards and energy cards, when used along with orchestration frameworks that are tuned to adhere to sustainability requirements, will be extremely important if we want practitioners to work toward sustainable AI.

The recipe for sustainable AI presented in this chapter is not exhaustive and has some limitations:

How is AI waste related to environmental debts? They seem very related; why not combine them?

Both these concepts are talking about environmental costs of AI systems. But AI waste is a more direct cost, whereas environmental debts are somewhat hidden and accrue over time.

"AI waste" refers to the immediate, observable inefficiencies in AI development and deployment—models trained but never used, excessive hyperparameter tuning, redundant inference, underutilized infrastructure, and so on (see "AI Waste" on page 53). These are direct energy and resource expenditures that yield little or no utility. We can often measure AI waste in kWh, compute hours, or carbon emissions wasted in obvious ways.

Environmental debt ("Environmental Debt of AI" on page 230), by contrast, captures the unseen, cumulative burden that accrues when organizations fail to account for the long-term environmental consequences of their ML practices. It is not just about the waste itself but the lack of transparency, tracking, and foresight that allows such waste to go unmitigated. Debt builds when emissions or energy usage are not reported or when systems are designed with no plan for sustainable maintenance. It is analogous to technical debt; what is easy today leads to compounded costs tomorrow.

The principles in green MLOps sound aspirational. Is it actually feasible to put them into practice?

When nothing else exists, aspirational principles are a good start. There are certainly gaps in putting them into practice—but we need to start somewhere.

In the absence of established norms, green MLOps provides a directional compass. Even if it's not always immediately feasible to implement every principle in full, these ideas offer a structured vision of what environmentally sustainable AI could look like. This kind of scaffolding matters: it helps align research, tooling development, institutional policy, and engineering priorities.

That said, the gaps are real. There is a shortage of standardized tools to track emissions at scale, few off-the-shelf orchestration systems are carbon-aware, and sustainability metrics still do not appear in most model evaluations. Organizational incentives often reward raw performance gains, not resource efficiency. So yes, implementation lags behind intent.

Energy labels seem like an easy way to rate ML algorithms. Why are they not used more broadly?

These are coarse labels and can drown nuanced discussions.

While energy ratings offer an accessible way to communicate the environmental efficiency of ML models, they risk oversimplifying a complex and context-dependent issue. Coarse labels, like "A" through "D" tiers, can obscure important nuances: what hardware was used, where the training occurred (and its energy grid), or whether energy-intensive phases like pretraining were included.

Such labels may also encourage rating optimization at the expense of holistic sustainability. Developers might tune systems to score well within a narrow metric, while ignoring broader impacts like embodied carbon in hardware, model lifecycle emissions, or real-world deployment efficiency. Moreover, without consensus on measurement standards, these ratings can mislead rather than clarify—especially if different organizations use inconsistent thresholds or measurement scopes.

Energy ratings should complement, not replace, detailed energy scores and transparent reporting. Without careful design, they risk reducing environmental responsibility to a checkbox—easy to display, but too blunt to drive meaningful change.

If we were to operationalize green MLOps entirely, would we achieve sustainable AI?

Unfortunately, no. Operationalizing green MLOps is a necessary but not a sufficient condition for achieving sustainable AI.

While green MLOps provides a foundational layer for operational sustainability, it does not address why we build AI systems or who benefits from them. For AI to be truly sustainable, green MLOps must be integrated into a broader framework that includes just, equitable, and mission-aligned design and governance. Only then can we talk seriously about sustainable AI in its full scope. This will be the focus of Chapter 10.

CHAPTER 10

Toward Sustainable AI

For much of our history, agriculture was constrained by the natural nitrogen cycle. Usable nitrogen was scarce, and farmers relied on manure, compost, and legumes to restore soil fertility.[1] These limits kept the yields modest, and food production was tightly coupled to ecological rhythms.

With the invention of the Haber-Bosch process (*https://oreil.ly/KEckM*) in the early 20th century, however, scientists unlocked the ability to produce synthetic fertilizer at industrial scale by synthesizing ammonia from atmospheric nitrogen. This had a transformative effect on food production and agriculture as crop yields soared, famine declined, and the *Green Revolution* brought this power to fields across the globe.[2]

But the efficiency gains that synthetic nitrogen unlocked came with unintended consequences. Figure 10-1 shows the historical trend of nitrous oxide (N_2O) in the atmosphere. Like other GHGs, N_2O levels rose sharply with industrialization beginning in the 19th century. What sets N_2O apart, however, is that the *vast majority* of its increase is from agriculture—primarily as a byproduct of the Haber-Bosch process, which underpins modern intensive industrial farming.[3]

1 C. C. Delwiche, "The Nitrogen Cycle," *Scientific American*, September 1, 1970 (*https://oreil.ly/rw119*).

2 Prabhu L. Pingali, "Green Revolution: Impacts, Limits, and the Path Ahead," *Proceedings of the National Academy of Sciences* 109, no. 31 (July 31, 2012): 12302–8 (*https://doi.org/10.1073/pnas.0912953109*).

3 Hannah Ritchie et al., "Breakdown of Carbon Dioxide, Methane and Nitrous Oxide Emissions by Sector," *Our World in Data*, June 10, 2020 (*https://oreil.ly/yMATi*).

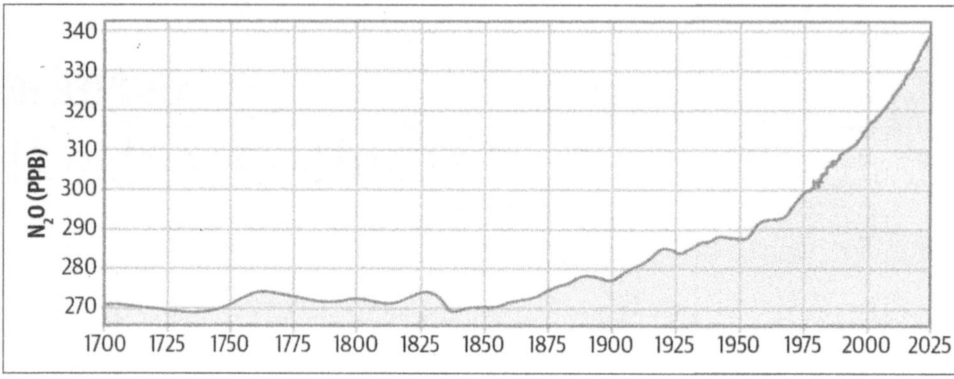

Figure 10-1. Historical trend of nitrous oxide levels measured in parts per billion (PBB). (Source: Two Degrees Institute (https://2degreesinstitute.org).)

Rather than reducing environmental pressures, the rapid scaling of agriculture introduced new forms of ecological strain.[4] Now, the Green Revolution is seen as a tipping point that has made industrialized agriculture one of the largest contributors to environmental degradation.

This an example of what economists call *rebound effect*: as a technology becomes more efficient, it often also becomes cheaper or more convenient to use, which can encourage people to use it more, offsetting or even reversing the intended savings. Rebound effect is also closely related to the Jevons paradox discussed in "Energy Efficiency, Sustainable AI, and the Jevons Paradox" on page 67.

Rebound Effects and AI

The techniques presented in this book have focused on improving the resource efficiency of AI systems. We have identified various forms of AI waste ("AI Waste" on page 53), introduced the concept of environmental debt ("Environmental Debt of AI" on page 230), and outlined numerous opportunities for making AI more efficient. If resource-saving techniques make AI extremely efficient, we must still confront the rebound effects.[5] This chapter will explore how to manage this paradox toward the goal of aligning efficiency with sustainability.

As I have hinted throughout, reducing carbon emissions through resource efficiency alone has only a limited effect on the sustainability of AI. As noted in Chapter 1 ("A

4 Harry M. Cleaver, "The Contradictions of the Green Revolution," *The American Economic Review* 62, no. 1/2 (1972): 177–86 (*http://jstor.org/stable/1821541*).

5 Alexandra Sasha Luccioni et al., "From Efficiency Gains to Rebound Effects: The Problem of Jevons' Paradox in AI's Polarized Environmental Debate," in *Proceedings of the 2025 ACM Conference on Fairness, Accountability, and Transparency* (FAccT '25), New York, NY, 76–88 (*https://doi.org/10.1145/3715275.3732007*).

Green Path to Sustainable AI" on page 16), we deliberately address the sustainability of AI using the narrow lens of resource efficiency. Confronting sustainability in all its dimensions—environmental, economic, and social—is a huge undertaking requiring efforts that go well beyond algorithmic improvements or efficiency hacks. I have used resource efficiency as a pragmatic entry point into the environmental dimension of AI's sustainability and to lay out the complexities that need to be addressed.

In this chapter, I will clarify why the focus on efficiency is a necessary but not a sufficient condition for achieving sustainable AI. Based on this critique, I will present suggestions based on frameworks that operate at higher abstractions (beyond algorithmic efficiency) to advance toward sustainable AI.

Efficiency Is Not Enough

The pursuit of resource efficiency is an important endeavor as it offers meaningful interventions during the development and deployment of AI systems at the level of an individual or small teams of developers.[6] However, solely obsessing over efficiency improvements by casting them as metrics to be optimized can have detrimental effects within the broader scope of sustainable AI. This is captured by the adage "When a measure becomes a target, it ceases to be a good measure," which is commonly known as Goodhart's law.[7] We need to address the broader environmental effects, economic viability, and the social impact of AI; to fully grapple with the sustainability of AI as efficiency alone is not enough.[8]

Broader Environmental Effects

In Chapter 3, we used the framework of resource pyramids (Figure 3-1) to illustrate the layered nature of resource consumption in AI models. Spanning from model complexity, we built the different levels of resource consumption leading up to the carbon footprint. As noted in the previous chapters, this carbon footprint corresponds to only the operational emissions due to the energy consumption. While we briefly touched upon the overhead due to networking costs and other IT equipment using the notion of PUE ("Estimating energy consumption" on page 64) and embodied emissions to account for the carbon emissions due to hardware manufacturing

6 Brian R. Bartoldson et al., "Compute-Efficient Deep Learning: Algorithmic Trends and Opportunities," *Journal of Machine Learning Research* 24, no. 122 (2023): 1–7 (*https://oreil.ly/o3Cyc*).

7 Adrian C. Newton, "Implications of Goodhart's Law for Monitoring Global Biodiversity Loss," *Conservation Letters* 4, no. 4 (2011): 264–68 (*https://doi.org/10.1111/j.1755-263x.2011.00167.x*).

8 The mantra "efficiency is not enough" in the context of AI is based on a paper of the same title by Dustin Wright et al. (2025) (*https://doi.org/10.1145/3724500*). I am the corresponding author on this paper, and several of the arguments from this work are echoed in this section.

("Embodied Emissions" on page 199), these do not fully capture the total environmental impact of AI.

To fully assess the environmental sustainability of AI, we need to look beyond operational and even embodied carbon emissions, which are mainly caused due to the energy consumed across the AI model lifecycle shown in Figure 1-6. Carbon footprint is only one factor that connects the AI model lifecycle to its environmental impact. There are multitudes of other factors that should be taken into account when discussing the true environmental impact of AI.

It is notoriously difficult to comprehensively measure the full environmental footprint of AI systems. The challenges of tracing the broader ecological consequences of AI arise not just from data scarcity but also from the sheer complexity of global supply chains and infrastructural systems.[9] For this reason, much of the existing research—including the focus of this book—has concentrated on the more readily quantifiable aspect: operational carbon emissions, or the emissions generated during the training and deployment of AI models. This approach only scratches the surface.

Beyond operational emissions, there are a number of other components that contribute to AI's environmental impact, and these are often overlooked precisely because they are harder to assess with precision. Consider, for instance, the embodied emissions associated with the manufacturing of the hardware required to run large-scale AI systems. This includes not just the energy consumed during the production of servers, GPUs, and networking equipment, but also the emissions embedded in the complex refinement processes for silicon, which are both energy-intensive and chemically hazardous.[10]

Water usage is another major factor, as large volumes are required to cool high-performance datacenters. This challenge is not easy to address directly through algorithmic improvements. While often treated as a local utility issue, the environmental costs of this water usage compound over time and are especially problematic in regions already facing water scarcity.[11]

Construction of datacenters themselves introduces yet another layer of environmental impact. The construction industry, widely recognized as one of the most carbon-intensive sectors globally, adds significantly to the AI footprint through the emissions

9 Alexandra Sasha Luccioni et al., "Estimating the Carbon Footprint of BLOOM, a 176B Parameter Language Model," *Journal of Machine Learning Research* 24, no. 253 (2023): 1–15 (*https://oreil.ly/G-rq_*).

10 Carole-Jean Wu et al., "Beyond Efficiency: Scaling AI Sustainably," *arXiv.org*, June 22, 2024 (*https://arxiv.org/abs/2406.05303*).

11 Pengfei Li et al., "Making AI Less 'Thirsty,'" *Communications of the ACM* 68, no. 7 (2025): 54–61 (*https://doi.org/10.1145/3724499*).

generated in producing concrete, steel, and other building materials, as well as through land use changes.

Moreover, the upstream extractive mining processes needed to supply rare-earth elements and other critical materials for AI hardware have serious ecological and human consequences. Mining for these materials not only depletes nonrenewable resources but often causes irreversible damage to ecosystems and poses health risks to local communities.

At the end of this hardware lifecycle lies another underexamined problem: e-waste (also see "E-Waste" on page 200). The disposal and breakdown of obsolete or nonfunctional electronic equipment contribute to both solid waste and toxic chemical pollution. And throughout the manufacturing and disposal stages, there are additional streams of chemical waste that are difficult to track and even harder to mitigate.

Taken together, these factors underscore how incomplete our current picture of AI's environmental cost truly is. Operational emissions may be the most visible and tractable aspect, but they are only the tip of a much larger, deeply interconnected system of ecological impacts. All these factors are considered to be the broader environmental impacts, and can help us better understand the actual environmental impact of AI. In Figure 10-2, these broader environmental effects are added as another layer on top of the resource pyramid introduced in Chapter 3 to form a more complete picture of the resource pyramid.

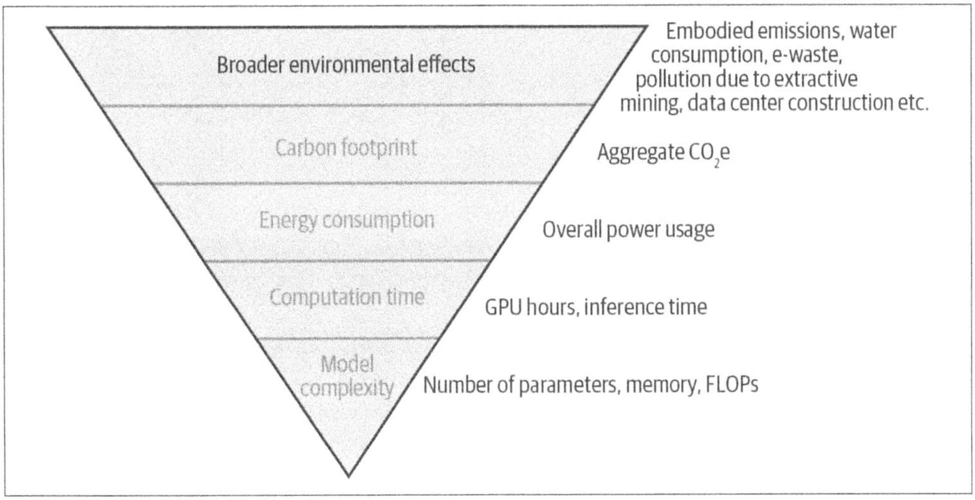

Figure 10-2. A resource pyramid with additional layers to take us closer toward the true environmental impact of AI.

The broader environmental effects are hard to measure but this does not make them any less real. If anything, their invisibility in dominant narratives about AI sustainability should raise more concern, not less.

Beyond Efficiency

Over the past decade, the energy efficiency of AI hardware has improved markedly. Figure 10-3 illustrates this trend, showing the amount of compute, measured in FLOP/s, delivered per watt of power consumed by various hardware accelerators. It shows a steady increase in energy efficiency of about 40% each year. These gains have made it more energy-efficient to train and run any *given* model. One might expect such improvements to translate into a reduction in the AI sector's overall energy footprint.

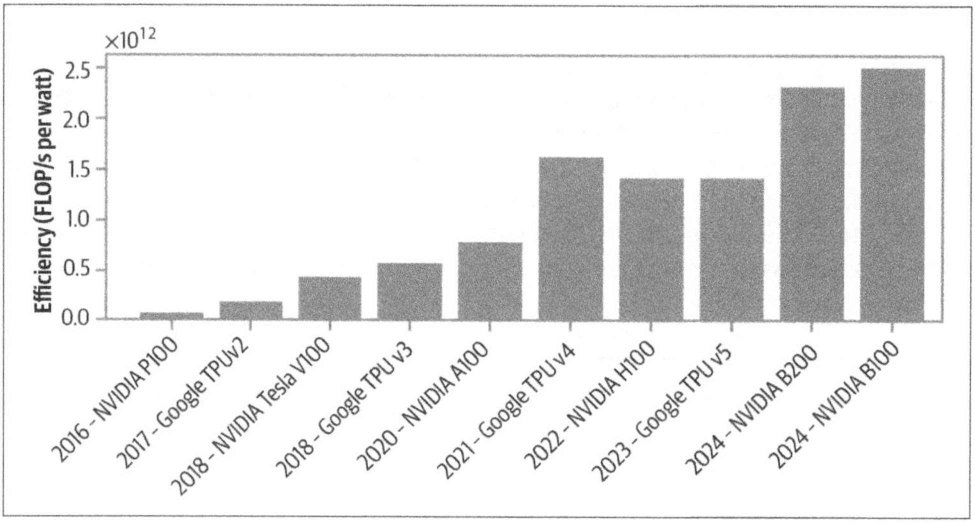

Figure 10-3. Energy efficiency improvements for different hardware accelerators. (Source: data derived from Robi Rahman, "Leading ML Hardware Becomes 40% More Energy-Efficient Each Year," Epoch AI [blog] (https://oreil.ly/8SUpC).)

However, in a classic rebound effect, the opposite seems to have occurred; the total resource consumption of developing frontier AI models has grown substantially (see Figure 6-2).[12] Rather than curbing energy use, gains in efficiency have encouraged the development of increasingly large models, trained on ever-larger datasets.

12 Ben Cottier et al., "The Rising Costs of Training Frontier AI Models," *arXiv.org*, February 7, 2025 (*https://arxiv.org/abs/2405.21015*).

The key question, then, is how we might retain the benefits of efficiency improvements without driving up the total resource consumption. This challenge lies at the heart of addressing the rebound effect and reconciling efficiency improvements with sustainability. To do this, I will draw upon the axes of agency and scope (adapted from Wright et al. (*https://doi.org/10.1145/3724500*)).

Figure 10-4 maps the landscape of sustainability in AI along two intersecting dimensions: agency, or the degree of control an individual or team typically has, and scope, the breadth and systemic depth of the impact. As one moves diagonally from the bottom left to the top right, the figure traces a shift from technical optimizations within reach of practitioners to far-reaching, systemic concerns that require collective, institutional, or political action. Improving the resource efficiency of AI methods by following the techniques presented in this book offers practitioners more agency; however, the scope of these measures can be limited when seen from an individual's point of view. To pursue sustainability that encompasses all aspects (environmental, economic, and social), a more concerted multistakeholder approach, such as by using systems thinking, is warranted.

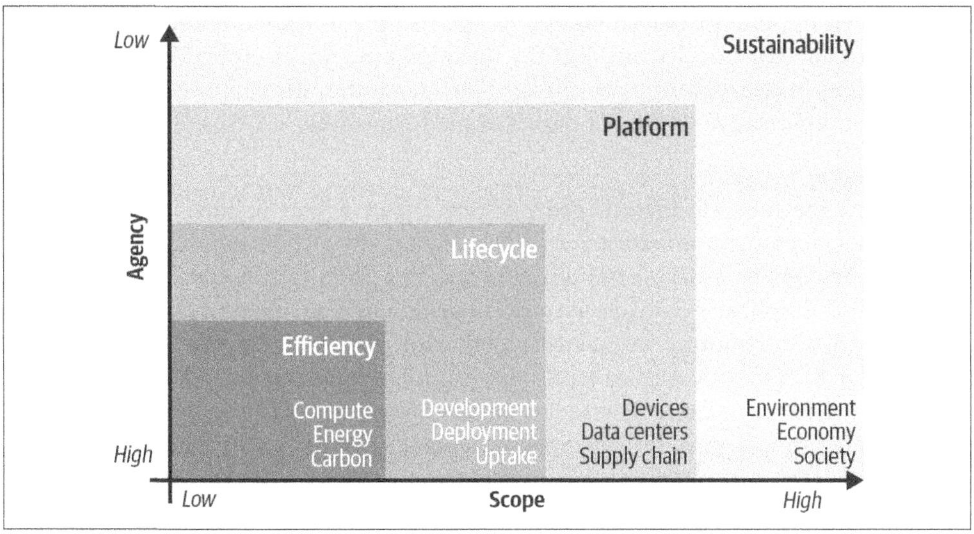

Figure 10-4. Sustainability of AI viewed along the axes of agency and scope. (Source: adapted from Wright et al.) (https://doi.org/10.1145/3724500).

The figure uses a layered approach comprising four levels:

Efficiency layer
: At the base lies the efficiency layer where most ML/AI practitioners begin, because it is where their agency is highest and the technical interventions are most straightforward. For example, performing dataset compression (Chapter 4) and using techniques like mixed-precision training to reduce training compute

load (Chapter 6) are decisions that can be made during model development. These optimizations are important, but their scope is narrow: they mostly affect localized resource use.

Lifecycle layer
: Above the efficiency layer is the lifecycle layer, which begins to encompass decisions around when and how models are trained, deployed, and maintained. Here, the agency of an individual practitioner starts to taper off. While developers can still control things like dataset size or model reuse, they begin to encounter broader consequences. For instance, the decision on how to allocate expensive compute resources along the model lifecycle can have far-reaching consequences, as discussed in Chapter 9. Using more compute in the model selection stage (Chapter 5) to search for an efficient model can reduce the resource consumption down the line, if the model is deployed to millions of users. However, this choice is not obvious for an individual developer as predicting the model uptake requires larger considerations.

  Predicting whether a given model will see significant uptake depends on a range of uncertain, often external factors. These include not just the model's technical performance or novelty but also the business model it is embedded in, the surrounding infrastructure, user engagement dynamics, distribution channels, and even timing relative to market trends or platform shifts.

Platform layer
: Beyond the lifecycle level is the platform layer, which includes infrastructure dependencies such as datacenters, devices, and the AI supply chain itself. The scope here is vast as the seemingly simple act of training a model on state-of-the-art GPUs implicates not just electricity grids but also the global supply chains responsible for mining rare earth metals and manufacturing the hardware (see Chapter 8). Practitioners generally have limited agency at this level. They may select a GPU or a cloud provider, but they have little say over how electricity is generated in a region, how servers are cooled, or how the mining for precious minerals is carried out by the hardware manufacturer.

Sustainability layer
: At the outermost level lies the sustainability layer in its broadest sense, encompassing environmental, economic, and social systems. The scope is enormous: for example, the deployment of automated decision systems in hiring may affect entire labor markets. But the ability of any one developer or research team to steer these systemic effects is reduced. This layer is often where the most meaningful sustainability outcomes reside, but they require collaboration across sectors, disciplines, and geographies.

To go from resource efficient or green AI to sustainable AI, we must fundamentally expand the scope of how we assess the sustainability impact of AI. The current emphasis in the AI research community, which is also echoed in this book, often centers around green AI, which prioritizes optimizing the efficiency of AI systems. Figure 10-4 can be seen as a road map for sustainable AI that urges ML/AI practitioners to transcend beyond the efficiency layer.

Economic Sustainability of AI

Throughout the book we've seen that developing the most recent class of AI models incurs massive resource costs. While we have primarily focused on the environmental costs, consuming resources at this scale also comes at a considerable monetary cost. This is reflected in the investment happening within the AI sector. Figure 10-5 (top) shows the growth of investments in AI from 2013 to 2024 and shows a steep growth over time. The bulk of these investments come from the private sector and happen in a handful of countries, such as the US and China, as shown in Figure 10-5 (bottom).

This is also reflected in the global distribution of high-performance computing infrastructure. Figure 10-6 illustrates the geographic distribution of the large-scale supercomputers capable of training and deploying the current generation of AI models. What emerges is a stark concentration of computational capacity within high-income countries (HICs), which Figure 10-5 also indicates. The development of hyper-scale datacenters, which are essential for cutting-edge AI research and deployment, demands substantial capital investment, both in terms of physical infrastructure and long-term energy commitments. In many cases, these investments are underwritten by the private sector (Figure 10-5 [top])[13] or state-backed initiatives with deep financial and technological resources.[14]

13 Nur Ahmed et al., "The Growing Influence of Industry in AI Research," *Science* 379, no. 6635 (March 2, 2023): 884–86 (*https://doi.org/10.1126/science.ade2420*).

14 Vili Lehdonvirta et al., "Compute North vs. Compute South: The Uneven Possibilities of Compute-Based AI Governance Around the Globe," in *Proceedings of the Seventh AAAI/ACM Conference on AI, Ethics, and Society (AIES-24)* 7, no. 1 (2024): 828–38 (*https://doi.org/10.1609/aies.v7i1.31683*).

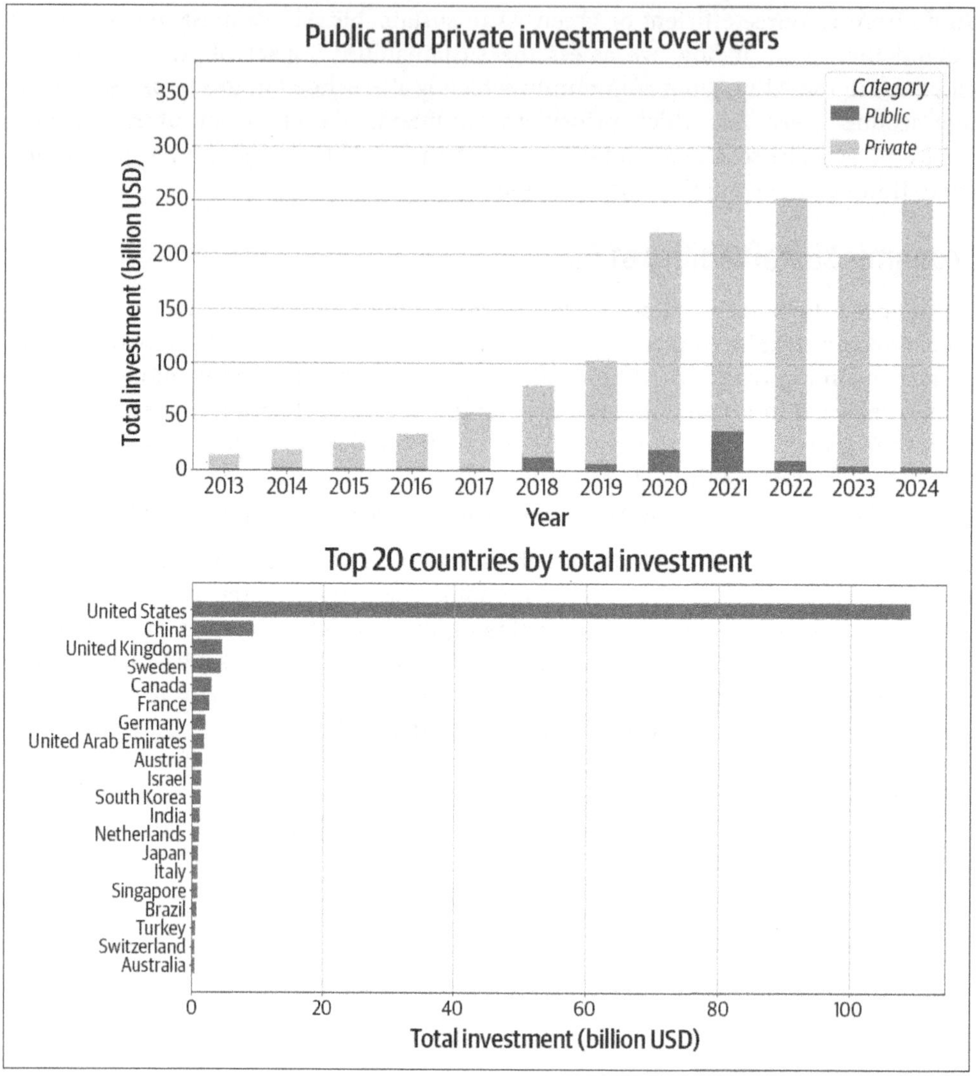

Figure 10-5. Investment in AI over time categorized into public and private contributions (top). Top 20 countries investing in AI (bottom). (Source: data from The AI Index 2025 Annual Report by Stanford University (https://oreil.ly/-rLw8).)

Figure 10-6 sorts the countries in decreasing order of the aggregate compute power in these clusters, measured in TFLOP/s according to the High-Performance Linpack

(HPL) benchmark.[15] Many regions are not even marked in this plot and even the shaded regions are close to the lower-end of compute capacity.

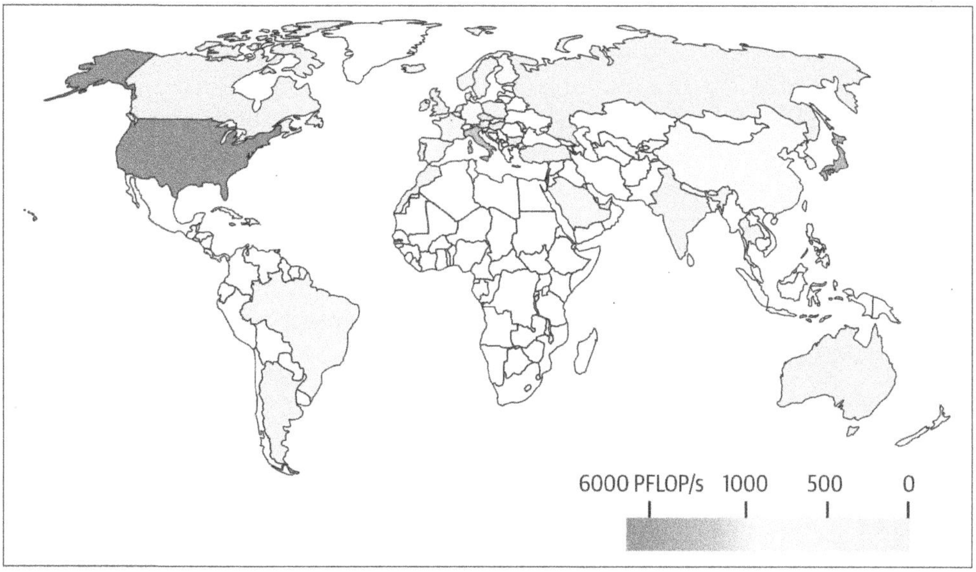

Figure 10-6. Distribution of the number of supercomputers listed in Green500 by country based on data from November 2024. (Source: data from Green500 (https://oreil.ly/VPo96).)

For low- and medium-income countries (LMICs), however, such investments often represent an economic burden that is simply untenable. The total investment in AI in 2024 was about 250 billion USD, which is more than the national GDP of 134 out of the 197 countries for which the data is available.[16] The cost of building and maintaining a competitive AI infrastructure could consume a nontrivial share of their GDP, which is a trade-off that few nations can justify when weighed against more immediate development needs like healthcare, education, or basic digital access.

As a result, many of these countries find themselves either reliant on external cloud services offered by a handful of dominant multinational tech firms or effectively sidelined from meaningful participation in the AI ecosystem. This asymmetry has both immediate- and long-term consequences. In the near term, the inability to control or shape AI systems locally means that these technologies often fail to reflect national

15 HPL (*https://oreil.ly/Zg3gO*) is a software package used to benchmark high-performance computers by solving a randomly sampled set of dense linear system equations in FP64 precision.

16 Based on the "World Economic Outlook" data for 2024 provided by International Monetary Fund (*https://imf.org/en/Publications/WEO*).

priorities, languages, regulatory environments, or cultural norms. It's not just a question of access, but of agency.

Over time, this dynamic threatens to exacerbate existing global inequalities by deepening the digital divide. The risk is not merely exclusion; it is entrenchment. As computational power, data infrastructures, and algorithmic design become increasingly concentrated in the hands of a few actors—mostly corporations and institutions headquartered in the HICs—LMICs risk being locked into a subordinate role. This emerging landscape has been described by some scholars as a new form of *digital colonialism*, in which technological dependence replicates and reinforces older patterns of economic and political domination.[17] As writer Naomi Klein has argued in the context of climate justice, such asymmetries are not accidental but are structured into the political economy of global technological development.[18] The same logic now applies to the geopolitical terrain of AI.

Investment in AI or Climate Change Adaptation?

The tension between investing in AI infrastructure and funding climate adaptation is a real and pressing dilemma for many LMICs. AI has clear potential to support climate resilience through better forecasting, smarter resource management, and faster disaster response, but developing these tools locally demands major up-front investments in compute infrastructure, data systems, and technical expertise.

Consider Bangladesh, which is already grappling with rising sea levels, erratic monsoons, and saltwater intrusion into freshwater reserves.[19] AI could directly support mitigation efforts: early warning systems for floods and cyclones, predictive models for crop yields, or intelligent allocation of relief resources. These are not speculative applications but urgent needs. Realizing them requires infrastructure that Bangladesh, like many LMICs, cannot easily afford. What exists is often confined to a few elite institutions and insufficient for broader national deployment.

This creates a harsh trade-off. Should Bangladesh direct scarce resources toward building large-scale AI capacity as part of the global AI arms race or prioritize immediate physical adaptation measures like strengthening embankments, relocating vulnerable populations, or safeguarding food systems? Both are vital. But the same limited funding

17 Samavia Zia, "Digital Colonialism: Reimagining Power, Identity, and Resistance by Decolonizing AI," *Yayasan Drestanta Pelita Indonesia* (2025): 129-147 (*https://oreil.ly/Gc-iT*).

18 Naomi Klein, *This Changes Everything: Capitalism vs The Climate* (Simon & Schuster, 2014).

19 Md. Arif Chowdhury et al., "Climate Change Adaptation in Bangladesh: Current Practices, Challenges and the Way Forward," *The Journal of Climate Change and Health* 6 (May 2022): 100108 (*https://doi.org/10.1016/j.joclim.2021.100108*).

pool must serve both ends. And while the risks of delayed AI development are abstract or long-term, the costs of climate inaction are immediate and concrete.

There are no easy answers to the dilemma posed here. But a truly sustainable vision for AI must also include economic sustainability—one that enables LMICs to access and shape AI technologies without sacrificing their capacity to confront urgent climate threats. Without this, the promise of AI for global climate resilience risks reinforcing the very inequities it claims to help solve.[20]

Social Sustainability of AI

The sustainability layer in Figure 10-4 lies at the outermost level, encompassing efficiency efforts, and consists of environmental, economic, and social sustainability. Among these three facets of sustainability, the social aspect is highly nebulous and hard to define concretely. This is simply because the interaction of AI with societies is still not fully understood, as AI and our relationship with it is evolving rapidly on a daily basis with each new technical development. Given this, in this book we will adhere to the definition of social sustainability of AI as the capacity of AI systems to support long-term societal well-being by promoting fairness, inclusivity, accountability, and equitable access to both the benefits and the governance of AI technologies.[21]

But recognizing these issues is only the first step. Measuring and optimizing for such criteria—particularly fairness, bias, and privacy—is far from straightforward. Take fairness, for instance. It's not a universal concept but a contextual one, and in ML it often requires explicit constraints or fairness-aware loss functions.[22] These criteria are frequently in tension with traditional performance metrics like accuracy, especially when data distributions reflect historical inequalities.

Furthermore, and more pertinent to this book, are the nontrivial computational implications of incorporating social sustainability. Techniques like differentially private learning, while crucial for protecting user data, introduce substantial training overhead.[23] This introduces a deeper tension between social and environmental sustainability: efforts to make AI systems more just and inclusive may paradoxically make them less environmentally sustainable.

---

20 Lynn H. Kaack et al., "Aligning Artificial Intelligence with Climate Change Mitigation," *Nature Climate Change* 12, no. 6 (2022): 518–27 (*https://doi.org/10.1038/s41558-022-01377-7*).

21 Aimee van Wynsberghe, "Sustainable AI: AI for Sustainability and the Sustainability of AI," *AI And Ethics* 1 (February 26, 2021): 213–18 (*https://doi.org/10.1007/s43681-021-00043-6*).

22 Sam Corbett-Davies et al., "The Measure and Mismeasure of Fairness," *Journal of Machine Learning Research* 24, no. 312 (2023): 1–117 (*https://oreil.ly/ofDs6*).

23 Zhiqi Bu et al., "Differentially Private Optimization on Large Model at Small Cost," *Proceedings of Machine Learning Research* 202 (July 3, 2023): 3192–3218 (*https://oreil.ly/Qxv5l*).

Equity Through Access

Social sustainability also involves *who* gets to develop, deploy, and benefit from AI systems. It encompasses questions of access: whether marginalized communities are represented in the datasets, whether they can shape how models are used, and whether AI tools are deployed in ways that reinforce or dismantle existing power structures.[24] Social sustainability thus can't be reduced to technical add-ons; it must be framed as a political and economic question about governance, participation, and accountability in AI development.

Socially sustainable AI is not just about protecting users from harm by improving model fairness or by making it private; it's about creating systems that meaningfully reflect and serve a broader range of social contexts. That requires more than fairness metrics—it demands rethinking where AI is built, whose values it encodes, and whose interests it ultimately serves.

The Way Forward

In trying to point out the narrow scope of resource efficiency improvements, the previous sections have been critical of solely focusing on algorithmic adjustments. While this might sound harsh, or even discouraging, the main point is to emphasize that sustainability in the context of AI or otherwise is a complex topic. The good news is that these difficult challenges can be addressed.

However, as individual ML practitioners our agency can be limited in affecting the broadest scope of sustainability. This requires a systemic view of these challenges and solutions that are rooted in multistakeholder efforts. And this should not come as a surprise to us, as the challenges posed by climate change, for instance, are at a planetary scale. Any, and all, efforts toward sustainable development should also be striving for global action.

We can formulate solutions to such challenging problems arising in complex systems using *systems thinking*, a policy framework that urges us to consider not individual components within a complex system but the entire system and its various interactions. For sustainable AI, this will require us to recognize that AI is a lot more than a sophisticated algorithm, as we have seen throughout the book where the material basis for AI has been formalized. AI should be viewed as an infrastructure, like electricity grids, which is increasingly becoming indispensable. Figure 10-4 is an attempt at laying out the different layers to the AI infrastructure.

24 Golnoosh Farnadi et al., "Position: Cracking the Code of Cascading Disparity Towards Marginalized Communities," *arXiv.org*, June 3, 2024 (*https://arxiv.org/abs/2406.01757*).

Risk of Greenwashing

When efforts toward sustainable AI stop at surface-level gestures like citing energy efficiency without addressing total energy use, or publishing carbon estimates without changing deployment practices, they risk becoming a form of *greenwashing*. By focusing on narrow metrics or isolated improvements, organizations may appear environmentally responsible while continuing to scale systems that remain fundamentally extractive, inequitable, or unsustainable.

This selective framing not only obscures real impacts but dulls public and institutional urgency. It creates the illusion of progress without confronting the harder structural questions: who benefits from AI, who bears the costs, and what kinds of futures we are building. Without a full-spectrum commitment—across the model lifecycle, supply chains, infrastructure, and access—sustainable AI risks becoming a branding exercise rather than a systemic shift. And in doing so, it delays the very changes it claims to support.

Systems Thinking

Systems thinking is an approach to understanding complex problems by seeing them as parts of an interconnected whole rather than isolated events or linear cause-and-effect relationships. Instead of asking, "What is the immediate outcome of this action?" systems thinking urges us to ask, "How does this action interact with other parts of the system over time?" It focuses on feedback loops, delays, emergent behaviors, and unintended consequences—all of which are common in dynamic systems like economies, ecosystems, and societies.[25]

Systems Thinking and the Crisis of Synthetic Fertilizers

Let's revisit the synthetic nitrogen example used at the beginning of this chapter to better understand how systems thinking can be used.

First, systems thinking allows us to understand synthetic fertilizer not just as a tool for boosting yields, but as a catalyst within a complex, interconnected system. Initially, more nitrogen meant more food and higher profits, which is basically a reinforcing feedback loop. But over time, a slower balancing loop emerged: soil degradation and ecological damage began to counteract those gains. Farmers responded with even more fertilizer, deepening the dependency.

25 Peter M. Senge and John D. Sterman, "Systems Thinking and Organizational Learning: Acting Locally and Thinking Globally in the Organization of the Future," *European Journal of Operational Research* 59, no. 1 (1992): 137–50 (*https://doi.org/10.1016/0377-2217(92)90011-w*).

Key delays in this system are the nutrient runoff accumulating in waterways or soil health declining over years, which masked the system's vulnerabilities. By the time problems surfaced, they were widespread and deeply entrenched.

Emergent behaviors, such as global monoculture farming and institutional reliance on chemical inputs, were not planned but arose naturally from the incentives the system created. And unintended consequences followed: water pollution, declining biodiversity, and the erosion of sustainable farming practices.

Systems thinking makes these patterns visible. It helps us see why efficiency gains, when isolated from the wider system, can backfire—not because the technology failed, but because the system adapted in ways no one initially anticipated.

A similar analysis can also be made about AI and efficiency improvements. One common storyline following efficiency improvements is that as models become more efficient, the environmental footprint of AI is shrinking.[26] Better algorithms, optimized architectures, and specialized hardware have reduced the energy needed per training run or inference task. On the surface, this looks like progress.

Making AI more efficient has not reduced its total energy use as established earlier in "Beyond Efficiency" on page 252; it has enabled rapid expansion. As costs drop, AI models are being deployed everywhere and models are growing larger.

This is a classic reinforcing loop: efficiency lowers barriers, demand rises, infrastructure expands, and the system accelerates. Any balancing feedback like energy limits or regulation lags far behind.[27] The result is a digital ecosystem that is more sprawling, more energy-intensive, and harder to govern. Emergent behaviors such as retraining for marginal gains, embedding AI in everything, and constant scaling, are not bugs but features of a system driven by cheap compute. The unintended consequences include rising emissions, hardware demand, and ecological strain, which follow naturally.

Putting Systems Thinking into Practice

We have seen how systems thinking can be used to analyze the effects of focusing on efficiency alone. But, it was demonstrated in a *post-hoc* setting to understand the larger systems effects after having pursued strategies for resource efficiency. We can also use systems thinking as a practical tool when developing a new AI model or when pursuing a new strategy that promises resource efficiency.

26 David Patterson et al., "The Carbon Footprint of Machine Learning Training Will Plateau, Then Shrink," *arXiv.org*, April 11, 2022 (*https://arxiv.org/abs/2204.05149*).

27 The closest legislation that even mentions the energy consumption of AI is the EU AI Act (*https://oreil.ly/Z7B88*). Although it doesn't have any concrete suggestions on standards for reporting or measures to curb it.

Sustainable AI Systems Assessment framework

Putting systems thinking into practice requires a holistic view of AI and its sustainability. As an attempt at this, I introduce the Sustainable AI Systems Assessment (SASA) framework in this book. Table 10-1 provides an overview of it. The SASA framework basically transforms the key concepts in systems thinking into a series of structured questions that can be used to anticipate the broader systems effects when developing AI systems. This is equally applicable for an individual trying to develop a new model or a company trying to develop a new AI product. The framework itself does not urge the users to pursue sustainable AI but helps them identify system-level effects that can be addressed to improve sustainability of their AI systems.

Table 10-1. SASA framework is a prototype for using systems thinking in practice.

Category	Guiding questions
1. Understanding the System Context	• What broader systems (infrastructure, user behavior, resource use) will our model interact with? • Are we creating a standalone tool or altering workflows, consumption patterns, or social expectations? • Could our product trigger downstream changes in how people or organizations operate?
2. Efficiency and Its Side Effects	• If we optimize for lower training cost or faster inference, will that lead us (or users) to run the model more often? • Are we using model efficiency to justify expanding features, retraining frequency, or scaling faster than needed? • Could making the model lightweight encourage unnecessary uses or integrations?
3. Behavioral and Usage Shifts	• Will users generate more content, queries, or interactions simply because the tool is fast and frictionless? • Are we replacing simple, lower-impact tools (e.g., search, static forms) with high-compute AI? • Could we be normalizing energy-intensive behavior (like constant generation or real-time interaction)?
4. Delayed and Hidden Costs	• Are we monitoring energy usage, cloud compute hours, or API load over time? • What hidden costs might emerge if we grow rapidly—server demand, data pipelines, storage, model versioning? • Are we building tracking systems to catch those trends early?
5. Scalability and Lock-In	• If our user base grows 10x, will our current architecture remain sustainable? • Are we designing in flexibility, or locking ourselves into a compute-heavy model? • Could a future update or feature dramatically increase resource intensity without us realizing?
6. Unintended Consequences	• Could our model be used in ways we did not intend—at scale, in automation chains, or in high-frequency tasks? • Are we unintentionally encouraging behavior that increases digital waste (e.g., AI slop, redundant tasks)? • What safeguards or usage guidelines are we providing to prevent overuse?
7. Building Internal Constraints and Signals	• Do we have internal guardrails for retraining frequency or model deployment volume? • Are we measuring compute and energy use per feature or model release? • Do we regularly review product scope and ask: *Are we building toward actual user value, or just scaling because we can?*

Category	Guiding questions
8. Designing for Sustainability as a Feature	• Can we offer lower-energy modes (e.g., batch processing, static outputs) for certain use cases? • Are we making our energy/resource use visible to users or partners? • Could we design incentives around efficient use—e.g., throttling, usage tiers, or opt-in compute budgeting?

The SASA framework should be used before the start of a new project and revisited throughout the lifecycle of an AI model. Doing this can help adjust and incorporate any system effects that were missed or exclude any other effects that become unnecessary.

Sustainable AI principles

The ML community has approached the complexity of looking beyond efficiency, primarily by urging for multiscale and multistakeholder efforts. These recommendations and suggestions are not as explicit as systems thinking (or the SASA framework in Table 10-1) but do urge AI practitioners to look beyond efficiency.

To illustrate, I'll highlight two frameworks that recognize the local nature of efficiency pursuits and urge for more coordinated efforts to tackle sustainability challenges:

GREENER principles
: Loïc Lannelongue et al., propose these principles in "GREENER Principles for Environmentally Sustainable Computational Science" (*https://doi.org/10.1038/s43588-023-00461-y*); they offer a comprehensive framework for guiding the development of environmentally sustainable AI (and do not focus on economic or social sustainability of AI). They emphasize not just technical efficiency but the need for clear governance structures, ethical responsibility, transparency, and innovation—all grounded in an awareness of environmental impact. GREENER principles encourage stakeholders to move beyond isolated optimizations and instead adopt a more integrated, accountable, and forward-looking approach to AI sustainability. (Figure 10-7 elaborates on the GREENER acronym.)

CARAML (Climate And Resource Aware Machine Learning) framework
: Outlines a multilevel approach to AI sustainability, emphasizing both climate responsibility and resource equity. The CARAML framework in "Climate and Resource Awareness Is Imperative to Achieving Sustainable AI (and Preventing a Global AI Arms Race)" by Pedram Bakhtiarifard et al. (*https://arxiv.org/abs/2502.20016*) argues that achieving sustainable AI requires coordinated action across five levels: individual, community, industry, government, and global. Their key points are illustrated in Figure 10-8. I have overlaid these guidelines to resemble Figure 10-4, which laid out the challenges of focusing only on efficiency.

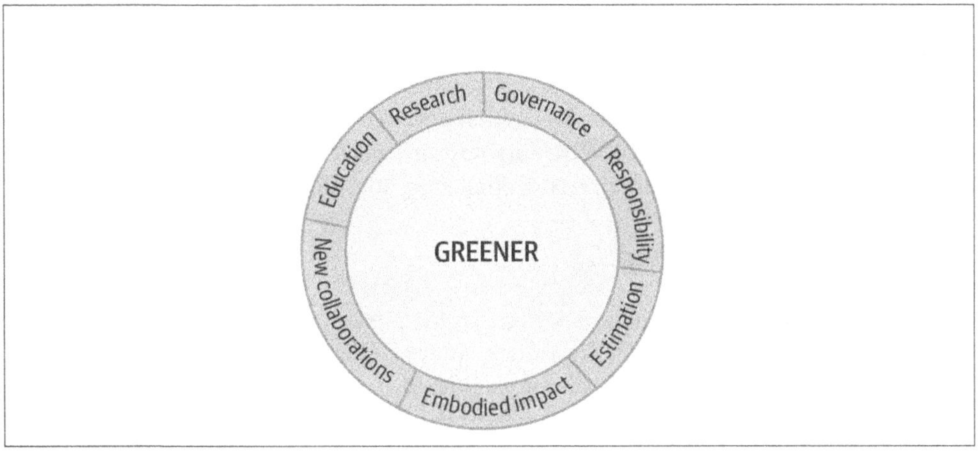

Figure 10-7. Lannelogue et al.'s (https://doi.org/10.1038/s43588-023-00461-y) GREENER principles.

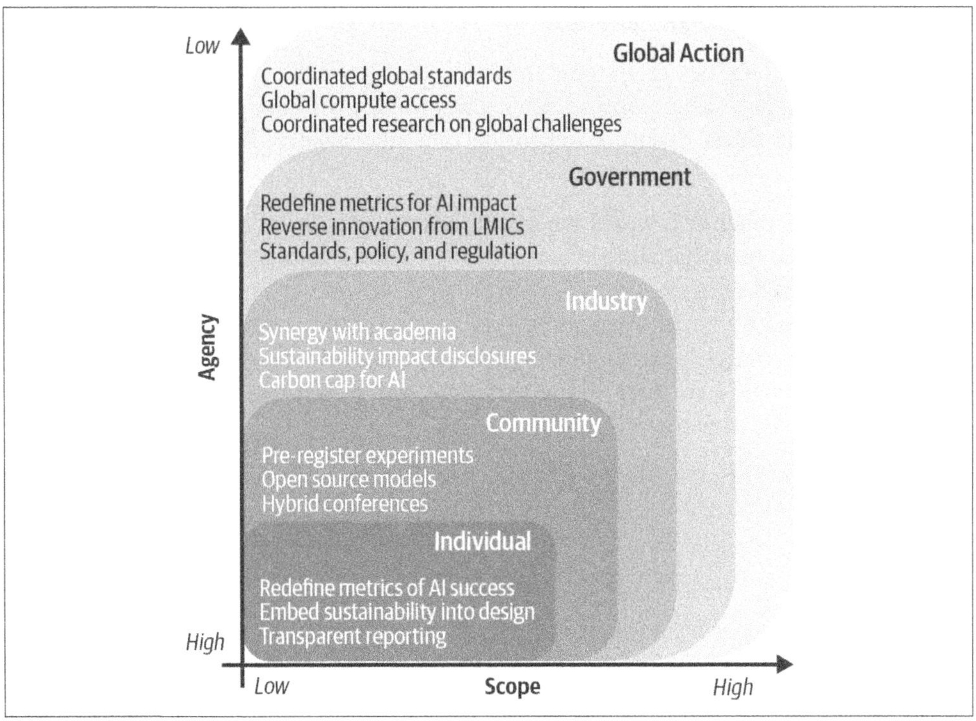

Figure 10-8. Bakhtiarifard et al.'s (https://arxiv.org/abs/2502.20016) CARAML framework.

Use guidelines such as those in Figures 10-7 and 10-8 as high-level road maps for thinking about improving the environmental impact or sustainability of AI. Developing sustainable AI systems requires careful considerations at many levels on top of all the technicalities of improving resource efficiency. While it does take additional effort to embed sustainability into AI, achieving sustainable AI can have a huge impact in how AI can help us tackle more pressing challenges like climate change.

Impact of Sustainable AI

This chapter provides a critical perspective on the pursuit of resource efficiency in AI systems. The tools and methods to reduce AI waste and improve the resource efficiency that I have presented in this book should be considered first steps toward sustainable AI. In this chapter, leveraging the rebound effect and systems thinking, I argue for a sustainable AI that requires extensive, multistakeholder engagement.

It is crucial to acknowledge that algorithmic improvements and efficiency measures alone will not deliver truly sustainable AI. I hope that this understanding will inspire, not discourage, our collective efforts.

Given all the complexities of systems thinking, if sustainable AI seems like a dream, then I can only invoke astronomer Carl Sagan to make the case for me when he said, "Imagination will often carry us to worlds that never were. But without it we go nowhere."

And I want us to imagine a world where all technology can be truly sustainable, and in particular AI to be sustainable because it is the most transformative technology we have at our disposal right now, when we are also faced with the greatest challenge as a civilization—climate change. We will need all the tools at our disposal to mitigate and adapt to climate change, and AI can be extremely useful—only if AI itself does not hamper these efforts. I sincerely hope the tools and insights presented in this book can be of use as we strive toward sustainable AI.

Epilogue

Every few days during the course of writing this book, a new model or method was touted as the next big thing. As a researcher in the domain, it was quite difficult not to be swayed by such excitement and to refrain from including each shiny new technical development and trend. This does not mean the book is stale; it has all the essential you need to understand even the most recent AI methods. None of the arguments I had from the outset for pursuing sustainable AI changed at all; if anything, they became even more pertinent with each new model or AI product.

When a new model or method is published tomorrow that is not *rooted in sustainability*, I urge you to use the tools presented here to assess and grapple with its true sustainability. As I see it, at least in the near future, sustainable AI will have to play catch-up until we have a systemic shift in how technology is developed. And that requires deep concern, persistent effort, and education of all the involved stakeholders. I have laid out the challenges, discussed several technical tools, curated a rich collection of literature (*https://github.com/raghavian/sustainable_ai*), and presented relevant conceptual frameworks in this book, with the hope that it will serve as a useful resource in understanding and realizing the full potential and implications of building sustainable AI.

Index

B

C

D

E

F

G

H

I

J

K

L

M

Q

R

S

T

U

V

W

Y

About the Author

Raghavendra (Raghav) Selvan is an assistant professor at the University of Copenhagen. His research spans sustainable machine learning, machine learning for sciences, medical image analysis, and graph neural networks. He holds a PhD from the University of Copenhagen and is affiliated with Pioneer Center for AI (Denmark) and the pan-European AI network ELLIS. Raghav was born in Bangalore, India.

Colophon

The animal on the cover of *Sustainable AI* is a barn swallow (*Hirundo rustica*), the most common swallow. Barn swallows have six subspecies and can be found on every continent around the world. They thrive in open land, such as pasture, meadow, and savanna, and build nests in human constructions.

Barn swallows are insectivores, endearing them to their human neighbors, and are known for hunting while in flight. Their long, pointed wings, forked tails, and slender bodies enable them to glide for long periods. The distinctive tail streamers, backs, and breast bands are steely blue, and the underparts are white or off-white. Above and below their short, wide beaks, barn swallows have rusty red feathers.

Many of the animals on O'Reilly covers are endangered; all of them are important to the world.

The cover illustration is by Monica Kamsvaag, based on a black-and-white engraving from *Lydekker's Royal Natural History*. The series design is by Edie Freedman, Ellie Volckhausen, and Karen Montgomery. The cover fonts are Gilroy Semibold and Guardian Sans. The text font is Adobe Minion Pro; the heading font is Adobe Myriad Condensed; and the code font is Dalton Maag's Ubuntu Mono.

www.ingramcontent.com/pod-product-compliance
Lightning Source LLC
Jackson TN
JSHW060019021125
93500JS00014B/305
* 9 7 8 1 0 9 8 1 5 5 5 1 3 *